Fundamentals of Ohio
Real Estate Law

Fundamentals of Ohio Real Estate Law

Wm. Bruce Davis

Associate Professor of Legal Studies
University of Cincinnati, Clermont College

CAROLINA ACADEMIC PRESS
Durham, North Carolina

eBook ISBN 978-1-5310-0218-3

Library of Congress Cataloging-in-Publication Data

Names: Davis, Wm. Bruce, author.
Title: Fundamentals of Ohio real estate law / Wm. Bruce Davis.
Description: Durham, North Carolina : Carolina Academic Press, [2016] |
  Includes bibliographical references and index.
Identifiers: LCCN 2016027857 | ISBN 9781611634013 (alk. paper)
Subjects: LCSH: Vendors and purchasers--Ohio. | Real property--Ohio. | Real
  estate business--Law and legislation--Ohio.
Classification: LCC KFO126 .D38 2016 | DDC 346.77104/3--dc23
LC record available at https://lccn.loc.gov/2016027857

Carolina Academic Press, LLC
700 Kent Street
Durham, North Carolina 27701
Telephone (919) 489-7486
Fax (919) 493-5668
www.cap-press.com

Printed in the United States of America
2022 Printing

Contents

Preface

I have taught Ohio real estate law for more than a dozen years to paralegal students and those who are preparing to take the Ohio real estate license exam. Students seem to relate to real estate law, because they all have a connection to real estate in some way. Perhaps they have rented an apartment, bought a house, or lived at home with their parents. Real estate is simply part of their lives.

Ohio has some unique twists when it comes to real estate law, partly because of its role in the westward expansion of the United States following the Revolutionary War. For example, we find more than 20 different survey systems used in Ohio, and the development of the rectangular coordinate system that is used in most of the states to our west. Yet we still have surveys that use long-forgotten trees, fences, and rocks as corners. Ohio is truly a unique place when it comes to real estate law.

I have written this book in a conversational style, which is intended to make the material less dry and more accessible to students. During the drafting process, I imagined that I was having a one-on-one discussion with a student in a tutoring session. I have tried to anticipate typical student questions and provide answers as they arise in the text. The numerous examples throughout the text are designed to place concepts within easy grasp of students. I have made rather extensive use of tables to present material that lends itself to that format so that concepts can be compared to one another.

The text is arranged in the logical order I present material in my classes and includes an appendix of practical forms, such as a sample lease, promissory note, and mortgage. In my experience, walking students through these documents and pointing out particulars of various clauses can make an otherwise dull class more relevant to them.

This book is divided into two parts. Part I contains the material that is typically used in a general undergraduate real estate law course, such as one taught to paralegal students. Part II adds three chapters that are required as part of an Ohio real estate salesperson prelicensing course.

I have included only a very few case references in this text but discuss a few of those that are of major significance, such as the *Kelo* decision. The text does not include sidebar excerpts of court cases for a couple of reasons. First, students generally tend to simply skip over them when they read the text. Second, when they do read the cases, they often fail to grasp the importance of them. Finally, I frequently find that an author's choice of cases to include does not match my view of their relevance. However, the instructor materials include a chapter-by-chapter list of citations to relevant Ohio and US Supreme Court cases that the instructor can use as he or she best sees fit.

Speaking of instructor materials, the supplement to this book includes a model syllabus, discussion questions, PowerPoint presentations for each chapter, quizzes, suggested assignments, and sample tests with an answer key. All of these materials are practical ones that I have actually used in my classes.

To all of you—instructors, students, and future real estate moguls—I bid you *bon voyage* on your journey into the fascinating world of Ohio real estate law.

Acknowledgments

"No man is an island."
—*Devotions upon Emergent Occasions*, John Donne, 1624

This book may have my name listed as the author, but many people were involved in creating it. I am most grateful for all of the people who have tolerated reading early drafts of the manuscript, whose comments and corrections have made the text better. Magistrate Barbara Antell, Drexanne Evers, Christian Gaitskill, Della Martin, Catherine Neumann, Greg Traynor, Laura Traynor, and Lisa Wharton all provided more help than I could have reasonably expected. I am grateful for the friendly people at the Clermont County Recorder's Office, including Recorder Deborah Clepper, Marsha Collier, and Romain Walker, all of whom demonstrated exemplary patience and a willingness to open the office on their day off to accommodate my class, which is absolutely above and beyond the call of duty.

I have a special fondness for the students in my Fall 2015 Real Estate Law class, who endured this book in manuscript form as the text for their class. These intrepid students helped me to solidify many parts of the book into the form you now hold—Devon Altman, Michele Anderson, Nancy Brooks, Mackenzi Carrington, Nikki Dickson, Amy Dziech, Leslie Jaggers, Allison June, Adrienne Troy, Michael T. Votel, and Miriam Wehner.

These wonderful people only helped to make this book better. Any errors are solely my own.

Part I

Basic Ohio Real Estate Law

Chapter 1

Introduction to Real Estate

What Is Property?

Intuitively, I think we all immediately understand what property is. It is our stuff, right? Well, mostly right. Your car, your textbooks, your computer, your clothes are all your stuff. But, property is more than just stuff. Property is also about rights associated with your stuff.

What does it mean when you say you "own" your house—which is certainly property? It means that you have some rights associated with the house—the right to be there, the right to exclude others, the right to sell it, the right to give it away, the right to leave it in your will, the right to change it, the right to quiet enjoyment (whatever that is), the right to receive profits from it, and many others.

These rights are what make up property. In fact, it would not be too bold to say that property is a collection of rights. Now, these rights are somehow attached to a particular piece of stuff, like your house, your car, and so forth, but in many ways, the *rights* are indeed the property.

From this moment on, whenever someone refers to "property," you should not think just about the thing, the stuff, but also focus on the *rights*. Often, you will hear lawyers and judges talk about "property rights"—in essence, they are talking about property in this sense—the rights associated with the stuff.

Often, these property rights are described as being a "bundle of rights." In fact, I like to think about property as a handful of pick-up sticks, with each stick representing a particular right—such as the right to be there, the right to exclude others, and so forth. If you have all of the available sticks in the bundle, then you have the most complete possible ownership of the property.

It is entirely possible to split up the bundle into its component parts and transfer some of the rights to another person. Indeed, that is exactly what happens, for example, when a landlord rents out a house. The landlord transfers some of the rights to the tenant, such as the right to be there, the right to ex-

3

clude others, and the list goes on. At the same time, the landlord retains some of the rights in the bundle—the right to receive rent from the tenant, the right to sell the property, the right to give it away in her will, and others.

As we will see later in this book, different ways that property can be held are merely different ways that the bundle of rights can be divided among several people. The sooner you grasp the idea that *property* is equivalent to *rights*, the sooner you will understand some of the more obscure ways that these rights can be divided up.

I mention all of the *available* sticks in the bundle because there is one very special stick in the bundle that you can never own—that which is held by the government. This is a very powerful stick, as it gives the government the right to tax property, impose certain restrictions on it, and even force it to be sold to the government under certain circumstances. Keeping with the pick-up sticks analogy, I refer to this as the *master stick*—the property rights that are held by the government. You might ask, How did the government obtain the master stick? In Ohio, it is actually pretty simple; the government had the master stick from the beginning. The federal government transferred land in Ohio to individual owners, often in the form of large land grants as part of the federal Land Ordinance of 1785. Because the federal government held the property beforehand, it simply held on to the rights associated with the master stick.

There is a long history of some rights to property being held by various governmental bodies—federal, state, and local. This dates back to the days of William the Conqueror in England after the Battle of Hastings in 1066. When William came to power, he was deemed to "own" all of the land in England. Having just defeated the Saxons, William needed to maintain an army to defend his claim to the kingdom. In order to do so, he granted large parcels of land to his favored and loyal subjects in exchange for supplying knights for his army, referred to as "knight servitude." These lords and barons[1] then further divided the land into smaller parcels, until it reached individual families, who were required to provide sons to serve as knights. For those who had no suitable male offspring, their servitude was extracted in the form of so many bushels of wheat, so many sheep, and so forth. Thus, the individual parcels of land were subject to a duty to supply goods or services to their higher-ups. This duty could never be extinguished—just as one today can never hold all of the sticks in the bundle because the master stick always belongs to the government.

---

1. The terms *landlord* and *land baron* seem to evolve from these terms.

What Is "Real Property"?

Simply put, real property is a location on the planet Earth and everything that is more or less permanently attached to that location. In fact, some lawyers talk about real property law as "dirt law." Indeed, that reduces the concept to its essence. Real property is a specific spot on the planet, everything that is sufficiently attached to that location, and perhaps more importantly, all the rights associated with that place.

Real property includes rights associated with the land itself, permanent buildings on the land, sidewalks, driveways, parking lots, barns, and everything else that is attached to the land, including growing things such as trees.

On the other side of the coin, **personal property** is everything that is not real property. Anything that is not more or less permanently attached to real property is personal property, sometimes referred to as **personalty** in the same way that real property is sometimes referred to as **realty**. Another name for personal property is **chattels**. Real and personal property should be distinguished for several important reasons. For example, if a person enters into an agreement to purchase all of another person's real property, what is included? It certainly includes the land, buildings, trees, driveways, and sidewalks. But what about things inside the building? What will be included? The drapes? The built-in refrigerator? The large oriental rug in the dining room? To answer this question, we need to first understand the concept of fixtures.

Fixtures

Earlier, I mentioned the phrase "more or less permanently attached" to the land. I did this to allow for the special category of **fixtures**. A fixture is simply an item of personal property that has been attached to the real property in such a way that it becomes a part of the real property. For example, built-in kitchen cabinets in a house will almost certainly be fixtures, and thus part of the realty. In Ohio, the courts use a three-part test to determine if an object is a fixture and therefore part of the realty, or not a fixture and thus an item of personalty.

We've all seen the scales of justice, a balance with pans on each side, which are figuratively used by the courts to weigh the outcome of a particular case. Consider each part of the test as placing pebbles in one pan or the other in these scales. After all the pebbles have been placed, we will look at the scales to see which way they are leaning.

The first part of the Ohio test is **attachment.** How permanently is the item attached to the realty? The more permanent the attachment, the more pebbles will be placed in the side of the scale favoring realty. For example, a battery-powered wall clock that is held up by a single small nail is not very permanently attached. On the other hand, a sink in the kitchen will likely be more permanently attached to plumbing and countertops. But, do not just look at the method of attachment alone—as many people mistakenly do. The other two parts of the test need to be considered.

The second part of the Ohio test is **adaptation**. To what extent was the item adapted for use in this real property, or to what extent was the real property adapted for this item? The more the adaptation, the more pebbles in the side of the scale favoring realty. For instance, if the refrigerator in a kitchen has wood inserts installed to match the rest of the cabinets and is placed so that it looks like part of the cabinetwork, it is adapted. On the other hand, a refrigerator that merely rolls into a standard-sized cubbyhole is not at all adapted. Likewise, if the realty has been specially adapted to accommodate the item, it is likely a fixture and thus part of the realty. For example, if a built-in big-screen television in the family room fits into a specially designed wall alcove, where the alcove has been built especially to house this particular television, the realty has been adapted for the item and it is likely a fixture.

The final part of the Ohio test to determine if an item is a fixture, and thus a part of the realty, is the **intent** of the person attaching the item. Did the person intend the item to become part of the realty at the time of attachment? If so, we must put more pebbles in the side of the scale favoring the item as a fixture. On the other hand, if the person attaching the item intends to remove it before leaving the realty, more pebbles go on the side of the scale favoring a determination that the item is not a fixture. Courts often say that the *intent* at the time of the attachment is the most important test.

For example, imagine a crystal chandelier in a dining room. In this case the chandelier has been in the owner's family for decades, handed down to each successive generation. The owner hangs it in the dining room to enjoy but intends to take it with him if he sells the house. Is this a fixture?

Using *attachment* test, we will put pebbles in the scale favoring the chandelier as a fixture, because it is quite well attached to the building—after all, we don't want the chandelier to come loose from the ceiling. The *adaptation* test will probably require us to put pebbles in the pan favoring the item as not a fixture, because neither the room nor the chandelier was specially adapted for this use. Finally, the *intent* test will definitely favor the chandelier as a fixture. The owner intends to take the item with him when he sells the house. Thus, I think we must conclude that the chandelier is not a fixture, and therefore, personalty.

Here's why categorizing an item as a fixture or personalty is so important. Suppose a buyer and seller agree to purchase and sell a house, and the agreement says nothing about whether or not the chandelier is included in the sale. If the scale tilts in favor of a fixture, it is part of the realty and thus included in the sale. On the other hand, if it tilts in favor of personalty, it will not be included. Of course, the purchase agreement could deal with this problem directly by stating that the chandelier will or will not be included. That's all well and good, but the problem arises when the agreement omits to say anything about the chandelier. Then, we must look to the test to determine whether it is included in the sale or the seller gets to take it with him.

Mobile Homes in Ohio

Are mobile homes real property? The previous discussion on fixtures would seem to suggest that the more permanently attached they are to the realty, the more likely it is that they are part of the realty. If the wheels are removed, a concrete foundation is constructed, and the mobile home is fastened to the foundation, surely it would become part of the realty, right?

Well, this may be the case in several other states, but not in Ohio. Here, mobile homes fall outside the tests for fixtures. It really doesn't matter how permanently attached they are, how adapted they are to the realty, or what the intent was at the time of the attachment. A completely different rule applies to mobile homes in Ohio.

When a person purchases a mobile home in Ohio, a certificate of title is issued from the Bureau of Motor Vehicles, just like that for a car, truck, motorcycle, or another kind of trailer. The certificate of title identifies the owner, and in order to transfer ownership of the mobile home, the owner must fill out the transfer information on the back of the certificate of title and then have it notarized and recorded with the Bureau of Motor Vehicles. Then ownership of the mobile home will transfer to the new owner.

However, the owner of the mobile home can make it a part of the realty. This is a fairly simple process where the owner surrenders the certificate of title to the county auditor. Then the mobile home becomes part of the realty and will now be taxed as part of the realty. Of course, it must still be permanently attached to the realty, with the wheels removed. But contrary to what may people think, merely removing the wheels and attaching the mobile home to a permanent foundation does not make it part of the realty.

This has caused some interesting legal battles in Ohio. Imagine someone purchasing a farm, complete with house, barn, storage buildings, well house, and mobile home where the ranch hand lives. If the purchase agreement doesn't specifically mention the mobile home as part of the sale of the realty, and the title to it has not been surrendered to the county auditor, the mobile home will remain personalty and will not be included in the sale. When the purchaser arrives at the farm from the closing and sees that the mobile home has been removed, the time is too late to deal with this problem.

Problems and Solutions in Sales of Personalty

The mobile home problem and the previous one dealing with the chandelier point to a couple of problems and their solutions. Most of these problems can be solved by being careful in preparing the purchase and sale agreement for the realty. If the buyer wants an item of personalty to be included in the sale, the buyer should be sure to specifically mentioned this in the agreement. Likewise, if the seller does not want to include the item in the sale, the seller should ensure that the agreement states that the item is not included. Otherwise, the defaults provided by Ohio will kick in to determine if an item is part of the realty or part of the personalty.

That's the legal answer, but there is a more practical solution. Before offering realty for sale, the seller should simply remove anything that is not to be included in the sale. Take down the heirloom chandelier, carefully put it in storage, and replace it with another light from a home center. If the buyer never sees the chandelier, the buyer will not know he wants it. Instead, if the buyer sees it, he will want it as part of the deal. The old adage applies here: "Out of sight, out of mind."

Types of Land

Real property can be categorized by the way it is used. The most basic categories are **unimproved land** and **improved land**. Unimproved land is just that—land that is more or less in its natural state. Grasslands, vacant lots, forests, and the like are examples of unimproved land. On the other hand, improved land has some structure on it. Houses, barns, shopping centers, and schools are illustrations of improved land. Keep in mind that for purposes of identifying real estate, the buildings are part of the realty. Thus, when we say that a house is an example of improved land, it naturally includes the entire real property—the land and the building. Unimproved land can be converted into improved land simply by building a structure on it.

Don't be confused by the term *improved*. Suppose I take vacant land, construct the world's ugliest house on it, and then paint the house purple with green stripes. Surely that will be understood to lessen the value of the property. Indeed, the property may well have been more valuable before I built the ugly house than afterward. Yet the property is still said to be improved, because it is no longer vacant land. From an aesthetic standpoint, I did not improve the beauty of the property; but from a real estate law standpoint, this is now improved land because it now has a structure on it.

Residential property consists of places where people live—places of **domicile**. Single-family houses, duplexes, apartment buildings, town houses, time-shares, condominiums, and co-ops are examples of residential property. As we will see later in this book, residential property is afforded some special treatment under the law.

Commercial property is land that is used for business. Commercial property includes a wide variety of purposes, such as stores, office buildings, shopping malls, and other places where goods are sold or services rendered.

Industrial property is land that is used for manufacturing and fabrication. Factories, industrial parks, and the like are examples of industrial property. This is frequently further divided into light industrial and heavy industrial. The primary difference between these two is the degree to which noise, smells, and other annoyances are discharged.

Agricultural property, as the name indicates, is land that is used to raise crops and animals. Typically, we think of this in terms of farms, ranches, and similar uses.

One thing to keep in mind as we consider the various uses of land is the concept of **zoning**. As we will see in Chapter 5, zoning divides land into different areas that are classified according to use. Zoning is intended to keep like uses of land together and improve the conditions of an area by limiting the permissible uses within a particular zoning district. As you might imagine, having a lead-smelting factory in the middle of a residential area would not be well received by the local residents. The power of the government to zone derives from the rights associated with the master stick. Just because you own a piece of property, you cannot use that property however you would like. Land can be used only in a way that is compatible with its zoning.

Discussion Questions

1. Why is it important to distinguish between real property and personal property?

2. For each of the following items, identify whether it would probably be a fixture and why. Some items may be arguable. Make your argument using the three-part test. How well you state your position is more important than the answer you choose.

  a. "Clicker" for garage door opener
  b. Wall-mounted big-screen television
  c. Front door key to house
  d. Portable dishwasher
  e. Washing machine
  f. Built-in oven
  g. Bathroom mirror
  h. Throw rug in family room
  i. Wired security system
  j. Refrigerator

3. Why is it important to determine if an item is a fixture?

4. Briefly describe how a mobile home can become realty in Ohio.

5. I just bought a parcel of vacant land and built the world's ugliest shack on it. I also dumped a load of scrap metal in a huge pile on the land. I started to dig a swimming pool but stopped halfway through, and the hole is now filled with stagnant water and algae. I abandoned four rusted-out cars on the land. I haven't mowed the grass in three months and it is about three feet high. Please explain to me why this is "improved" land.

Key Terms

Adaptation test
Agricultural property
Attachment test
Chattels
Commercial property
Domicile
Fixture
Improved land
Industrial property
Intent test
Personal property
Personalty
Property rights
Real property
Realty
Residential property
Unimproved land
Zoning

Chapter 2

Rights in Real Property

Property as a Bundle of Rights

In Chapter 1, we started looking at real property in terms of a bundle of rights, such as the right to be there, the right to exclude others, the right to sell it, the right to give it away, the right to leave it in your will, the right to change it, and other rights. Not all property has all of these rights. As a quick example, if you are renting an apartment, you certainly have the right to be there, the right to exclude others, and several more rights. However, you do not have the right to sell the apartment building, give it away, or leave it to someone else in your will. The more rights that a person holds in his or her bundle, the higher the quality of ownership that person has. Ohio recognizes several different kinds of ownership—for example, the one described briefly in this paragraph is called a **leasehold** interest. This and other types of ownership will be developed more fully in future chapters.

Land is generally thought of as starting at the center of the earth, moving through the subsurface of the planet, through the property boundaries, and extending through the atmosphere of the earth, in theory, forever. From this we can divide the property into surface rights, subsurface rights, and air rights. We will examine each of these in turn.

Surface Rights

Some rights are connected with a physical part of the land, such as surface rights. As the name implies, these rights deal with using the surface of the land. You certainly have the right to be present on the surface of your property. You may also allow others to enter your land, giving them some surface rights also. For example, if you have a party at your house, your guests will have the right to be there—a form of surface right. As we will see later in this chapter, these rights may be temporary or permanent. Allowing your party guests onto your property is clearly a temporary right. After the party is over and everyone has gone home, the guests no longer have the right to be on your property. On the other hand, you could permanently allow a neighbor to use a part of your private road to reach their property. We will discuss these concepts in more detail later in this chapter.

Water Rights

Water rights refer to rights associated with water on, under, or adjacent to real property, including (1) how a boundary is determined when the property uses a body of surface water to describe the edge of the property and (2) the right to use the water in that body. This can include lakes, ponds, streams, rivers, and underground water. An owner's rights with respect to this water depend on the type and source of the water.

Moving water, such as a stream, creek, or river, can be further divided into navigable and nonnavigable water. If the waterway adjacent to a landowner's property can be used for navigation (for example, the Ohio River), it is considered a public waterway, and the land underneath the water belongs to the state.[1] If a property is bounded by a navigable waterway, the high water line of the waterway is typically used as the property boundary. On the other hand, if the property is bounded by nonnavigable water, the property owner typically owns the submerged land up to the centerline of the water.

Riparian rights are those associated with nonnavigable moving water. A landowner whose property borders moving water may make use of the water so long as he or she does not interfere with the rights of those downstream. Thus, a farmer whose land borders a nonnavigable stream could use water from the stream for irrigation. However, the farmer could not dam up the stream or pump all of the water out of the stream, because this would interfere with the rights of downstream property owners.

Littoral rights are associated with nonmoving water, such as lakes, seas, and oceans. Ownership of land that uses a littoral body of water as a boundary runs to the mean (average) high-water mark of the body of water, with

---

1. With respect to the Ohio River, where Ohio is separated from Kentucky by the Ohio River, the Kentucky border starts at the northern shore of the river. Therefore, much of the Ohio River is actually in Kentucky.

the rest of the property being held by the government. Landowners may make unrestricted use of the water, subject to the rights of the government.

Both riparian and littoral rights are attached to the land itself and not personal to the landowner. Thus, when a property with riparian or littoral rights is sold, those rights pass to the new owner and cannot be retained by the seller. Such rights are said to be **appurtenant** to the property—that is, attached and part of the land. Think of appurtenant rights as yet another stick in the bundle.

A property owner whose land is bounded by water can see the property boundary change over time. **Erosion** of the soil as it is carried downstream can result in the property becoming smaller. **Accretion** is the exact opposite—as soil is deposited onto the banks of the body of water, the property can become larger.

Subsurface Rights

Because the property is considered to start at the center of the earth and continue through the property boundaries, an owner of land also owns everything between the surface and the center of the earth. Thus, mineral rights, oil and gas rights, and the like are all considered to be **subsurface rights**. Keep in mind that the bundle of sticks representing property rights includes subsurface rights. Therefore, a landowner could sell or lease mineral rights to a gold-mining company to remove gold ore from underneath the property. Naturally, if the mining company wanted to come onto the property to remove the gold, the company would also need to get surface rights to do so. However, if the mining company has surface rights on adjacent land, it could dig down there and tunnel underneath the property. As is the case with all rights, the mining company's right could not interfere with the other rights of the property owner. So the mining company must take care to not allow the property under which they are mining to sink, or *subside*.

Groundwater

Groundwater is water that is found beneath the surface of the earth. Groundwater is considered part of the property and can be used by the property owner, so long as the use does not harm adjacent property owners. Thus, a property owner can drill a water well on his or her property and use the water for irrigation, domestic, or other uses.

Air Rights

As mentioned earlier, ownership of real property includes everything from the surface of the land upward forever. In essence, this means that property ownership includes the clear blue sky above the land. However, just like all of the other rights, this is subject to the master stick—the rights held by the government. Thus, you cannot keep airplanes from flying through your airspace, because the governmental rights include the right to define navigable airspace. Likewise, you cannot build your personal Tower of Babel to the heavens, because the government can place building restrictions on your property.

Incorporeal Rights: Easements, Licenses, and Profits

Easements

Suppose Jim owned a large parcel of land, which included a house, garage, and driveway, as shown in Figure 2.1. At some point, Jim divided the parcel in two, constructed a house on the rear parcel, and sold the house to Chris. In order to gain access to Chris's house, it is necessary to use Jim's driveway (see Figure 2.2). Jim can accomplish this with an **easement**. An easement is a permanent property right (one of the sticks in the bundle) that is transferred from Jim to Chris. This gives Chris the right to use the driveway for access to her property. This right is said to **run with the land**, which means that when Chris sells her property, the right to use Jim's driveway will pass to the new owner.

Easements have some special terminology associated with them. In this case, Chris's property would be called the **dominant tenement** and Jim's would be referred to as the **servient tenement**. The dominant tenement is the one that has easement rights to use another's property, whereas the servient tenement is the one that is burdened by the easement. Jim's property is burdened by having to allow Chris's use of his driveway for access to her property. This kind of easement is known as an **appurtenant easement**. Thus, when the property is sold to subsequent owners, the easement will pass to the new owners as well. Just as the appurtenant riparian and littoral rights are connected to the property itself, so are appurtenant easements.

Easement in gross, on the other hand, refers to easements held by a person and not connected to any particular parcel of land. An example is an easement held by the power company to run electric lines over the airspace of an owner's land or to place utility poles on the property. Likewise with water, sewer, nat-

Figure 2.1—Easement 1

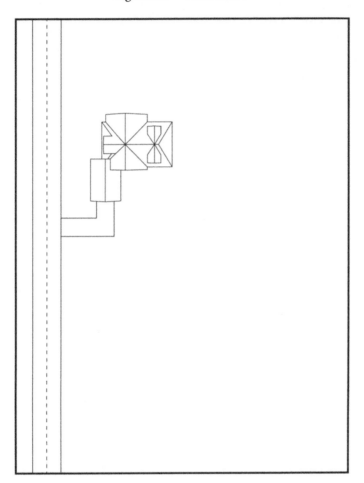

ural gas, telephone, and cable easements. These are held personally and not associated with any other particular parcel of land. Unlike appurtenant easements, easements in gross can be transferred to others as a separate right apart from a parcel of land. Thus, when another power company acquires the local electric company, the power line easements can be easily transferred to the new owners. An easement in gross will have a servient tenement but no dominant tenement, as there is no particular real property associated with the easement rights.

Figure 2.2—Easement 2

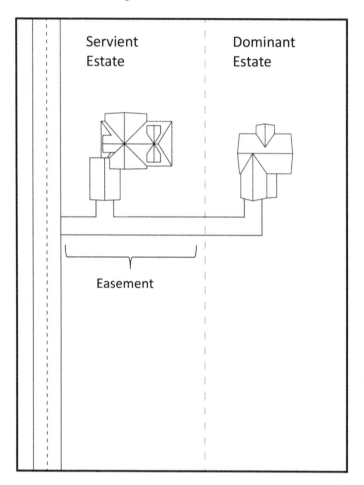

Creation of Easements

Easements can be created in a number of ways. Perhaps the simplest is to create an **easement by deed,** for example, Jim's creating a driveway easement for Chris. Likewise, an easement can be **retained** when transferring property to another. In the example above, Jim could just have easily decided to move into the new house and sell the original one to Chris. In doing so, Jim would retain an easement to use the driveway on the property now owned by Chris.

A third way is **easement by prescription.** In essence, a person who trespasses long enough across land held by another, in the same way as a person who holds a legitimate easement, would eventually hold an easement by prescription. Please note that easements by prescription (or prescriptive easements) are difficult to create. In particular, the trespassing used to create the easement by prescription must continue for a very long time. In Ohio, the use must continue for 21 years. The tests used to determine if an easement by prescription exists will be discussed in more detail in Chapter 8 when we examine the topic of adverse possession.

Finally, it is possible for an **easement by necessity** to be formed when an owner sells part of a parcel of land that has no access to it except over the seller's remaining property. A court order granting the easement is needed to create an easement by necessity. Remember the term *necessity* here. Just because a particular route of access is inconvenient will not suffice; there must truly be no other way to reach a public road except over the seller's property. One cannot create "landlocked" real property in Ohio, with no means of access except perhaps by helicopter. The parcel must have a surface means of access.

Termination of Easements

An easement can be terminated in a number of ways, all of which share a common theme—the easement is no longer needed. First, an easement can be terminated if it contains an expiration date or if it specifies an event that will cause it to be terminated. The situation of an expiration date is pretty obvious, but termination upon the occurrence of a specific event may yield to an example. Suppose a property owner obtains an easement to cross an adjacent parcel while a driveway is being replaced. When the driveway is completed, the easement will be terminated.

An easement can also be **abandoned**. If the easement holder stops using the easement and intends to never use it again, the easement will be terminated. It is up to the owner of the servient estate to prove that the holder of the easement has that intention; the mere fact that the easement is not being used is not enough. The parties can also agree to terminate an easement for a variety of reasons.

Finally, an easement can be terminated through the concept of **merger**. If the same person winds up owning both the dominant and servient estates, that person would surely have the right to use the entirety of both parcels. Thus, the easement would no longer serve any purpose. However, in some circumstances merely owning both the dominant and servient estates will not terminate an easement. For example, the dominant estate might be a rental property that uses the easement for access. A tenant could still need the easement to cross the dominant estate. In this case, the easement would not terminate due to merger.

Licenses

A **license** is a temporary, revocable right to go onto the real property of another. When you go to a football game, your ticket gives you a license to enter the property and watch the game. A license is temporary, so when the game is over, your right to be at the stadium ends and you must leave. Camping out in your seat overnight is not an option. Licenses are also revocable, so you can be ejected if you misbehave. We see examples of licenses all around us, and we frequently do not recognize them as such. When you park your car in a paid lot, you have a license. When you go to a concert, you have a license. When you go to visit your friends, you have a license. You have a license to be in the classroom at college. Just like the football game license, each of these rights to be on someone else's property is temporary and revocable.

Note that the driveway problem that Jim solved by creating an easement could also be solved by a license to use the driveway, but Chris would probably not like this solution. Because the right to use the driveway could be revoked by Jim at any time, Chris would not have the comfort of knowing that the driveway would always be available. Unlike a license, an easement is permanent and cannot be merely revoked later. Clearly, the preferable solution is an appurtenant easement, which will pass to subsequent owners when Chris sells the property.

Profits

A **profit** is very much like a license but with one important difference—the right to take away something from the property. For example, if a landowner agreed to allow a timber company to enter the land, cut down trees, and remove them from the property, a profit would be necessary. The trees are part of the *realty* while growing on the property but become *personalty* when severed from the land. The profit would allow the timber company to cut down the trees and haul them away. (Naturally, the landowner would expect to be compensated for this.) Allowing someone to enter your property and take away something, such as gravel from a pit or rocks from a quarry, would be accomplished by a profit.

Limits on Property Rights

As we will see in Chapter 5, the rights contained in the bundle of sticks are not absolute. Through the exercise of powers held by virtue of the master stick, state, federal, and local governments can impose restrictions on the use of real property. Eminent domain, zoning, building codes, and environmental and other regulations place limits on what can be done on the realty and may even force an owner to sell his or her property.

A landowner can also transfer some of the rights in the bundle by contract or by deed. For example, many residential communities are now subject to a set of rules, sometimes called **covenants, conditions, and restrictions,** or CC&Rs. These can dictate such things as what color you can paint your house, how many flowers you can plant, and what you can park in your driveway, to name a few. These restrictions are considered private land-use restrictions. They were created not by governmental dictate but rather by agreement among home-owners or by a developer. The CC&Rs run with the land and are binding on any subsequent owner of the property. Private land-use restrictions will be more fully explored in Chapter 5.

Discussion Questions

1. Why do landowners have subsurface rights to the land they own?
2. The following parcels of land are adjacent to bodies of water, and the body of water determines the border of the property. For each of the following, describe (1) where the parcel border is located and (2) to what extent the parcel owner can use the water:
    a. A small creek
    b. A private lake
    c. The Ohio River
    d. Lake Erie
3. The text says that property rights extend upward from the borders of a parcel forever. Explain then why a landowner cannot prohibit airplanes from flying over his or her property.
4. Why do you think that the law allows for easements by prescription?
5. Explain the difference between easements, licenses, and profits. Give an example of a situation where each would be the appropriate incorporeal right to use.
6. Why does the power company have an easement in gross and not an appurtenant easement?

Key Terms

Abandoned easement
Accretion

Air rights
Appurtenant
Appurtenant easement
Covenants, conditions, and restrictions (CC&Rs)
Dominant tenement
Easement
Easement by necessity
Easement by prescription
Easement in gross
Erosion
Groundwater
Leasehold interest
Licenses
Littoral rights
Merger
Profit
Riparian rights
Run with the land
Servient tenement
Subsurface rights

Chapter 3

Ownership of Real Property

We have looked at property as a bundle of rights. The right to be there, the right to exclude others, the right to profit from it, the right to sell it, the right to give it away, the right to use water, the right to things above and below the surface, and others, all make up the bundle of rights that we now know as property. We also know about the "master stick"—those rights that are held by federal, state, and local governments that can never be held by anyone else. What's more, we now understand that it is impossible to make an exhaustive list of all the property rights because new ones are being recognized all the time. For example, suppose a new industrial use is discovered for a rare mineral—let's call it "squirdlump." If your property contained the squirdlump mineral, you would have a stick representing squirdlump rights. You could sell, lease, grant a profit to mine squirdlump, and so forth. This is not just a fanciful possibility—not that long ago, having crude oil under your land was considered a nuisance instead of a boon.

In this chapter, we will look at the ownership of property from the perspective of the bundle of rights—especially which sticks in the bundle are being held. In Chapter 1 we briefly described a thing called a leasehold estate, whereby the bundle of rights is divided between the landlord and tenant. Indeed, the differences in the various forms of ownership described in his chapter basically boil down to which sticks in the bundle are held by whom and how those sticks are transferred.

Fee Simple Absolute

When you think of owning real property, you probably are automatically thinking of **fee simple absolute**. In Ohio, the highest form of realty ownership is known as fee simple absolute, sometimes referred to as "fee simple" or just "fee." This is the most complete set of rights that can be held—all of the sticks in the bundle *except* the master stick. The name *fee* comes from the feudal system of landholdings and is derived from the term *fief*, which deals with the concept of holding property in exchange for allegiance and service to the king—which we are alluding to with the master stick.

Remember William the Conqueror and the knight (and other) servitudes? Because all properties came with some duty of service or allegiance, some method of transferring ownership of the property to another—while preserving the servitudes—was necessary. This system would have to create a collective memory of the transaction, together with the servitudes that were attached to the property. Very few people in the 11th century could read (other than the clergy and a few others), so this was accomplished by a form of ritual known as a **feoffment with livery of seisin. Livery of seisin** from the feoffment ceremony can be roughly equated to "delivery of possession." The new owner thereby is able to "seize," or hold, the property.

Imagine people in the village gathering together for a ceremony occurring on the land being transferred. The seller would announce to the audience the boundaries of the property—"running from the river in the north to the edge of the forest in the south, and from the mountains in the east to the sea in the west." Next, the seller would announce the servitudes attached to the land. "You must provide 150 bushels of wheat to the king each year." Then the seller would pick up something representing the land, such as a clod of dirt or a few twigs, and hand it to the buyer. This symbolic transfer indicated the moment at which the ownership of the property passed. The record of this transfer was made in the collective memory of those present at the ritual, because a written record would not be possible. Some have suggested that a baby present at the ceremony may have been spanked at the moment of the transfer to instill in that person a more lasting memory of the event. "When Jacob sold his land to Cravat, you were the one who was spanked to signify the event." This would thus be passed down through the generations: "I was the one who was spanked," and so forth. The moment the clod of dirt was handed to the buyer symbolized the instant the transfer was effective. Because the land was subject to the servitude, the land always had to have an owner who could be specifically known and who was responsible for honoring the servitude.

In a sense, we still perform a feoffment ceremony when we transfer real property, except we now call it a **closing**. The moment of transfer is now indicated by the delivery of the deed. Recording the deed now preserves the collective memory of ownership. A legal description of the property is indicated on the deed. Finally, the "servitudes" of taxes and limits on the property are noted among the documents signed and exchanged at the closing. The closing accomplishes the same purposes as the old ritual. Indeed, many people who go through the closing process feel as though they have been subjected to a confusing and perhaps ancient ceremonial process.

One important concept that emerged from all this is that *real property always has an owner and the owner can be determined with specificity.* Unlike personalty, which can be discarded or abandoned, thereby potentially belonging to no one, real property always needs an owner who is expected to honor the servitude. A visit to the county recorder's office will often disclose the owner of any particular parcel. In those instances where ownership is in dispute, eventually the courts will resolve the issue. In the end, all realty has an owner who can be specifically determined.

As the most complete ownership of realty, fee simple absolute gives the owner the exclusive right to use the property, enjoy the profits from it, change it, sell it, give it away in a will—indeed, do anything on the land that is not restricted by the master stick. Remember that a property owner can impose private land-use restrictions—for example, in the form of covenants, conditions, and restrictions (CC&Rs)—on their own land, and these private restrictions can pass to future owners of the property. Such limitations on the use of land do not change the property from fee simple absolute ownership to something else. The view is that the owner has agreed to the restrictions and will be bound by them, and that does not change the type of ownership of the property. Indeed, much of the land in Ohio is subject to some private land-use restriction.

Generally, when someone purchases real estate, they expect to receive a fee simple absolute interest in the land. However, this is not the only way that real property can be held in Ohio, as we will shortly see. The collection of rights represented by the bundle of sticks can be divided in several ways, each denoting a different form of ownership.

Life Estates

Imagine a house that has been in a family for generations. The current owner, Linda, is a divorced woman who has a daughter from her previous marriage. She now marries Fred, who also has children from his own previous marriage. Linda wants to continue owning the house and to live there with her new husband, and she wants him to continue living there if she should die first. However, when he dies, she will want the property to pass to her own daughter and not to Fred's children.

If Linda were to simply leave the house to Fred in her will, the house would then be his to do with as he pleases, including leaving it to his own children. This would not be a good solution because she would have no assurance that her daughter would eventually wind up with the house. And Linda certainly would not want to die without a will, because Ohio laws would then determine who receives the house. What to do?

A simple solution would be to create a **life estate** for her husband in her will, with her daughter holding the **remainder**. Fred would then be able to stay in the house for the rest of his life, and upon his death, ownership would automatically and instantly pass to Linda's daughter. This could be as simple as the will saying, "I leave my house at 235 Elm Street to my husband, Fred, for his life, and then to my daughter, Catherine."

This would create both a present possessory interest in the property (held by her husband) and a future interest, called a remainder, held by her daughter. The bundle of sticks would be divided between the two. Fred, who would hold the **life interest**, would have the right to be on the property, the right to exclude others (including her daughter during his lifetime), and many of the other rights that we would otherwise associate with fee simple absolute ownership, with some important exceptions. For example, he would not have the right to leave the property in his will, as the property would automatically and instantly pass to Catherine on his death. Any attempt on his part to leave the house to his children would therefore be ineffective. And he could not do whatever he wanted to do while he was in possession of the property. Primarily, he would have a duty to not commit **waste**. That is, he would be obligated to maintain the property, not take anything away from the property (no mining or timber cutting), and preserve the property for the benefit of the person holding the remainder, the daughter.

The duty to maintain will be somewhat limited, however. The life tenant must make necessary repairs but does not have to improve the property. For example, if the roof is leaking, the life tenant must repair the leak but has no obligation to replace the entire roof. In essence, the life tenant must maintain the property in same condition as when the life tenant received the it, less **ordinary wear and tear**. The following are a few examples of ordinary wear and tear versus **damage** to the property:

Ordinary Wear and Tear	Damages
Small nail holes for hanging pictures	Large holes in the walls
Faded or chipped paint	Permanent marker writing on the walls
Carpets faded by the sun or slightly worn	Torn or burned carpets
Dirty curtains or carpet that can be cleaned	Stains or odors that are permanent
Worn countertops	Burns or cuts in countertops
Dusty blinds	Broken, bent, or missing slats in blinds
Water stains on bathroom or kitchen floors	Uncleanable tile or grout

In short, ordinary wear and tear includes those things that one would naturally expect to occur on real property as a result of using the property as it is intended to be used. Damages, on the other hand, are those things that go beyond that.

As you think about things that could happen to real property while the life tenant has possession, you are sure to come up with instances where the delineation between ordinary wear and tear and damages is not so clear as the examples shown above. As is the case with many legal concepts, ordinary wear and tear is easy to understand at the extremes but becomes murky in the middle. In some ways, this is the beauty of the law and something you will grow to appreciate throughout your legal career. I often tell my students, "When you are finished with this course, you may not know many answers, but you will really understand the questions." By this I mean that it is often difficult to determine how the court or jury would rule about a particular issue, but we can come to more fully appreciate the factors that go into their decision.

At first, you may think that one who holds a life estate interest in property could not sell their interest. In our example, where the will simply left the house to Fred for life, there were no restrictions. Thus, Fred could sell his interest to Jim, who would also have the duty to maintain the property for the remainder person. Jim can remain there only while *Fred* is alive, not while *Jim* is alive. This is called a **life estate pur autre vie**. *Pur autre vie* means for the life of another, who is sometimes referred to as the **measuring life**. Thus, if Fred (the measuring life) dies before Jim, all of the rights in the property would immediately and automatically transfer to Catherine, and Jim would have no more right to remain on the property.

A general rule dealing with real estate is that one can always transfer their rights to another, so long as nothing can prevent the transfer. In this case, the will that created the life estate in Fred did not contain any restrictions; thus Fred would be free to sell his interest—the right to be there while he is alive. But beware; Fred can only sell that which he holds—the right to be there for Fred's life. In real estate law, people frequently try to sell more than they hold. Any restrictions or limitations on the property will pass to the next owner. It is important to always investigate and understand any restrictions that may exist on the property when you are working on a transfer of interests in real estate.

An interesting question may arise here. How much is Fred's life estate worth? What would be a fair value for Jim to pay? The short answer is, whatever is agreed between Fred and Jim. But, keep in mind that one of the factors at play here will be Fred's expected longevity. If Fred is 26 years old and in good health, his life estate interest would certainly be more valuable than if he is 86 years old and in poor health. In the case where Fred is older, the risk to Jim is greater as to how long he would be able to stay in the house. As a general rule in real estate, *risk* and *value* are directly related.

Keep in mind that it may be quite difficult, if not impossible, for Jim to borrow money to purchase Fred's life estate. Because Jim would have the right to remain on the property only while Fred is alive, a lender would be reluctant to loan money to Jim for this transaction. Remember, you can only transfer that which you own—thus, the lender could only get a **lien** on the property (the right to recover against the property in the event of a default) to guarantee payment that would be effective during Fred's life. Because the proverbial beer truck could run over Fred at any time, the risk to the lender would likely be too great.

So, it may be difficult for Fred to find a buyer for his life estate interest. But one person may be quite motivated to purchase his life estate—daughter Catherine, who holds the remainder interest. Think this through—when the life estate was created, the bundle of rights relating to the property was split in two. Fred had part of the bundle, and Catherine held the rest. If Catherine purchases Fred's rights, she would then hold all of the rights in the bundle and thus hold the property as fee simple absolute. Anytime a person winds up holding all of the rights in the bundle, that person will hold the property as fee simple absolute. Similarly, when Fred dies, Catherine would have all of the rights in the bundle and a fee simple absolute interest in the property.

Qualified Fee Estates

As the name suggests, **qualified fee estates** involve holding something less than all of the sticks in the bundle of rights. These come in a variety of flavors, and we will look at two of them in this chapter. In general, a qualified fee estate is created by transferring most of the bundle of rights but placing certain qualifications on how the realty can be used—as well as possible forfeiture of the property if the qualifications are not met. This will become clearer as we look at the qualified fee estates in more detail. A few different kinds of qualified fee estates exist—for example, fee simple determinable, fee simple on condition subsequent, and fee simple defeasible—but they differ only slightly in the way they work. For the purposes of this text, we will group them together and speak of them in general. Qualified fee estates are sometimes called **defeasible fee estates**. This is the same thing with a different name.

Suppose you owned a large parcel of vacant land and you wanted to donate that land to the county to be used as a public park. Suppose further that you wanted to ensure that the land would always be used as a public park and never sold by the county to a developer or used in any other way. How could you transfer this realty to the county and make sure that it is so used? A qualified fee estate would do the trick rather nicely. Simply placing restrictive language in the deed transferring the property to the county could create it. "I hereby grant to Larrabee County all of my right, title, and interest in Blackacre,[1] so long as the property is used for a public park." This would create a present possessory interest in Larrabee County and a future interest (called a **reversionary interest**) in you (and your heirs). Clearly, Larrabee County could use the property as a public park, but what would happen if the county attempted to use it otherwise? The reversionary interest would then give the holder of that interest the right to recover the property. The basic distinction between the different types of qualified fee estates is how the holder of the reversionary interest recovers the property. In some of the qualified fee estates, the realty would immediately and automatically be transferred to the holder of the reversionary interest. In other qualified fee estates, the holder of the reversionary interest would have to go to court to complete their right to possess the property.

Naturally, without further restrictions, the county could sell the property to another, but the duty to use it as a public park would transfer as well. Note that the reversionary interest represents a real property interest and part of the bundle of rights, which can be passed from generation to generation. Note that a qualified fee estate could be used to restrict use of land to a particular purpose, or to prohibit certain activities on the land, such as hunting.

Present and Future Interests

We sometimes speak of **present interests** and **future interests** in land. As you might expect, a present interest is one that gives the interest holder the right to possess the property right now, in the present. Conversely, a future interest gives the interest holder the right (or potential right) to possess the property in the future. We have seen examples of both of these. With a life estate, the life estate holder will have a present interest in the property during his or her life, and the person holding the remainder will have a future interest in the property. When the life estate holder dies, the remainder interest holder will obtain a present interest in the property.

---

1. *Blackacre* is a term for a generic and fictitious parcel of land. Real estate professors have used it since at least the 17th century, and I shall continue the tradition.

With qualified fee estates, the present interest can last indefinitely, so long as the property is used as designated. The reversionary interest associated with a qualified fee estate will be a future interest. Note that the reversionary interest may never become a present possessory interest, as the holder of the qualified fee could continue using the property as designated. But that does not extinguish the reversionary interest — the mere *possibility* that the property could be used contrary to the conditions placed on it by the qualified fee will be enough to keep the reversionary interest in place.

Rule in Shelley's Case

Perhaps no principle of real estate law has confused more law students than the **Rule in Shelley's Case**.[2] I think the somewhat arcane language used in this centuries-old case has created much of the confusion. However, the essence of the rule is actually easy to understand.

In the 16th century, whenever the fee simple absolute interest in realty was transferred, a tax had to be paid on the transfer. (This practice is still in effect today in the form of a transfer tax paid to the county auditor.) To avoid this tax, clever lawyers would transfer a life estate to the buyer and a remainder to the buyer's heirs, like this: "I hereby transfer Blackacre to A for life, then to A's heirs."

Since neither A nor A's heirs received a fee simple absolute interest in the property, the transfer was not taxed. As is often the case in tax avoidance schemes, the tax collector did not favor this practice and sued. The court looked at the transfer and reasoned that this was exactly the equivalent of granting a fee simple absolute interest to A, since a life estate plus a remainder interest equaled all of the sticks in the bundle and thus a fee simple absolute. If the transfer had been to A in the form of a fee simple absolute, A could use the property during A's life and A's heirs would inherit it after A's death. The court reasoned that between A and A's heirs, a fee simple absolute resulted. So, any transfer of a life estate to a person with the remainder interest going to that person's heirs became the transfer of a fee simple interest to the person.

You probably are thinking that there are differences between a life estate in A with a remainder to A's heirs and fee simple absolute in A. For example, A will have some duties that would not exist in a fee simple absolute, such as the duty not to commit waste. And indeed there are differences. Ohio abolished the Rule in Shelley's Case in 1953[3]. So, in Ohio, it is possible to create a life es-

---

2. *Wolfe v. Shelley*, 1 Co. Rep. 93b, 76 Eng. Rep. 206 (1581).
3. Ohio Rev. Code § 2107.49.

tate in A with a remainder interest in A's heirs and have it function as intended. So, if this is no longer the rule in Ohio, why did I include this section? Actually, the reason is fairly simple. As you work in your real estate career, you may indeed run across a transfer of property that occurred before October 1, 1953, when the rule was abolished, which would trigger the Rule in Shelley's Case. You will then need to remember that the transfer will be treated as a grant of a fee simple absolute and not a life estate with a remainder.

In this chapter we have examined the various ways that real property can be held, as well as the various restrictions that can accompany them. In the next chapter we will look at how property can be held by more than one owner simultaneously.

Discussion Questions

1. Explain why a baby was spanked at a feoffment with livery of seisin ceremony. What modern concept is now used for the same purpose?

2. Describe why some rights may not be held by a landowner who holds property in fee simple absolute.

3. Barney and Betty were married and the live in a house that Barney owned before the marriage. In Barney's will, he left the house to Betty in the form of a life estate, with the remainder to his son BamBam. After Barney died, Betty sold her interest to Wilma. Explain what interest in the house Wilma has, what duties she owes to BamBam, and what happens to the house when Betty dies.

4. Explain why an elderly widow might want to change ownership of her house such that she holds a life estate with the remainder being held by her children. Assume that this occurred after 1953, so you need not consider the Rule in Shelley's Case.

5. Suppose a rich landowner left 1,000 acres to the State of Ohio on the condition that it be used for a college. The State constructed some buildings and opened a college on the land. Many years later, the State decided to close the college. What happens to the land and the buildings? Assume that the rich landowner died before the college closed.

Key Terms

Closing
Defeasible fee estate
Fee simple absolute

Feoffment
Future interest
Life estate
Life estate pur autre vie
Life interest
Livery of seisin
Measuring life
Present interest
Qualified fee estate
Remainder
Reversionary interest
Rule in Shelley's Case
Waste

Chapter 4

Concurrent Ownership of Real Property

In the previous chapter, we looked at various ways that property can be held in Ohio. We looked at fee simple absolute, where the owner holds all of the rights, represented by sticks in a bundle; ownership that has associated future interests in another person, such as a life estate or a qualified fee; and adverse possession, by which a trespasser can become an owner of real property.

In this chapter, we will examine how multiple people can simultaneously own real property. Not surprisingly, more than one person frequently owns a particular parcel of real property. Married couples, for example, may want both the husband and wife to be owners of their residential home. Brothers and sisters may inherit a particular parcel of real estate. We are also increasingly seeing condominiums, cooperatives, and other forms of joint ownership of real estate.

Severalty as Contrast

"The law is an ass."[1] Just when everything starts to make sense, legal jargon comes along and throws everything out of kilter. The word *severalty*, as applied to real property ownership, would naturally suggest that several people simultaneously own property at the same time. That is both logical and wrong. When real property is held in **severalty**, it means that only one person owns the property. However, let's not stop there. If a corporation, a partnership, or some other joint enterprise owns the realty, it is still held in severalty. This is because the corporation, partnership, or joint enterprise is considered to be one "person," albeit an artificial one indeed. So even though there may be several shareholders of a corporation, perhaps even millions, if the corporation owns

---

1. Charles Dickens, *Oliver Twist* (1838).

real property in its own name, it is held in severalty. The law considers these joint enterprises to be separate from their owners. Thus, the ownership is in severalty. Don't try to reason this one out—just accept it as one of the odd twists in the law of real property.

Tenancy in Common

The most common way for more than one person to simultaneously own real property is by **tenancy in common**. In fact, this is the default situation when an interest in real property is conveyed or devised to two or more persons.[2] It is possible to create other types of joint interests in real property, as will be seen later in this chapter; however, unless special steps are taken to create a different type of joint ownership interest, a tenancy in common will result.

If property is held as a tenancy in common, each owner has an undivided interest in the property and has the right of full ownership and possession of the entire property. So, if Phoebe and Don own a 50-acre parcel of real estate as tenants in common, this does not mean that Phoebe owns 25 acres and Don owns 25 acres. That would be a divided interest. They both together own the entire 50 acres—an undivided interest. What's more, they each have the right to use the entire parcel. Think of it this way—if Phoebe and Don each owned 50 percent of a horse, it is not as though one of them owns the left side and the other the right, or the front and back, or however you might divide the horse. They together own the whole horse. Phoebe has the right to ride the entire horse, as does Don.

This is not to say that tenants in common have to own equal interests in the property. The division could just as easily be 75 percent owned by Phoebe and 25 percent owned by Don. In this case, suppose that the property is a rental house. Phoebe would be entitled to 75 percent of the profit and Don's share would be 25 percent. If Don decided to sell his share of the property, he could sell only his 25 percent interest, not the entire ownership interest. Of course, Phoebe and Don could act together to sell the entire parcel to someone, who would then own all of the interest in the property.

It is not necessary that all tenants in common acquire their interests at the same time. Suppose Phoebe decided to sell her interest in the property to Greg. After the sale, Greg and Don would be tenants in common. A tenant in common interest can be sold, given away, left in a will, mortgaged, or otherwise

---

2. Ohio Rev. Code§ 5302.19.

conveyed to another person without the consent of the other co-owner, so long as doing so does not negatively impact the other co-owner.

Suppose Jennifer's will says, "I leave my house to my two children, Andy and Karen," and the will says nothing more about how the property is to be held. Upon Jennifer's death, Andy and Karen would become tenants in common in the house, each holding an undivided 50 percent interest. Again, a tenancy in common is the default way for more than one person to own real property.

Ohio Statutory Survivorship Tenancy

What happens to a person's interest in real property when that person dies? Remember from Chapter 1 that one characteristic of real property in Ohio is that it always has an identifiable owner. So who then becomes the owner?

I frequently say that the correct answer to every legal question is, "It depends." Of course, that is only the first half of the answer. The second half of the answer is all about the "depends" part. What happens to a person's interest in real property when that person dies? It depends on how the property is held. In the previous chapter, we examined life estates, in which a life tenant has certain rights to possess and use real property during their life, and when they die, the interest in the property automatically passes to the person holding the remainder interest in the property. We will see other ways for an interest in real property to pass upon the death of the person with a present possessory interest in the property.

At the end of the previous section, "Tenancy in Common," Jennifer left her interest in her house to her two children. When a tenant in common dies, that person's interest in real property passes either by the terms of a will or by **intestacy**, where the laws of the state determine how a person's possessions are passed on in the absence of a will. Every state has specific laws that govern how the property of a person who dies without a will is inherited. Of course, all that can be changed by a will. This subject will be examined in more detail in Chapter 14.

But for now, suppose two people (say, brother and sister) want to own real property together, and when one of them dies, the ownership automatically passes to the other. That is, each owner would have an undivided interest in the property, with the right to possess and use the entire property, but when one owner dies, the property would pass to the other. In Ohio, this is particularly easy to accomplish with a **statutory survivorship deed**.[3] The following language will create a statutory survivorship tenancy in Ohio real property:

---

3. *See* Ohio Rev. Code § 5302.17.

I hereby grant Blackacre to Andy and Karen, for their joint lives, remainder to the survivor of them.[4]

When either Andy or Karen dies, his or her ownership interest in Blackacre will automatically pass to the other. Neither Andy nor Karen need to mention anything in their wills—no need to worry about the laws of intestacy, and no need to be concerned about dealing with probate. The transfer occurs instantaneously upon death of one of the survivorship tenants. This is the primary advantage of a statutory survivorship. As we will see in Chapter 14, in order for the survivor to be able to convey clear title of the property to another person, the fact that it has automatically transferred will need to be presented to the county auditor and county recorder in the form of a **certificate of transfer,** or an affidavit and death certificate.

There are some significant differences between a tenancy in common and a statutory survivorship tenancy. Unlike a tenancy in common, where the tenants in common can hold different percentage interests in the property, each statutory survivorship co-tenant holds an equal share of the property. Thus, with three co-owners, each will hold one-third of the interest. When one of the three dies, the surviving two would each hold one-half of the interest. Finally, when one of the two remaining co-owners dies, the sole survivor would hold the property in severalty.

If one of the survivorship co-tenants sells his or her interest in the property, the survivorship aspect is terminated and the owners will become tenants in common. Similarly, if both of the survivorship co-tenants convey all of their interests to a third person, that person will hold the property in severalty. Likewise, if all of the survivorship co-tenants except one convey their interests to the remaining survivorship co-tenant, that person will hold the property in severalty.

Joint Tenancy with Right of Survivorship

In the previous section, we discussed Ohio's statutory survivorship tenancy. The Ohio legislature created this in 1971 to supplant the common law **joint tenancy with right of survivorship** (or JTROS). In a JTROS, just as with an Ohio statutory survivorship tenancy, a co-tenant's share of the property will pass to the surviving co-tenant or co-tenants. In fact, a JTROS functions exactly the same as an Ohio statutory survivorship tenancy. The only real difference is in

---

4. Some additional formalities would be required in a valid deed, which will be discussed in more detail in Chapter 10.

how it is created. With an Ohio statutory survivorship tenancy, specific wording from the statute is required.[5] To form a JTROS, we must look more carefully at the circumstances of the ownership.

To form a JTROS, the co-tenants must share four **unities—unity of time, unity of title, unity of interest, and unity of possession**. These are often remembered by the acronym T-TIP.

Unity of Time	All owners must acquire ownership of the property at the same time.
Unity of Title	All owners must have the same title to the property; if a condition applies to one owner, it must apply to all owners.
Unity of Interest	Each owner must own an equal share in the property. If there are two owners, each must have a one-half interest in the property. If there are three owners, each must have a one-third interest in the property, and so on.
Unity of Possession	All owners must have the right to possess the entire property—that is, an undivided interest in the whole property.

If even one of these unities is not present, a JTROS will not be created even if it was intended, and the result will be a tenancy in common, the default coownership form in Ohio. For example, suppose Jennifer's will had said, "I hereby grant Blackacre to Andy and Karen, to be held jointly." This language would have to be interpreted by a court to determine how the property was held. The court might determine that the language of the statutory survivorship tenancy was not used and therefore a statutory survivorship tenancy was not created. What's more, the court could find that one or more of the unities are not present, thus creating a tenancy in common for Andy and Karen.

Ohio's statutory survivorship tenancy avoids the complexities required for a JTROS and the need to be careful with respect to the four unities. You may

---

5. Actually, the statute reads, "in substance following the form set forth in this section." This would seem to give some leeway as to the exact wording required. However, most careful real estate professionals use the exact wording specified in the statute: "to XXX and YYY, for their joint lives, remainder to the survivor of them...." Using the exact wording from the statute will avoid the possibility of accidentally forming something other than an Ohio statutory survivorship tenancy.

wonder then why we even bother to look at the law of JTROS when a statutory survivorship tenancy exists in Ohio. There are a couple of reasons. First, for conveyances that occurred before 1971, when the statutory survivorship tenancy went into effect, a JTROS was the norm, and you may still encounter them in Ohio. Second, if a conveyance used language other than that required by the statutory survivorship law, perhaps a JTROS could be created instead.

Tenancy by the Entirety

Also in 1971, the Ohio legislature created **tenancy by the entirety**. The original legislation was not clear as to how these forms of co-tenancies worked, so it took a number of court cases to flesh them out. A tenancy by the entirety was available only to married couples. The easiest way to understand these co-tenancies is to think about them as if the *marriage* is the owner of the property, and not either spouse. The husband and wife each hold an undivided half interest in the entire estate, and neither can convey or encumber the property without the consent of the other. Upon the death of one spouse, the property automatically and immediately becomes the property of the surviving spouse in severalty.

In 1984, the Ohio Supreme Court held that a creditor of either husband or wife could not reach property held as tenancy by the entirety. Because the property was essentially being held by the marriage, neither spouse had a personal interest in the property. Thus, the property could not be foreclosed upon to satisfy a debt owed solely by either individual spouse. This is in contrast to a statutory survivorship tenancy, where a creditor can obtain a judgment lien against an individual spouse, which will attach to that spouse's interest in the property. For all of its characteristics, a tenancy by the entirety was highly favored by married couples.

However, the 1984 Ohio Supreme Court decision was not well liked by creditors, who could then not reach what was often the most valuable asset of the couple in order to satisfy a judgment lien. Creditors almost immediately lobbied the state legislature to repeal the law, which it did. Thus, no new tenancies by the entirety could be created after April 4, 1985. I suppose creditors have a better legislative lobby than do marriages.

This does not mean that the existing tenancies by the entirety were eliminated, but only that new ones could not be created. Any tenancy by the entirety that was in place before April 4, 1985, remains valid.[6] Some property in Ohio

---

6. Ohio Rev. Code § 5302.21.

is still held in tenancy by the entirety, so you may very well run into this during your career. Do not be misled into thinking that property held in a tenancy by the entirety is beyond the reach of creditors. If both spouses are responsible for an unpaid debt, creditors may attach liens on the property held by the entirety and sell it to satisfy the joint debt.

Ohio Dower Rights

You may find this section to be the most surprising in the entire book. So, pay careful attention. Almost all states have laws that are intended to protect the rights of married people in their spouse's real estate. Essentially, they are intended to prevent one spouse from financially cheating on the other. These are commonly in the form of **community property**, **curtesy**, and **dower** rights.

Ohio does not recognize community property rights, but these rights automatically exist in a few states, as listed below. In a community property state, all property acquired during the marriage is owned by the community—with each spouse having an undivided one-half interest. The only exceptions are property acquired before the marriage, gifts, and inheritances, which are considered **separate property**. The rules about converting separate property into community property, and vice versa, are rather complicated. Because our focus is on Ohio law, we will not go into further detail.

Community Property States
Arizona
California
Idaho
Louisiana
Nevada
New Mexico
Texas
Washington
Wisconsin
(Alaska allows couples to enter into community property arrangements, but they are not automatic.)

Ohio does recognize dower rights[7]—the right of a spouse to a potential life estate in all real property held by the other spouse in a form that could be inherited and sold during marriage upon that spouse's death.[8] Essentially, dower rights work in the following way: Each spouse holds an **inchoate** (incomplete) interest in all real property that could be inherited that is held by the other spouse at any time during the marriage. For this inchoate dower right to become complete, the owner spouse has to sell the property during the marriage without the non-owner spouse's consent, and then the owner spouse has to die and be survived by the non-owner spouse. At that point, the dower rights become currently **possessory** (meaning that the surviving spouse could then possess the real property), and the surviving spouse would automatically have a one-third life estate in all of the real property sold during the marriage without consent.

Perhaps an example will help here. Suppose Howard and Bernadette are married, and Howard already owned a valuable piece of vacant land before the marriage. Also suppose that after they were married, Howard sold the property to Raj without Bernadette's consent, and Howard died shortly afterward. In the meantime, Raj developed a shopping center on the land. As soon as Howard and Bernadette were married, Bernadette had an inchoate dower interest in the vacant land. Bernadette now has a one-third currently possessory life estate interest in the property, even though Raj currently owns it. Poor Raj—he thought he was purchasing the vacant land from its owner, Howard, but he managed to acquire only part of the sticks in the bundle.

Let me assure you, however, that all of the competent real estate attorneys, agents, brokers, banks, and title companies in Ohio know about dower rights and work to prevent the problem encountered by Howard, Bernadette, and Raj. A release of dower is part of the sales contracts, deeds, and other forms used in real estate transactions. About the only way a dower problem such as the one described above could actually occur would be if Howard sold the vacant land to Raj for cash, used a deed form that Howard found online somewhere, and Raj never bothered to record the deed. Doing so would put the transaction outside the reach of real estate professionals, who would surely see the issues that would be raised.

If a married person has sold real property without the consent of the other spouse, the inchoate dower essentially renders that property unmarketable;

---

7. In some states, the term *dower* refers exclusively to rights held by a wife and *curtesy* refers exclusively to rights held by a husband. In 1953, Ohio abolished use of the term *curtsey*, and *dower* is now used to describe rights held by either spouse.

8. Ohio Rev. Code § 2103.02.

that is, no informed future purchaser could receive good and clear title to the property without resolving the dower issue. Untangling this snarl would surely involve a lawsuit, writing checks to the surviving spouse, or both.

On occasion, the non-owner spouse will discover that they can use their agreement to release dower rights as a lever to extract something from the other spouse. Perhaps that spouse now has power, when none existed in the marriage—to prevent the sale of the real property unless the owner spouse agrees to certain conditions. This can rather obviously get quite ugly.

Condominiums

You have probably heard of a **condominium** (sometimes simply called a **condo**). A condo is a similar to an apartment building or group of buildings where the property is divided into units. However, with a condo, the residents own their own living space. The owners hold their particular unit individually, and the so-called **common area** is held as a tenancy in common with all of the other owners. Typically, a unit consists of the individual living space, sometimes referred to as everything from the "interior paint inward." The common area makes up of the rest of the condominium: the building exteriors, shared hallways, the land itself, together with any shared space, such as a clubhouse or pool. Ownership of a unit in a condominium allows a person to own their own living space without the burden of maintaining a building and grounds.

Chapter 5311 of the Ohio Revised Code controls condominiums. Condominiums are formed solely under state law, and they are created by a **declaration of condominium**, which lays out the covenants, conditions, and restrictions (**CC&Rs**) that govern the development, appearance, usage, and maintenance of the condominium units and common area. The CC&Rs are a form of **private land-use restriction**, which will be discussed in more detail in Chapter 5. Restrictions in the CC&Rs can range from relatively benign conditions, such as the use of a clubhouse or pool, to such detailed things as the color of curtains as seen from the outside of the building, and the number and kind of flowerpots that can be placed on the unit's balcony or patio. Since the purchase of a unit in a condo includes agreement to abide by the CC&Rs, a potential buyer is well advised to carefully read them before purchase to ensure no surprises after the fact.

Management of a condo is typically carried out by a **homeowners' association**, which usually is overseen by a board, which is elected by unit owners. Each owner is assessed a monthly assessment, or dues, which is used to pay for maintaining the common area and managing the property. The home-owners' association has the power to place a lien on units that fall into arrears with their dues. Each individual unit owner is responsible for real estate taxes on their unit.

Because each unit in a condo is individually owned, each owner can mortgage his or her unit in order to finance the purchase or upgrade of it. These mortgage liens cover only the individual unit (and its associated common area) and do not affect any of the remaining units. Thus, if a condo owner defaults on his or her mortgage, only that particular unit is at risk for foreclosure, and the neighboring units are not part of the foreclosure action.

Cooperatives

At first, a **cooperative** (sometimes called a **co-op**) looks a lot like a condo. A co-op is a group of residence units where each resident has an ownership interest in the property, but the similarity stops there. Unlike a condo, a corporation owns a cooperative, and the residents are shareholders in that corporation. The corporation then has a **blanket mortgage** on the entire property, and the residents cannot mortgage their individual living units. The corporation leases living space to the residents in the form of a **propriety lease**. A propriety lease is very similar to a more typical landlord–tenant relationship, except that the lease is for a much longer term (often many years), and the tenant may have much greater rights than under a usual lease. Similar to condo owners, residents of a cooperative share in the management, taxes, and maintenance of the building and grounds. Because the building has a single owner (the corporation), the corporation is responsible for the real estate taxes, and the residents are not taxed on their individual unit.

You may ask why anyone would go to the trouble to set up an odd arrangement like a cooperative—and that would be a good question. The answer is simply the ability to control the selection of persons who are to be residents. Since the entire property is subject to one blanket mortgage, a deadbeat cooperative tenant could put the entire property at risk of default. In a condo, if an owner defaults on making mortgage payments, only that owner's individual unit is at risk of foreclosure. Thus cooperative owners have an interest in only allowing people who are financially able to afford living in the property, to help ensure that the entire property is not at risk of foreclosure. This does not mean that cooperative residents can be completely arbitrary in selecting persons to live in the facility; they are still subject to fair housing laws and rules.

Discussion Questions

Scenario for questions 1 and 2: Tracey wants to transfer ownership of her house, which is located in Ohio, to her three daughters, Sarah, Casey, and Amanda. She wants them to have an equal ownership interest in the property—Blackacre—and not be able to sell their interest without the consent of the others. Tracey would like to keep Blackacre in the hands of her three daughters, such that when one of them dies, the property is automatically owned by the remaining daughters, with the last surviving daughter owning Blackacre by herself.

1. What form of ownership should Tracey use to accomplish these wishes?

2. Write the language that could be used on a deed to accomplish this transfer. (You can use an example from the text as a starting point.)

3. Explain the four unities required for joint tenancy with right of survivorship, and how the Ohio statutory survivorship simplifies things.

4. Describe a situation in which a unsuspecting property purchaser could run into problems with the Ohio dower laws. Describe how to avoid this problem.

5. Describe the difference between a condominium and a co-op. Describe a person who might be interested in living in each of them.

Key Terms

Blanket mortgage
CC&Rs
Certificate of transfer
Common area
Community property
Condominium
Cooperative
Curtesy
Declaration of condominium
Dower
Homeowners' association
Inchoate
Intestacy
Joint tenancy with right of survivorship
Possessory
Private land-use restriction
Propriety lease

Separate property
Severalty
Statutory survivorship deed
Tenancy by the entirety
Tenancy in common
Unity of interest
Unity of possession
Unity of time
Unity of title

Chapter 5

Restrictions on Use of Real Estate

Some people believe that in a free country, they can do anything they would like to do on their own land, so long as it is not a crime. While it is possible to be the outright owner of real property, that does not give the owner the right to do whatever he or she pleases on or with the property. Remember the master stick? It represents the interest that the government has in all real property. The master stick is very powerful and allows for a wide variety of **public land-use restrictions**, such as zoning, health regulations, environmental regulations, and even the power to force a sale of the property for the greater public good. Likewise, an owner of real property can agree with other people to place restrictions on the use of property. These **private land-use restrictions** can take a wide variety of forms. You have already seen one sort of private land-use restrictions in the form of covenants, conditions, and restrictions (CC&Rs) that are associated with condominiums.

Zoning

Would you like to live in a house next door to a lead-smelting factory? How about sending your children to an elementary school adjacent to a sewage treatment plant? Do you think that retail shops should be clustered together in a business district, or scattered around town haphazardly? I think the answers to these questions are self-evident. And if you think about a typical town in Ohio, you will probably recognize that similar uses of land are bunched together — residential housing is located in neighborhoods, shopping areas have compatible stores located near one another, and heavy industrial concerns are off by themselves. To a large extent, zoning is responsible for this.

Zoning divides a municipality into areas, called zones, and defines the type of use that can be made of property in each zone. You may see areas set aside to be used for single-family residences, multi-family residences, commercial busi-

43

nesses, industry, and agriculture. Zoning is mostly a local function and not mandated by the state or federal government. Often, the rules for land-use will be rather complicated. For example, an area zoned R-2 (Residential 2), might have the following requirements:

- Single-family detached dwellings only
- A minimum lot size of one-fourth acre
- A minimum of 50 feet from the street to the front of the house
- Side yards at least 10 feet wide
- A rear yard at least 30 feet deep
- Fences can be no more than 6 feet high
- And many more

Are these restrictions on land-use constitutional? They almost certainly are. Under the state (and local) government's so-called **police power**, so long as the zoning restrictions are a reasonable and nondiscriminatory effort to promote safety, public health, and general welfare, the zoning regulations will be upheld. Under the Equal Protection Clause of the US Constitution, the courts will likely presume the zoning scheme to be valid. While landowners can, on occasion, successfully challenge zoning regulations, it is quite an uphill battle.

Conforming and Nonconforming Uses

As the name suggests, a **conforming use** is one that obeys the zoning regulations. Most real estate will comply with zoning regulations and therefore be a conforming use.

However, suppose the local zoning board decided to expand a residential zone to accommodate an increase in demand for single-family homes in the town. What if an already existing bar and grill is located in the new single-family zone, and it was a conforming use before the zone was expanded? Does the business have to close, be torn down, or converted into housing? Or is there another solution? Wouldn't your innate sense of fairness make you feel that it would be appropriate to allow the bar and grill to continue to operate? For once, the law makes common sense. Under the Due Process and Equal Protection Clauses of the US Constitution, the bar and grill can continue to operate as a **nonconforming use**. This is sometimes referred to as **grandfathering**.

A nonconforming use is one that was in full compliance with the zoning regulations but is no longer in compliance due to a change in the regulations. The nonconforming use can continue, but the eventual goal is that the property converts to a conforming use. Several restrictions are imposed on the continued nonconforming use of the property:

- The property must continue to operate in its present use—that is, it cannot be converted to another nonconforming use. Our bar and grill cannot be converted into a music store, for example.
- The nonconforming use cannot be expanded or altered. Thus, the bar and grill cannot add an outdoor deck for patrons to use in good weather. However, existing structures on the property can be repaired.
- If the owner abandons the nonconforming use for a substantial time (typically two years in Ohio), it cannot be restarted and must become a conforming use.
- If a nonconforming use building is destroyed by fire, flood, wind, or otherwise, only a conforming use can be built to replace it.
- The property can be sold to another owner, who can continue the nonconforming use, but finding a bank to finance the purchase of the property may be quite difficult.

As is understandable, banks may be reluctant to loan money to purchase nonconforming use property because of the risk associated with the ability of the nonconforming use to continue if a structure is destroyed. What's more, if a nonconforming use becomes a **public nuisance**, the local zoning board may terminate the nonconforming use. A public nuisance is something that threatens public safety, health, welfare, or morals or becomes a public annoyance. For example, if our bar and grill plays loud live music every night until 2:00 am, this may not be compatible with nearby conforming single-family housing and would constitute a public nuisance, justifying termination of the nonconforming use.

Exclusive v. Cumulative Zoning

As mentioned before, areas can be zoned in several different categories. Most zoning schemes have multiple versions of each zoning type, with different permissions and restrictions in each one. For example, the township where I live has five different residential zones, including mobile home parks. Zone R-1 is for single-family residences with a lot size of roughly one-half acre; Zone R-2 is for single-family residences with a lot size of roughly one-fourth acre; Zone R-3 is for two-family residences (duplexes); Zone R-4 is for apartment buildings; Zone T is for mobile home parks; and so on. Commercial and industrial zones are similar to this.

Zoning schemes come in two flavors—**exclusive zoning** and **cumulative zoning**. Exclusive zoning, as the name suggests, requires that property be used exclusively in accordance with the zoning scheme. Using the zoning scheme mentioned in the previous paragraph, if an area is zoned R-3 for duplexes, only duplex residences can be placed in that area, and no single-family housing would be permitted. This creates homogenous land usage within a particular zone.

Cumulative zoning, on the other hand, divides property zones into layers, or strata. In this zoning scheme, R-1 is in a higher layer than R-2, which is in a higher layer than R-3, and so on. Property can be used to comply with the current zoning layer as well as any higher layer. Using the previous example, in a cumulative zoning scheme, an area zoned R-3 for duplexes could also be used for single-family residences (as allowed in zones R-1 and R-2). But the converse is not true—if an area is zoned R-2 for single-family residences, that area could not be used for R-3 duplexes, because R-3 is in a lower layer. The following chart shows the difference between exclusive and cumulative zoning.

Zone	Exclusive Zoning	Cumulative Zoning
R-1	Single-family residence with a lot size 1/2 acre or more	Single-family residence with a lot size 1/2 acre or more
R-2	Single-family residence with a lot size 1/4 acre or more	Single-family residence with a lot size 1/4 acre or more
R-3	Duplex	Duplex or single-family residence with lot size 1/4 acre or more
R-4	Apartment building	Apartment building or duplex or single-family residence with lot size 1/4 acre or more

Variances

Suppose you owned a parcel of land measuring 104 feet by 104 feet that was zoned R-2 in our scheme, which requires a minimum lot size of one-fourth acre. Your parcel contains 10,816 square feet, which comes out to about 0.248 acres—just under one-fourth acre. Does that mean you are completely out of luck and cannot build a house on the property? Perhaps not—you could seek a **variance** from the zoning board. A variance is an allowed deviation from the strict rules of zoning. To obtain a variance, you would need to show to the zoning board that strict compliance with the zoning rules would cause practical difficulties and that granting the variance would not cause substantial detriment to the public good. You are almost in compliance with the one-fourth acre rule, being short by only 74 square feet, an area about 8.5 feet by 8.5 feet. You would have an excellent chance of being granted the variance and thus being allowed to build your house on the parcel. The property must still be used in the same way as other properties in the zoning area. For instance, you could not use the variance mechanism to put a factory in a residential zone.

Variances come in two flavors—**use variance** and **area variance**. A use variance seeks to use the property in a way that is not in compliance with a particular zone—putting a commercial establishment in a residential zone, for example. An area variance seeks to bend the rules regarding lot size, building size, setback, and so forth. It is substantially easier to be approved for an area variance than it is for a use variance.

It is easy to confuse variances and nonconforming uses. A variance is a permanently allowed deviation from the zoning requirements that attaches to a particular parcel of land. After a variance is granted, it becomes a conforming use and the law will seek to defend it. Future owners of the land will enjoy the benefit of the variance, which can last *ad infinitum*. On the other hand, a nonconforming use is one that was conforming at one time, but a zoning change caused the property to no longer be in compliance. The property is allowed to continue being used exactly as it was before the zoning change, but the goal is to eventually eliminate the nonconforming use.

Exclusionary Zoning

Suppose a community wanted to have only high-end, single-family homes owned by wealthy residents. Could the zoning board put zoning regulations into place that would restrict property use in the entire area to single-family residences? Could the zoning board require a minimum lot size of, say, 5 acres to keep property values high and thus exclude less well-to-do families? The answer to these questions is a resounding maybe.

Enacting such zoning regulations to exclude certain people is known as **exclusionary zoning**. In general, zoning plans, including exclusionary zoning, have been upheld as a valid exercise of a state's police power. What's more, courts have routinely ruled that people do not have the right to live wherever they choose—indeed there is no fundamental constitutional right to housing.

Surely a zoning plan that created a particular area that was exclusively reserved for persons of a particular nationality would not be compatible with concepts of fair housing. This is an example of **disparate treatment**—where protected classes such as race, color, national origin, religion, gender, age, or disability are treated differently on the basis of membership in the class. However, if the exclusionary zoning has a **disparate impact** on a protected class, the exclusionary zoning plan may violate fair housing laws. A discriminatory impact occurs in zoning when a zoning plan does not discriminate on its face but effectively excludes a protected class. For example, if an entire community's zoning plan allows only for higher-end housing and does not provide for multiple-family residences, this may have a disparate impact on some racial groups, who might not be able to afford housing. In this instance, a court may find that the zoning plan violates fair housing laws by creating a segregated community.[1] Note that exclusion based solely on economic status is not discriminatory on its face and thus does not constitute disparate treatment; but if the effect is to exclude a protected class, it may be disparate impact. This difference is important to understand.

Spot Zoning

Spot zoning occurs when a zoning board acts with respect to a particular parcel of land in a way that is not compatible with the use of the surrounding area. Spot zoning may either benefit or restrict a particular parcel and is an illegal use of the state's police power. As a rather obvious example, rezoning one parcel as industrial to allow for a lead-smelting plant in an otherwise residential area is certainly illegal spot zoning.

Do not confuse spot zoning with use variance, sometimes called **conditional use**, which allows land uses that are strictly inconsistent with a zoning plan but otherwise benefit the area. Conditional use permits allow such things as churches, schools, hospitals, and perhaps even gasoline stations to be located in what would otherwise be residential or other noncommercial areas. These conditional uses are unlike spot zoning in that they are entirely compatible with the use of the surrounding area and are beneficial to the community as a whole.

Building Codes

Building codes are another restriction on the use of real estate. They establish construction standards for structures in a community. Building codes specify such things as the type and use of material, how plumbing and electrical systems are to be installed, and so forth. They are typically enforced by permitting and inspection systems. Before a new structure can be built or an old structure substantially remodeled, plans for the project need to be presented for approval and a building permit issued for the project. A building inspector will then examine the construction at certain points along the way. If the

---

1. *See, e.g., U.S. v. City of Parma*, 661 F.2d 562 (6th Cir. 1981).

inspector detects flaws in the construction, these must be corrected before the project can move to later stages. The purpose of the building codes is to further safety and to help ensure that local structures meet at least minimum standards. Building codes and their enforcement are a valid exercise of the state's police power.

Some property owners ignore the permitting and inspection process and attempt to bypass the system by not getting a building permit when one should be obtained. This is rather foolhardy. In some jurisdictions, if this is discovered, the structure must be torn down at the owner's expense. What's more, many insurance companies will deny a claim for damage to unpermitted structures, so even if everything was constructed properly, a casualty loss might have to be totally borne by the owner—this can create a double whammy. If an unpermitted building is destroyed by fire, the owner not only loses the building but also discovers that the insurance company will rightfully refuse to pay for the damage. And many banks simply refuse to loan money to a buyer of an unpermitted structure. If the property is later sold, the seller must disclose the fact that construction was done without the required permits, which can easily scare away some buyers. Finally, property taxes are based on valuation, and the county assessor uses building permits to be made aware of increased value of property as a result of improvements. Failure to obtain a building permit and the required inspections may be seen by the county as a form of tax evasion—with the attendant fines and penalties. It is far better to simply get the required permit and inspections.

Health Department Regulations

Many locations in Ohio do not have access to a public sewer system. In such cases, wastewater is handled by a septic system. The local health department must approve the septic system and issue a permit before it can be installed and used. The permit will typically include specifications as to where the system is located, its size, requirements for pumps, and so forth. What's more, the health department will periodically inspect the septic system, and the property owner must correct any deficiencies.

Environmental Regulations

Near where I grew up was an old farmer who had quite a few farm machines—tractors, trucks, harvesters, and other such things. Whenever he changed the oil in his equipment, he would simply pour the used oil along the fence line to kill weeds. His attitude was, "They pump the oil out of the ground, so I'm just putting it back."

I think most of us would be a bit taken back by this attitude. We have become more environmentally aware. Today, extensive environmental regulations restrict the right to release material into the air, water, and ground. The farmer's oil disposal and weed abatement program would certainly not pass muster under current standards.

One particular concern is leaking underground storage tanks; sometimes referred to by the rather amusing acronym LUST. For many years, gasoline station fuel and home heating oil was stored in steel tanks buried in the ground. Over time, these steel tanks would rust and begin to leak, sometimes even contaminating the local water table. It is entirely possible that a leaking underground storage tank will do such extensive environmental damage that the cost to remediate exceeds the value of the property. This renders the property unmarketable. Today, tanks made from fiberglass and other materials that do not rust have supplanted steel tanks. Frequently, the newer tanks are of a double wall, tank-within-a-tank design to minimize and control leaks.

A complete discussion of environmental laws and regulations and their impact on real property is far beyond the scope of this book and could easily constitute a text and course by itself. Just be aware that environmental considerations are widespread, and an attorney who practices environmental law should examine concerns that arise in this area.

Eminent Domain

Remember the master stick—representing the rights held by the government? One of the powers held by local, state, and the federal governments is the right to force the sale of private property for public purposes, referred to as **eminent domain**.[2] Indeed this power is so fundamental that it can be found in the US Constitution: "nor shall private property be taken for public use, without just compensation."[3] So what is **public purpose** and **just compensation**?

For many years, public purpose was generally understood to be those things that benefited the public in general. Such things as a road, a sidewalk, an air-

---

2. Eminent domain is sometimes referred to as a "taking" or "condemnation."

3. U.S. Const. amend. V. Even though this is written in the negative, it means that private property *can* be taken, so long as (1) it is for a public purpose, and (2) the property owner is justly compensated.

port, a library, a school, and so on clearly serve a public purpose. But in 2005, the US Supreme Court took this area of jurisprudence in a rather unexpected direction in a case involving a neighborhood in Connecticut.[4]

The City of New London exercised its eminent domain powers to acquire residential property from homeowners, including a landowner named Kelo, and transfer the property to a private developer.[5] The developer did not plan to open the land to the general public but intended to build a hotel, conference center, and upscale housing, among other things. The basic argument made by the property owners who refused to sell to the City was that the planned development was not a public purpose, as required by the Fifth Amendment to the US Constitution. This case eventually found its way in to the US Supreme Court, which essentially held that economic development was a public purpose. Keep in mind that the protection of property owners found in the Fifth Amendment to the US Constitution is a minimum. States can always create a higher standard that must be met.

Since *Kelo*, many states, including Ohio, have strengthened the rights of property owners. In 2007, the Ohio legislature passed Senate Bill 7, which includes the following language:

> "Public use" does not include any taking that is for conveyance to a private commercial enterprise, economic development, or solely for the purpose of increasing public revenue, unless the property is conveyed or leased to one of the following:
> (a) A public utility, municipal power agency, or common carrier;
> (b) A private entity that occupies a port authority transportation facility or an incidental area within a publicly owned and occupied project;
> (c) A private entity when the agency that takes the property establishes by a preponderance of the evidence that the property is a blighted parcel or is included in a blighted area.[6]

Having dealt with the issue of public use as it was expanded by *Kelo* and contracted by the Ohio legislature, we now turn to the question of "just compensation." If the taking under eminent domain is for a valid public purpose, what constitutes just compensation? This is an easy question to understand in concept but can be the subject of protracted litigation in eminent domain cases. In essence, because an eminent domain action is a forced sale, the question of

---

4. *Kelo v. City of New London*, 545 U.S. 469 (2005).
5. It should be noted that many of the property owners voluntarily sold their property.
6. Ohio Rev. Code § 163.01(H)(1).

just compensation is reduced to a determination of fair market value of the property taken. This is frequently resolved by testimony of experts—real estate appraisers and the like. Two different approaches can be used to determine fair market value—depending on how much of the property is taken by eminent domain. If the taking is of the entire parcel, the determination is the value that a knowledgeable and willing buyer would pay a knowledgeable and willing seller for the property, when neither is under any pressure to buy or sell. If the taking was less than the entire parcel, say, as a result of widening a road, then the determination is the diminution in value caused by the taking. In other words, what is the fair market value of the property before the taking and the fair market value after the taking? The difference between the two values is the value of what was taken—thus, the just compensation to be paid to the property owner.

Eminent domain actions are more common than you might think. So long as there is a legitimate public purpose (and there usually is), the real legal dispute is over what just compensation should be paid to the property owner. As you might imagine, emotions can run high when someone has property taken by the government for public use.

For what it's worth, as of the date I wrote this, the land taken by eminent domain that was the subject of the *Kelo* case has not been developed and remains vacant land.

Contractual Restrictions

So far, we have only looked at public land-use restrictions—these are essentially involuntary restrictions placed on the use of real property by governmental entities. Private land-use restrictions have their root in the voluntary right of a property owner to enter into contractual relationships with others and thereby restrict land use. As mentioned earlier, the CC&Rs associated with condominiums and homeowners' associations are an example of contractual land-use restrictions. Commercial developments frequently have their own set of CC&Rs, and property owners can be very inventive in imposing private land-use restrictions.

Often, private land-use restrictions are found in a deed. In addition to transferring ownership, the deed may include **deed restrictions**, such as the following:

- maintaining views
- constructing a certain type of fences

- cutting down trees
- adding garden sheds
- using specified paint colors
- allowing a certain number or kind of pets

In general, so long as the private land-use restrictions are not against public policy and not discriminatory against a protected class (such as a restriction against selling a property to a particular race), they will be upheld by the courts.

However, the concept of **laches** may come into play in private land-use restrictions. Laches is a concept in equity that is similar to statutes of limitation. If a person has a right but doesn't enforce it, the right will eventually go away. For example, suppose the CC&Rs of a particular development prohibit garden sheds on the property. If several property owners ignore that restriction and construct sheds anyway, and no other property owner or the homeowners' association does anything about the sheds, eventually the restriction against sheds will become unenforceable. The old adage applies here: if you don't use it, you will lose it. If you don't enforce the restriction, it will go away.

Discussion Questions

1. Explain the difference between a variance and a non-conforming use.
2. Explain how a non-conforming use can be eventually eliminated.
3. Give an example where a area variance might be given by a zoning board.
4. Explain why the situation in Kelo v. City of New London would not occur in Ohio.
5. Explain the difference between exclusive and cumulative zoning.

Key Terms

Area variance
Building codes
Condemnation
Conditional use
Conforming use
Cumulative zoning
Deed restrictions
Disparate impact
Disparate treatment

Eminent domain
Exclusionary zoning
Exclusive zoning
Just compensation
Laches
Nonconforming use
Police power
Private land-use restrictions
Public land-use restrictions
Public nuisance
Public purpose
Spot zoning
Taking
Use variance
Variance
Zoning

Chapter 6

Real Estate Contracts

Contract law is a huge topic, and we will hit only the high points in this chapter as they relate to real estate transactions. Indeed, Contracts is frequently an entire course by itself, so there is much more to learn and understand than can possibly be included in this chapter. However, you should have a basic understanding of contracts and a good overview of how they work in real estate transactions.

So what is a contract? Is it some special document full of legalese written in dense prose? Is it something that only lawyers can understand? Does it require pages and pages of complex terms? Or is it something else altogether?

Simply put, a contract is nothing more than one or more promises that can be enforced in court. Now, in order for the promises to be enforceable, certain things must be present, but they are not all that complicated. In fact, it is quite likely that you have entered into at least one contract already today. Did you purchase a cup of coffee? You entered into a contract. Did you buy gas for your car? You entered into a contract. Did you eat at a restaurant? You entered into a contract. Did you purchase something from a vending machine? You entered into a contract. Contracts are all around us—we don't always recognize them, but they are a natural part of our everyday life.

We can divide the subject of contracts into three main parts—**contract formation**, **contract performance**, and **contract breach**. Contract formation is all about creating a contract in the first place, which creates the enforceable promises, called **duties**. Contract performance deals with those duties being carried out, and contract breach is concerned with what happens when the duties are not performed.

Types of Contract

First, let's deal with some terminology. In much the same way as we can describe a person as having blue eyes or brown hair, we can describe a contract by some of its characteristics. Just as a person can have blue eyes and brown hair or brown eyes and brown hair, the characteristics of contracts can be mostly mixed and matched as they describe different aspects of the contract.

Executory and Executed

An **executory contract** is a contract where some duties have not been fully performed. For example, if I buy Girl Scout cookies from my neighbor and pay for them in advance, but they haven't yet been delivered to me, this is an executory contract. The duty of delivering the cookies has not yet been fully performed. In contrast, an **executed contract** is one where all of the duties have been fully performed. Using the previous example, when my supply of Thin Mints has been delivered to me, the contract for their purchase has been fully performed and this is now an executed contract. Unfortunately, the term *executed contract* can have two meanings—it can mean (as it does here) that all of the duties have been performed, or it can mean that all parties to a written contract have *signed* (or executed) the contract. You have to look at context to understand which meaning is intended.

Bilateral and Unilateral

A **bilateral** contract is one where each side has made promises about what they will do in the future. Remember that a contract is simply one or more promises that can be enforced in court. For example, suppose we enter into a contract for you to sell your car to me for $500. I promise to pay you $500, and you promise to sign over the title to the car. Bilateral is a promise in exchange for a promise—my promise to pay and your promise to give me title. On the other hand, a **unilateral** contract is one that requires some **performance** in exchange for a promise. The textbook example of a unilateral contract is a reward offer. Suppose my brand-new puppy has vanished and I offer a $100 reward to whomever finds and returns the dog to me. To collect the $100 reward, you must find and return the dog (a performance). Merely promising to find the dog will not do—you must actually find her and return her to me. A unilateral contract is one where it is impossible to exchange promises—instead there will be a performance in exchange for a promise.

Express and Implied

An **express contract** is one that has been stated in words, either written or oral. For example, the contract to purchase your car mentioned earlier is an example of an express contract. The basic terms were explicitly stated. Contrast this with an **implied contract** (sometimes called **implied at law**), where the contract is merely implicit by the actions of the parties. For example, if I go to see my doctor, I am implying that I will pay his fee, even though I don't say so expressly. After all, it would be a bit silly to say, "Doctor, if you promise to treat my broken arm, I promise to pay your fee." But that is exactly what our actions imply when I show up with a broken arm and he puts it into a cast. I think that purchasing something from a vending machine is another example of an implied unilateral contract. The implication made by the vending machine owner is, "If you put $1.50 into my machine, you will receive a cold beverage." Notice that this is indeed an implied promise because the promise to deliver the beverage is not stated. What's more, it is a unilateral contract in that I must actually make a payment (a performance) before I receive my beverage. It would be silly to stand in front of the machine and tell it, "I promise to give you $1.50 if you promise to give me a refreshing beverage," and expect a soda to magically appear.

Valid, Void, Voidable, and Unenforceable

We want to be creating **valid** contracts—ones that are legally binding and enforceable. A valid contract is one that contains all of the necessary elements of a contract—capacity, offer, acceptance, and consideration. These elements will be examined in more detail later.

A **void** contract is one that is a misnomer, because a void contract is simply not a contract at all. It never was a contract and will never be a contract. One or more of the elements of a contract are missing, for example, no consideration. Alternatively, a contract for an illegal purpose is also void. For example, a contract to kill someone in exchange for a payment of money is illegal and thus a void contract. This makes sense, because by definition, a contract is a promise that can be enforced in court. And I think we would certainly agree that no court would enforce such an arrangement.

On the other hand, a **voidable** contract is one that can be canceled by one or more parties. The classic example is a contract entered into between a minor and an adult. The minor can cancel the contract at any time before all of the performances are completed. For example, suppose a minor enters into a contract with a gym for a 12-month membership, with payments due each month. At any time before the end of the contract term, the minor can simply disaffirm the contract and walk away with no further obligation. Unfortunately, the gym does not have a reciprocal right—so long as the minor is paying the membership dues, the gym cannot cancel the contract. Needless to say, it is a foolish adult who enters into a contract with a minor. Some exceptions to this rule deal with necessaries and emancipated minors, but that discussion is beyond the scope of this text.

Finally, an **unenforceable** contract is missing something that is necessary to make it enforceable. For example, as we will see in the next section, certain contracts must be in writing to be enforceable, say, a contract for the conveyance of an interest in land. An oral contract to purchase a house generally will be unenforceable, unless some exception applies.

Written and Oral

Contracts can be **written** or **oral** (spoken). A written contract is just what it says, one that has been reduced to writing. Quite likely when you began thinking about contracts, you had a written contract in mind—one that is written on paper and signed at the end. If I go into a restaurant and order a burger and fries, no written contract is signed by the restaurant and me. Instead, I simply give my order, and a few minutes later, out comes my meal. This is still a valid contract and I will get nowhere trying to argue that I didn't expect to pay for it and that the restaurant must be making a gift of the burger and fries. I think it's pretty clear that this is a contract—even with some of the particulars created by implication. Here's how my interaction would most likely be interpreted by a court—"I promise to pay you the price stated on the menu for a burger and fries if you promise to bring them to me."

The problem with oral contracts is in proving that they exist and proving their terms, not in creating them. The old adage "An oral contract is not worth the paper it is written on" may be a bit humorous and does have an element of truth to it, but enforceable oral contracts are entered into all the time. The difficulty is frequently not so much in proving that the contract exists, but dealing with the particulars of the transaction. I think my restaurant example is pretty clear that the particular terms of the transaction will be taken from the restaurant menu. The problem becomes more troublesome when there is not something as handy as a restaurant menu to fill in the gaps of an oral contract. Courts, however, will frequently fill the gaps by looking at what a **reasonable person** would understand as the terms of the contract.[1] A reasonable

---

1. A "reasonable person" is defined as "a hypothetical person used as a legal standard ... a person who exercises the degree of attention, knowledge, intelligence, and judgment that society requires of its members for the protection of their own and of others' interests. The reasonable person acts sensibly, does things without serious delay, and takes proper but not excessive precautions." *Black's Law Dictionary*, 1050 (Bryan A. Garner, ed. abridged 9th ed. West 2005).

person would not expect to get a meal for free at a restaurant and would understand that the restaurant expected to be paid the stated price on the menu when ordering the food. Similarly, in other circumstances, courts will look to the normal practice in the particular situation and what a reasonable person would understand the missing terms to be.

Statute of Frauds

Certain contracts, however, must be in writing and signed by the parties in order to be enforced. These are covered by the **statute of frauds**, which details the contracts that must be in writing. An easy way to remember these particular contracts is with the mnemonic MYLEGS. Each letter refers to a particular kind of contract that must be in writing to be enforceable. Let's look at each of these in order:

M	Marriage—a contract in contemplation of marriage. For example, a prenuptial agreement must be in writing to be enforced.
Y	Year—a contract that, on its terms, is impossible to fully perform in less than a year. For example, a 5-year lease on a car must be in writing to be enforced.
L	Land—a contract for the conveyance of an interest in land. For example, a contract to purchase a house must be in writing to be enforced.
E	Executor—in a probate estate, if the executor (the person who manages the estate) agrees to personally pay for a debt of the estate. For example, a daughter probating her mother's estate may feel some personal responsibility to her mother's good reputation. If she agrees to pay some of her mother's debts, this must be in writing to be enforced.
G	Goods—any contract for the sale of goods for $500 or more must be in writing to be enforced.
S	Surety—an agreement to answer for the debts of another. For example, cosigning for a loan must be in writing to be enforced.

In the next chapter, we will look at leases, which have a contractual aspect to them. So, do leases have to be in writing to be enforceable? It depends. As we will discuss more fully there, a lease is not a *conveyance* of land; instead, it is a *transfer of rights*. Therefore, a lease does not have to be in writing to be enforced unless it is a lease for more than one year. The L aspect of MYLEGS does not apply, but the Y aspect does in a lease for more than one year. However, it is common practice to put leases in writing to make sure that the parties fully understand each other's rights and responsibilities.

Exception to the Statute of Frauds

Even though the statute of frauds requires certain contracts to be in writing, the **doctrine of part performance** provides an exception. If the parties have **substantially performed** the contract, then a court can enforce the oral contract. For example, if you and I enter into an oral contract for me to purchase your house for $120,000, and I move in with your permission and make repairs and other modifications to the property, such as replacing the roof, a court has the power to enforce the purchase contract, even though it is not in writing. However, please note that merely making payment, without anything more, will not be sufficient. In the example, you allowed me to move into the house, and I replaced the roof. Both of those represent substantial performances. The law is sometimes logical—an owner would not allow someone to merely move into a house and a purchaser wouldn't just spend a few thousand dollars to replace a roof without an underlying purchase agreement. Thus, the logical thing for the court to do is to cause me to pay you the purchase price and you to deliver a deed to the house to me.

Contract Formation: Elements of Valid Contract

Not every promise will create an enforceable contract. For example, if I promise that it will rain tomorrow, surely you can see that as an unenforceable promise. However, if I promise to pay you $120,000 to purchase your house— that creates an enforceable contract. To create a contract, we must find the basic elements of **capacity, offer, acceptance,** and **consideration.** We will look at each of these elements in turn.

Capacity

To form a contract, both parties must have **capacity,** that is, the right and power to enter into a contract. As discussed earlier, minors (in Ohio, under the age of 18) do not have capacity to enter into contracts. Likewise, people who have serious mental illnesses do not have the capacity to enter into contracts. If someone has been judged as incompetent and has a guardian appointed for them, they lack capacity to contract. Serious chemical dependency, including drugs and alcohol, *may* create a lack of capacity, but courts are fairly reluctant to declare a person who is voluntarily under the influence of drugs or alcohol to lack capacity, mostly because that person put himself or herself in that condition. Generally speaking, everyone else has capacity.

Offer

An offer is a proposal to enter into a contract, made by one known as the **offeror** to someone known as the **offeree**. An offer gives the offeree the power to create a contract by accepting the offer. An offer has the following elements:

Promise	An offer must include a promise to do something in the future. For example, "I promise to pay you $400 for your blue car." The promise can by implied. For example, if I order a meal at a fast-food drive-up, I probably will not use the word "promise," but I am certainly implying that I promise to pay for the food.
Communication	The offer must be communicated to the offeree. One cannot accept an offer that he or she does not know about. An offer is effective when received by the offeree.
"Enough" terms	For the court to enforce a contract, the offer must include sufficient specificity so that the court can work out what was intended. In the earlier example under "Promise," if the offeree owned two blue cars, the offer would be ambiguous and unenforceable, because the court would not be able to figure out which blue car was intended.
Intent to be bound	The offeror must have the intent to form a contract and be bound by that contract. Note that this is determined by an **objective** standard—would a reasonable person believe that the offeror intended to be bound? What the offeror **subjectively** intended doesn't matter. If you were kidding, but a reasonable person would understand you to be serious, you may create a legally binding offer. On the other hand, an offer clearly made in jest will not be binding. Suppose my car would not start in the parking lot of the mall, and I said, "For two cents, I'd sell this piece of junk." A reasonable person probably would not understand this to be a serious offer and present intention to sell the car for only two cents.

Offers do not last forever. When an offer has been terminated, it is no longer effective. An offer can terminate in any of the following ways:

Lapse of time	An offer can specify how long it will remain open. For example, the offer might state that it is valid for only 24 hours. If the offer does not state a termination time, it will remain open for a reasonable time. (See "Time Is Of The Essence" later in this chapter.)
Destruction of subject matter	If the subject of the contract is destroyed, the offer is terminated. For example, an offer to purchase your blue car will terminate if the blue car is destroyed in a fire.
Death or incapacity	An offer terminates if one of the parties dies or becomes incapacitated.
Revocation	Generally speaking, the offeror has the right to revoke an offer at any time before it is accepted. One major exception to this is an **option contract**, which is essentially an agreement not to revoke an offer for some period of time. A revocation is effective when the offeree receives it.
Rejection	If the offeree rejects an offer, that offer immediately terminates. The offeree cannot later change his or her mind and resurrect the offer. When an offer is rejected, it is finished. Consider the following series of communications between persons A and B:
	A1: "I will sell you my blue car for $300." B1: "That's too much. I'll pay $250." A2: "No way will I sell it for only $250." B2: "Ok, I'll pay the $300."
	You may be surprised, but there is no contract here. Let's look at the communications in order.
	A1—this is an offer to sell the car for $300. B1—this is a rejection of the offer and a new offer to purchase the car for $250 A2—this is a rejection of the offer to purchase for $250 B2—this is a *new offer* to purchase the car for $300. The original offer to sell the car in A1 was rejected by B1 and can no longer be accepted. B2 is simply a new offer to purchase the car for $300 and must be accepted by A to form a contract.
	The B1 communication is sometimes called a **counteroffer**. Sometimes confusion surrounds counteroffers. A counteroffer is simply a rejection of an offer along with a new offer with different terms. A counteroffer is not somehow more binding than the original offer. The fact that a counteroffer has been made may be an indication that the parties are getting closer to a deal, but the counteroffer is still nothing more than a rejection and a new offer.

Acceptance

An offeree has the power to form a contract by accepting the offer. An acceptance has the following elements:

Mirror-image rule	The acceptance must "mirror" the offer. In other words, the terms of an acceptance must be exactly the same as the terms of the offer. Any attempt to alter the terms of the offer acts as a rejection and a new offer (counteroffer). The parties must have a "meeting of the minds." If the offeror has communicated an offer to sell one car but the offeree believes that they are talking about a different car, there is no meeting of the minds and there is no contract.
Correct person	Only the person to whom the offer is made can accept the offer. You cannot accept someone else's offer.
Do what the offer requires	The offeror controls the offer. An offer to form a unilateral contract must be accepted by performing. Once again, the classic example of a unilateral offer is a reward offer. You cannot accept a reward to find a lost dog by promising to find the dog; you must actually find the dog. Likewise, an offer to form a bilateral contract must be accepted by promising to perform in the future.
Communication	The acceptance must be communicated to the offeror. While most communications in contract formation are effective when received, acceptances have a different rule. An acceptance is effective *when properly sent*. This is sometimes referred to as the "mailbox rule." The acceptance is effective, and a contract formed, as soon as an acceptance letter is dropped in the mailbox. Consider the following letters mailed between A and B:
	A1: "I will sell you my car for $300." This is effective when B receives it. B1: "I accept your offer to purchase the car for $300." This is effective when B mails it. A2: (Before receiving the acceptance letter from B) "I revoke my offer to sell my car."
	The contract between A and B was formed when B dropped letter B1 in the mailbox. Since a revocation is effective when received by an offeree, the A2 communication is of no effect, because the acceptance of an offer changes that offer into a contract. The original offer can no longer be revoked.
Silence as acceptance	Generally speaking, silence cannot indicate acceptance of an offer. The offeree must take some action to accept it. The following offer would not work: "I will sell you my blue car for $300. If I don't hear differently from you before 5 p.m. tomorrow, I will consider you to have accepted my offer."

Consideration

The final element in contract formation is **consideration**. In essence, this is what the parties have bargained for in the contract. Consideration is all about what each side gives up, not what they receive in return. Consideration is sometimes referred to as **legal detriment**. To have consideration, each side must either (1) do something that they have no duty to do otherwise, or (2) refrain from doing something that they have the right to do otherwise. In the example of selling a car for $300, the seller's consideration and legal detriment is giving up the car, and the buyer's consideration and legal detriment is giving up $300.

It is always better to look at consideration from the perspective of what is being given up, and not what is received. For example, I could agree not to ever travel to Timbuktu in exchange for $100. My consideration is my promise not to travel to Timbuktu, something I presently have the right to do. The other side's consideration is paying me $100, something they do not have any obligation to do. It does not matter that the other side does not receive anything other than my promise. They do not need to benefit from the transaction — what's required is that each side gives something up.

You may wonder how this would ever be enforced. When do I earn the $100? When I die, having never been to Timbuktu? No. I earn the $100 immediately with my promise not to travel to Timbuktu. I have given up my right to travel there — that is my legal detriment, my consideration. What happens if I indeed go to Timbuktu? This is now a breach of my promise not to travel there and thus a breach of the contract. This may give rise to damages, as we will discuss later.

So long as no other defect is in a contract, courts will not examine the **adequacy of consideration**. In other words, the parties to the contract strike their own deal and are bound by it. So, if a seller later believes that he sold his house for less than it was worth, the courts will not go back and change the terms of the contract. Any consideration, no matter how small, is adequate to form a binding contract. In fact, the classic example is that the exchange of one peppercorn is adequate consideration to purchase the Empire State Building.

Advertisements as Offers

Generally speaking, advertisements are not offers. Rather, they are invitations to make offers. Consider a For Sale advertisement in the newspaper for a house. If this were an offer, who could accept it? Anyone who reads the paper?

What if three people try to accept the offer, but there is only one house? Surely the same house can't be sold to three people simultaneously. The advertisement is merely an invitation for people to make offers to purchase the house.

As always, there is an exception to this general rule, but it requires some rather unusual facts. Suppose an advertisement read as follows, "The first person to enter XYZ store on Wednesday, July 18, can purchase a brand-new electric toaster for only $1.00." Now, we have clearly identified the person who can accept the offer—the first person to enter the store on that date. Likewise, only one person—the person to find the lost pet—can accept an advertisement for a reward offer.

Contract Performance

After a contract has been formed, the parties have a **duty** to perform the promises that were made as part of the offer and acceptance. This would seem to be simple enough, but some things can cause duties, or indeed entire contracts, to be set aside and become unenforceable. We will look at some of these in the following sections.

Conditions

Frequently, contracts contain certain **conditions** that affect the duties of the parties. For example, a residential real estate purchase contract may include a condition that the property passes a termite inspection. If the property does not pass the inspection, the condition is not met and the duty to purchase the house is discharged. In the language of real estate, these conditions are frequently referred to as contingencies. Other common conditions in residential real estate contracts include such things as obtaining financing to purchase the property and the sale of another residence, where the proceeds from that sale are needed for the purchase.

Impossibility of Performance

The law does not require people to do things that are **impossible**. Some things that can make performance impossible include destruction of the subject matter or death of someone who is to provide a personal service that cannot be provided by someone else—for example, the death of an artist who was hired to create a piece of art for a building. If a house is destroyed by a tornado, it is impossible for the seller to deliver the house to the buyer. Note that this requires absolute impossibility, not mere difficulty or even extreme hardship. Unforeseen additional costs to perform do not constitute impossibility. Impossibility requires that *no one* could perform the duties under the contract.

Fraud, Duress, Undue Influence, and Mutual Mistakes

Grounds for voiding a contract include fraud, duress, undue influence, and mutual mistakes. **Fraud** is basically lying (or failing to disclose something you have a duty to disclose), intending that someone will rely on it; they do rely and are harmed. For example, if the seller tells a potential buyer that the basement of a house never floods, but it regularly does so during the spring months, and the buyer purchases the house relying on this lie, the buyer will certainly be harmed when the basement fills with water the next spring.

Duress and **undue influence** are similar in that a person exerts some force or power over another to enter into a contract. Threatening physical harm unless a person agrees to sell their house would be an example of duress. Undue influence is similar, in that someone uses a position of power to cause someone to act. For example, a caregiver might exert undue influence over an elderly person in their care.

Mutual mistakes go to the heart of the contract. If both the offeror and offeree are mistaken about a material aspect of the contract, there was no meeting of the minds and the contract is void. For example, *both* the buyer and seller incorrectly believe that a particular horse is a valuable racehorse. They enter into a contract for the purchase and sale of a valuable animal, but the mutual mistake can make the contract voidable. Note, however, that if only one party was mistaken, that does not excuse performance. Using the same example, if the buyer mistakenly believed the animal to be a valuable racehorse and purchased it thinking he would turn a quick profit, this is only a **unilateral mistake** and the buyer would be obligated to live with his error. Likewise, if the seller mistakenly believed the animal to be only ordinary when in fact it was quite valuable, this unilateral mistake on the seller's part would not be sufficient to void the contract. Courts do not generally look at the intrinsic fairness of a transaction but hold the parties to the bargain they have made. Otherwise, the courthouse would be flooded with people who did not like the deal they struck.

Contract Breach: Damages

What happens if a party to a contract does not fulfill the duties required by the contract? This is a **breach of contract** and gives rise to damages. The ordinary measure of contractual damages is **compensatory damages** and is a simple subtraction problem:

	What the party should have received under the contract
MINUS:	What the party actually received
EQUALS:	Compensatory damages

The goal of compensatory damages is to compensate the person who did not receive what was agreed in the bargain. The parties should be compensated for any losses they incurred. So, if a party was to have made a profit on the transaction, that profit would be included in the losses.

The nonbreaching party has a duty to **mitigate damages**. That is, to take actions to prevent the damages from getting any larger. For example, if a renter breaches an apartment lease contract by moving out earlier, the landlord is entitled to damages equal to the amount of unpaid rent for the remainder of the lease term. However, the landlord has a duty to mitigate damages by taking actions to rent the apartment to another tenant. If the landlord rents the apartment to a new tenant, the compensatory damages will not be for the entire remainder of the original lease term, but only for the period while the apartment was actually vacant.

Ordinarily, **punitive damages** (damages designed to punish) are not awarded in breach of contract cases. Instead, the courts try to put the parties in the position they would have been in had the breach not occurred. Punitive damages are sometimes awarded for intentional torts, but not for contracts. However, it is possible to commit a tort in connection with a contract. For example, if someone held a gun to a seller's head to force the sale of a house, the contract would be void for duress, but a separate tort of assault will result from the gun being used this way. The court may award punitive damages for the tort of assault, but not for the voided contract.

Liquidated damages are an amount of money that the parties agree upon and write in the contract in the event of a breach of the contract. These damages are an amount that the breaching party will pay to the nonbreaching party. Courts will generally uphold a liquidated damage provision in a contract only if it is difficult to calculate actual compensatory damages and the court does not construe the liquidated damage amount as a penalty. Note that liquidated damages are *instead of* and *not in addition to* compensatory damages.

Specific performance is a remedy that the court can use in certain instances to order the parties to perform their duties under the contract. Specific performance requires that the subject matter of the contract be unique and money damages would not be adequate. For example, suppose a museum contracts with the Louvre to purchase the Mona Lisa painting for $500 million, and on the day that the closing is to occur, the Louvre reneges and refuses to deliver the painting. Because the Mona Lisa is unique and money damages would not adequately compensate the other museum (because the museum couldn't go buy another Mona Lisa), the court could order the Louvre to deliver the Mona Lisa and the other museum to pay the $500 million. Interestingly enough, real property is *always* considered to be unique. So, if a seller reneges on delivering a deed in connection with the purchase of a house, specific performance may be an available remedy for the buyer.

Earnest Money

In residential real estate transactions, it is quite customary for the buyer to pay some **earnest money** at the time the buyer makes an offer to purchase a home. The earnest money is simply a payment made to demonstrate the buyer's sincerity in wanting to purchase the property. The earnest money is typically held in trust by the buyer's real estate broker and will be applied to the purchase price at closing. Note that earnest money is not an element of contract formation but is intended to show to the seller that the buyer is serious about buying the house.

If the deal does not close and the buyer is not at fault for the failure to close, the buyer should receive a refund of the earnest money. Some sellers believe that if the deal does not close because of something the buyer has done wrong, the seller gets to keep the earnest money. Perhaps that is so, but the seller should approach that concept with caution. The court could look at the seller's keeping the earnest money as *liquidated damages*, and that will be seller's only remedy. Consider the following example of why keeping the earnest money may be foolhardy:

> Suppose Buyer and Seller have contracted for the sale of Seller's house for $200,000, and Buyer has paid earnest money in the amount of $1,000. Before the closing, Buyer backs out of the transaction without any valid reason. This is a breach of contract, and Seller will be entitled to receive damages. Remember, Seller has a duty to mitigate damages, so Seller immediately puts the house back on the market. In the meantime, the housing market takes a downturn, and despite serious efforts on the part of Seller, the house eventually sells for

$190,000. Remember the basic formula for contract damages—the difference between what Seller should have received under the contract and what Seller actually received, or in this case, $200,000—$190,000 = $10,000. So, the normal measure of compensatory damages would be $10,000. If Seller had merely kept the $1,000 earnest money, the court could treat that as liquidated damages and that would be Seller's sole remedy. I think Seller would much rather receive $10,000 in damages than $1,000.

Time Is of the Essence

Ordinarily, contract performance is expected to be completed in a *reasonable time* (there's that *reasonable* word again). However, if the words **time is of the essence** are included in a written contract, any dates or timing in the contract are considered to be an essential and material part of the transaction and will be strictly enforced. For example, imagine a real estate purchase contract that includes the following provision:

> The transaction contemplated by this agreement shall close no later than midnight June 15, 2016. Time is of the essence.

If either side causes the transaction not to close by that date, this will be a material breach of the contract and the other side may be entitled to damages. Without the "time is of the essence" clause, the general rule is that the transaction must close within a reasonable time after the deadline, and that will not be a material breach of the contract.

Parol Evidence Rule

Parol evidence is oral testimony offered to contradict or supplement a final, complete written contract. Generally speaking, parol evidence is not allowed in a contract dispute. However, parol evidence may be allowed to show that the contract is not final or complete or that there was some defect in forming the contract, such as fraud. But courts are not rigid, unthinking institutions. If the written contract is ambiguous and does not clearly state the parties' intentions, parol evidence may be allowed to untangle the ambiguity. Wise legal professionals work diligently to avoid ambiguity, as any piece of litigation can have unexpected outcomes. One should not rely on the possibility that a future court case would resolve issues created by poor drafting.

Assignment

Assignment occurs when one party to a contract transfers rights under the contract to someone else. For example, a bank may sell a mortgage loan to another financial institution, a fairly common practice. The bank would then assign their mortgage loan contract to the other financial institution. The new financial institution would then have the right to receive the mortgage payments and could exercise all of the original bank's rights under the contract, including the right of foreclosure.

Technically speaking, one *assigns* rights and *delegates* duties. However, the usual use of the term *assignment of contract* includes both assignment of rights and delegation of duties. It is possible to split rights and duties apart and transfer only one or the other—in such a case, it should be made clear exactly what is being done.

In Ohio, *all* contracts can be assigned, with only two major exceptions. First, if a written contract includes a statement that it cannot be assigned, any attempt to assign the contract will not work. Second, **personal service** contracts cannot be assigned at all. A personal service contract is one where the essence of the bargain is that a specific person will perform the contract. For example, a concert promoter may contract with a particular musician. The bargain is for this particular musician to perform, and the musician cannot assign the contract to another person. Surely the concertgoers would not be happy to pay to hear one performer but find out at the concert that someone else will be playing.

The party assigning the contract is known as the **assignor**, and the party to whom the contract is assigned is known as the **assignee**. When a contract is assigned, the assignor remains secondarily "on the hook" for duties and liabilities under the contract. So if the assignee breaches the contract, the other party can seek damages from both the assignee and the assignor. Merely assigning a contract does not extinguish one's duties under it. The next section will discuss a couple of ways to relieve the original contracting party from duties under the contract.

Novation, and Accord and Satisfaction

A **novation** occurs when the parties *agree* to substitute someone else for a party who wishes to withdraw from the contract. This is different from an assignment, because no agreement is necessary to assign a contract—contracts are freely assignable, but the assignor remains liable for the performance of the assignee. Even if the contract includes a statement that it cannot be assigned without consent, consent to assignment does not relieve the assignor of liability under the contract. A novation accomplishes this by an agreement to substitute a new person to the contract and relieve the original person of any further liabilities or duties under the contract.

The term *novation* can also refer to substituting a new and different contract for an old one. The original parties may remain on the new contract, or new parties may be substituted.

An **accord and satisfaction** is an agreement to substitute new performances for those originally contained in the contract. Performance of the new obligations relieves the parties of duties under the original contract. For example, suppose a buyer and seller have contracted to purchase and sell a house for a particular price. If a termite inspection reveals the need for costly repairs, the buyer and seller could agree to a reduced purchase price in an accord and satisfaction — the agreement to the reduced purchase price being the *accord*, and the payment of it being the *satisfaction*.

Discussion Questions

1. Give an example of a unilateral contract other than a reward offer.

2. Grace recently orally agreed to purchase Marsha's house. Grace moved in, replaced the furnace in the house, resurfaced the hardwood floors, and made two payments to Marsha. Last week, Marsha told Grace that because there was no written contract, as required by the statute of frauds, that the oral agreement for the sale of the house was unenforceable.

Discuss this situation, and what would you tell Grace?

3. You received the following letter in the mail from one of your friends:

"I am considering buying your car and am willing to pay as much as $1,000 for it, if my wife likes the car. Unless I hear differently from you by noon next Thursday, I will consider that you have accepted this offer."

Is this a valid offer? Why or why not? Discuss each potential problem.

4. Discuss the difference between the following:

a. An offer and a counteroffer

b. A rejection and a counteroffer

5. Bob bought an oil painting at Fred's garage sale for $50. He thought it was a valuable piece of art and planned to sell it to his art collector friend. When the art collector saw the painting, he told Bob that it wasn't even worth $10.

Bob went to Fred and demanded his $50 back, saying he would sue if Fred did not refund his money.

Discuss the law and probable outcome in this case.

6. You saw an advertisement in the local newspaper placed by a Lexus dealer, which read:

> "Brand new 2016 Lexus RX, VIN number 1LM2253KL36J4. Saturday only, $2,000. This is not a misprint. Only one available at this price to the first person with cash money."

You were the first person to arrive at the Lexus dealer on Saturday and had 20 crisp $100 bills with you. The salesman said that because advertisements are invitations to make an offer, they were rejecting your offer of $2,000.

Is the salesman right?

7. Give an example with enough detail to explain the outcome as to why performance might be excused for each of the following reasons:
   a. Mutual mistake
   b. Nonoccurrence of a condition
   c. Undue influence
   d. Impossibility

8. Explain why it might be a bad idea for a seller to insist on receiving the earnest money deposit when a buyer wrongfully breaches a real estate purchase contract.

9. Describe a situation where a liquidated damages provision would be appropriate in a real estate contract.

10. Explain the difference between (a) a novation and (b) an accord and satisfaction.

Key Terms

Acceptance
Accord and satisfaction
Adequacy of consideration
Assignee
Assignment
Assignor
Bilateral contract
Breach of contract
Capacity
Compensatory damages

Consideration
Contract breach
Contract formation
Contract performance
Counteroffer
Doctrine of part performance
Duress
Duty
Earnest money
Executed contract
Executory contract
Express contract
Fraud
Implied at law
Implied contract
Impossibility of performance
Legal detriment
Liquidated damages
Mitigate damages
Mutual mistake
Novation
Objective standard
Offer
Offeree
Offeror
Option contract
Oral contract
Parol evidence
Performance
Personal service
Punitive damages
Reasonable person
Specific performance
Statute of frauds
Subjective standard
Substantially performed
Time is of the essence
Undue influence
Unenforceable contract
Unilateral contract

Unilateral mistake
Valid contract
Void contract
Voidable contract
Written contract

Chapter 7

Landlord–Tenant Law

Chances are good that you have been part of a landlord–tenant arrangement at some point. You may have rented an apartment or a room in someone's house. You may even have informally agreed to stay in someone else's apartment or home and paid something for the right to stay there. In any of these cases, you have been subject to Ohio's landlord–tenant law, even if you did not sign a lease or rental agreement.

There is also a great possibility that many of the stores you shop at on a regular basis are rented by the storeowner from a commercial landlord. Likewise, much office space, including many law offices, are located in rented space in an office building.

Leases basically come in two flavors—residential and commercial. This chapter will begin with a discussion of **residential leases** (sometimes called a **rental agreement**).[1] Residential leases, as the name implies, deal with the rental of places where people live, as opposed to **commercial leases**, which are concerned with renting real property of every kind other than places for people to live.[2]

Because residential leases are concerned with places that people live, more laws are in place to protect the residential tenant. Commercial leases do not offer the same degree of tenant protection. An entire chapter of the Ohio Revised Code deals with landlord–tenant laws.[3]

Nonfreehold Estates

Leases are referred to as **nonfreehold** estates. This means that the tenant has possession but not ownership of the underlying realty. Nonfreehold es-

---

1. A sample residential lease is included in Appendix A.
2. Agricultural leases, which deal with renting farmland and buildings, have their own special set of concerns. But, they are essentially commercial leases and will be lumped together with them in this chapter.
3. Ohio Rev. Code Chap. 5321.

tates come in several varieties, each of which will be discussed in more detail below.

Estate for Years

You probably are thinking of an **estate for years** when you picture a real property lease in your mind. An estate for years (also called a **term tenancy**) is a lease of real property for some specific period of time, with definite beginning and ending dates. So, a lease that begins on January 1, 2015, and ends on December 31, 2019, is an estate for years. Once again, legal terminology may trip you up here. This five-year lease is certainly an estate for years, but an estate for years means *any* real property lease that has definite beginning and ending dates. Thus, a lease that begins on January 1, 2015, and ends on June 30, 2015, is still an estate for years, even though it is only for six months, because it has definite beginning and ending dates. The term *year* in this context means any fixed time period, and not just one year.

Estate from Year-to-Year

An **estate from year-to-year** is one that continues from one time period to successive time periods. Here again, the term *year* means any fixed time period. An estate from year-to-year is sometimes called **periodic tenancy**. Unlike an estate for years, which expires at the end of the lease, an estate from year-to-year automatically continues at the end of each period for an additional period. Either the landlord or tenant can terminate an estate from year-to-year by notifying the other party at least one month before the end of the current period. Sometimes, term leases include a provision to turn the arrangement into an estate from year-to-year at the expiration of the term. An apartment lease for two years that then goes month-to-month at the end of the two-year period is an example of this arrangement. Please note that this arrangement to automatically convert a term tenancy into a periodic tenancy is not always the case but must be spelled out in the lease agreement.

Tenancy at Will

A **tenancy at will** is one that exists so long as the landlord and the tenant desire the relationship to exist, with no specific beginning date and no specific ending date. Either the tenant or the landlord can terminate a tenancy at will at any time for any reason, or for no reason. A tenancy at will arrangement may be desirable to tenants and landlords who wish to have the flexibility to change rental situations easily. For example, suppose Dan owns a vacant rental house and his granddaughter has just started college. Dan might very well say to his granddaughter, "If you pay me $300 a month, you can stay in the rental house." This would create a tenancy at will, as there is no specific term.

Do not be concerned that the lease was not in writing, as this particular example *could* be fully performed in less than a year if the granddaughter stayed in the house for only nine months of the school year. Thus, the statute of frauds would not be an issue and the arrangement need not be made in writing. So long as Dan allows his granddaughter to stay in the house and she pays the rent, which is accepted by Dan, it is difficult to believe that she does not have the right to be there. This is an example of a valid oral lease.

Tenancy at Sufferance

A **tenancy at sufferance** is a bit of an odd situation. It occurs when a tenant who once had the right to be on the rental property no longer has the right to be there but remains anyway. This is sometimes called a **holdover tenancy**. For all practical purposes, the tenant looks just like a trespasser, because he or she no longer has the right to be there, but the holdover tenant has a few more rights than a mere trespasser. The holdover tenant must continue to pay rent, and the landlord's acceptance of the rent does not destroy the holdover tenancy. To remove the holdover tenant from the property, the landlord must go through the **eviction** process, discussed later in this chapter. The landlord cannot use self-help and change the locks, remove the tenant's possessions, or otherwise interfere with the tenant's possession of the rental property. If the landlord does so, the landlord will be in the wrong and may be subject to a lawsuit from the holdover tenant. In a tenancy at sufferance, the landlord is the one suffering.

Tenant's Fixtures and Trade Fixtures

Back in the first chapter, we discussed fixtures and looked at the three-part test used in Ohio to determine if something is a fixture—attachment, adaptation, and intent. This test is used to determine if a particular item is part of the realty, and thus included in the purchase of real estate. This all works very well when the *seller* attaches the item, but what if a *tenant* does?

The basic rule is this—if a renter attaches something that would become a fixture, and thus part of the realty, therefore belonging to the landlord, the tenant can remove the item and keep it at the end of the rental term. This is called a tenant's fixture. So, anything that the tenant attaches to the realty does not become a part of the realty but instead remains the property of the tenant.

For example, a tenant may want to replace the standard thermostat with an automatic setback thermostat to save energy. Under the normal tests, this would probably become a fixture and thus part of the realty. However, since the property is rented, the setback thermostat is a tenant's fixture and remains the personal property of the tenant and can be removed (and the original thermostat replaced) at the end of the lease term.

Most leases require the premises to be returned to the same condition as it was at the start of the rental term, except for ordinary wear and tear. So a tenant can attach things, so long as they are removed at the end and any damage is repaired. This can include painting a bedroom, replacing a shower head, hanging a flat screen TV on the wall, installing a setback thermostat, and so forth. If a room is painted, the tenant should repaint it at the end of the lease back to the original color, usually something off-white.

This rule about tenant's fixtures is the general law in Ohio. However, a written lease can change the general rule. A tenant should carefully read the lease before relying on the tenant's fixture rule. For example, a lease may specifically prohibit painting walls, or using anything larger than a picture hanger to mount something to the wall. If there is a conflict between Ohio's tenant's fixture law and a written lease, the lease will prevail. In residential leases, it is somewhat common to find restrictions against tenant's fixtures.

For commercial leases, the rules are a bit different. Anything that is used in a trade or business that is placed on the premises remains removable, without regard to the fixture rule. Such items are referred to as **trade fixtures**. However, anything that is not used in the trade or business and is attached as a fixture becomes part of the realty and cannot be removed at the end of the lease. The distinction is quite simple—if an item meets the three-part test for fixtures and is used in the trade or business, it is a trade fixture and can be removed by the tenant; if it is only ancillary to the trade or business, the item becomes part of the realty.

Perhaps a couple of examples will help. Imagine a manufacturing company that has leased factory space from a landlord. The manufacturer installs a large piece of production machinery that needs to be attached to the concrete floor with several large bolts, which requires the concrete floor to be specially reinforced to accommodate the machine. Looking at the fixture test, the machine certainly is quite permanently attached to the realty, and the realty is adapted to the machine.[4] But, since it is used in the business, it remains a trade fixture and does not become part of the realty at the end of the lease. In contrast, if the commercial tenant were to install a replacement toilet in the employee restroom, it would probably be only ancillary to the business and not a trade fixture.

The topics of tenant's fixtures and trade fixtures can become an issue when rental property is sold. In the trade fixture example in the previous paragraph, a potential purchaser who does not understand the issues may think that the production machine is part of the realty and be unpleasantly surprised at the end of the lease when it has been removed.

Eviction

Eviction is the legal process by which a tenant who no longer has the right to be on the rented property is removed. In Ohio, eviction is called **forcible entry and detainer**. To evict a tenant, including a holdover tenant, the landlord must take specific steps and do so precisely as spelled out in the Ohio Revised Code.[5] This includes providing a notice (referred to as a **three-day notice**), which must be delivered to the tenant by certified mail, return receipt requested; by physically giving it to the tenant; or by leaving a copy of the notice at the premises or at the tenant's residence. Three days afterward, the landlord has the right to file a claim in municipal court seeking a forcible entry and detainer.

Keep in mind that if the lease requires a termination notice, that notice must be given before the three-day notice. So, if Gary is renting an apartment from Janet on a month-to-month basis, and Janet wishes to terminate the lease, Janet will be required to give Gary a one-month notice. If at the end of the month, Gary remains in the apartment, Janet will need to provide a three-day notice before starting a forcible entry and detainer action. The first notice terminates the lease, and the three-day notice is the "key" to the courthouse for the forcible entry and detainer suit.

If the lease is for a residential property, the three-day notice must include the following statement: "You are being asked to leave the premises. If you do not leave, an eviction action may be initiated against you. If you are in doubt

---

4. The intent test would favor the machine not being a fixture, but because of the rule for trade fixtures, it is irrelevant here.

5. Ohio Rev. Code § 1923.04.

regarding your legal rights and obligations as a tenant, it is recommended that you seek legal assistance."[6] Otherwise, the three-day notice will not be effective.

So what happens next? There is a municipal court hearing on the case, which typically is docketed sooner than other matters in municipal court. Only a couple of findings of fact are necessary: (1) that the tenant no longer has the right to be there, and (2) that the three-day notice was properly provided. Often, the landlord will make another claim for unpaid rent, because this is frequently the reason for terminating the lease and starting the eviction. The court hearing is usually very quick, and the tenant only rarely shows up for it. If all goes well, the court will issue a **writ**, or court order, to the county sheriff for forcible entry and detainer, and may also award the landlord damages for unpaid rent.

Does the landlord *now* have the right to physically remove the evicted tenant, change the locks, or remove the tenant's property? No. Believe it or not, the tenant still has some rights—for a while. Remember the writ issued by the court to the sheriff? The sheriff, or more likely a deputy, will show up at the property and remove the tenant, by force if necessary. The tenant's property will be removed by the sheriff and placed at the edge of the property, typically on the curb. What if it's raining or snowing that day, or if someone steals the tenant's property from the curb? Too bad—the tenant's possessions are left outside. Obviously, this is a rather harsh remedy, and having the sheriff's office confront the tenant and do the physical removal is better than the landlord doing so. The sheriff is far better equipped to handle a belligerent tenant who doesn't want to be removed. Not surprisingly, often the tenant leaves of their own accord after the court hearing and before the sheriff shows up.

Fundamentals of Leases

A lease is a bit of an odd thing. It is simultaneously a contract and a real property transaction. The contract portion of a lease spells out the terms and conditions of the rental agreement—things like what the rental payment will be, when it will be due, what can and can't be done on the premises, and so forth. Standard contract law applies to the contract portion of the lease and all of the normal contract formation, performance, and breach mechanisms apply. The usual concepts of offer, acceptance, and consideration are necessary to form a lease, and after the lease is formed, each side has rights and duties that arise. The contract can have conditions that are either satisfied or excused, and

---

6. Ohio Rev. Code § 1923.04 (A) ¶ 2.

Figure 7-1 — Landlord–Tenant

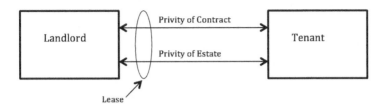

duties can be discharged or breached. Everything you learned in Chapter 6 about contracts applies here.

However, a lease is also a **transfer** (but not a **conveyance**) of rights in real property. Remember the sticks representing real property rights? A lease transfers some of these rights from the landlord to the tenant. These rights include the right to be there, the right to exclude others, the right to quiet enjoyment, and others. I say that this is a transfer of rights but not a conveyance. In a conveyance, real property rights are permanently transferred from one person to another. For example, if I sell you my house, I permanently convey real property rights to you. In a lease, the transfer of rights is temporary in that the tenant possesses these rights only during the term of the lease. So, the tenant holds these rights only temporarily. At the end of the lease term, the property rights revert back to the landlord.

So, a lease creates a contractual relationship between the landlord and the tenant, which is referred to as **privity of contract**, as well as a transfer of real property rights, referred to as **privity of estate**. (See Figure 7-1.) Note in Figure 7-1 that the arrows point to both the landlord and the tenant. With privity of contract, contractual duties are owed both ways. The tenant has duties to the landlord to pay the rent, not damage the property, and others. The landlord has duties to the tenant to not interfere with the tenant's use of the property, maintain it, and so forth. For privity of estate, the landlord transfers certain of the bundle of rights to the tenant, and the tenant has the duty to return the rights at the end of the lease term. So, there are rights and duties flowing both ways under both privity of contract and privity of estate.

Abandonment of Premises

What happens if a tenant decides that he or she no longer need the rental premises, but the term of the lease is not yet up? Can the tenant merely walk away and stop paying rent? Well, this would be a breach of the contract portion of the lease, in which the tenant promises to pay rent for the full term of the lease in exchange for the right to occupy and use the premises. The landlord is counting on the rental income, and the tenant who simply walks away has breached the lease. The landlord is entitled to damages, measured in the usual contractual way—the difference between what the landlord should have received under the lease and what the landlord actually received. Keep in mind, however, that the landlord will have a duty to **mitigate damages**—that is, take steps to reduce the damages. This means that the landlord must actively try to re-rent the premises to a new tenant. When and if the property is re-rented, the damages to the landlord will be the difference between what the landlord would have received under the original lease, minus what the landlord receives under the lease with the new tenant. So, if the property is re-rented two months later for the same rental amount, the landlord's damages will be the lost rent for the two months (in addition to any damages to the property caused by the tenant and any extraordinary costs associated with finding a new tenant).

Subletting and Assignment

Can the tenant do anything to avoid paying these damages on rental property that the tenant no longer needs? Perhaps there is. The two basic approaches are **subletting** and **assignment**. We will look at these each in turn.

In a sublet (sometimes called a **sublease**), the original tenant essentially becomes a landlord and rents (sublets) the premises to a new tenant (referred to as a **subtenant**). The original tenant is still in both privity of contract and privity of estate with the landlord, so the original tenant is "on the hook" for all of the obligations under the lease and must still make timely rental payments to the landlord.

Additionally, the original tenant is now a landlord to the subtenant, and both privity of contract and privity of estate exist also between the original tenant and the subtenant. (See Figure 7-2.) Note that the privity of contract and privity of estate still exists between the landlord and the original tenant. Subletting the property does not reduce the original tenant's rights and duties at all. But, privity of contract and privity of estate now exist between the original tenant and the subtenant. So, the subtenant now has rights and duties to the original tenant, who is now the landlord in the sublease. Notice that no privity of estate or privity of contract exists between the original landlord and the subtenant.

What this means is that if the subtenant fails to pay rent, which causes the original tenant to default on rent payments to the original landlord, the land-

Figure 7-2—Sublet

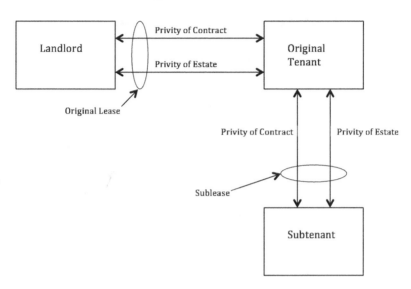

lord's remedy is to sue the original tenant and not the subtenant. Likewise, if the landlord does not perform some duty under the original lease, the subtenant cannot sue the landlord directly, as they are not in privity of estate or privity of contract. The subtenant would, however, have a cause of action against the original tenant—the landlord in the subtenancy.

Subleases are pretty common in commercial situations. Imagine a situation where Steve owns an office building and leases the entire building to Bob. Bob could then lease individual offices in the building to others, say, Mary, Leslie, and Chuck. Mary, Leslie, and Chuck are subtenants in this arrangement and see Bob as their landlord. They pay rent to Bob, and Bob is responsible for duties under the subleases to Mary, Leslie, and Chuck. Bob, in turn, owes rent payments to Steve for the entire office building. If Mary defaults on her office lease, Bob (but not Steve) could evict her. This eviction would be under the sublease.

In an **assignment**, the original tenant transfers the entire lease to a new tenant, called an **assignee**. In this case, the assignee essentially takes over the rights and duties under the lease and is in privity of estate and privity of contract with the landlord. (See Figure 7-3.) Notice that the landlord and tenant are still in privity of contract, as this portion of the original lease splits, with the original tenant still having some contractual duties to the landlord. Remember from the previous chapter when we talked about assigning contracts? As we

Figure 7-3—Assignment

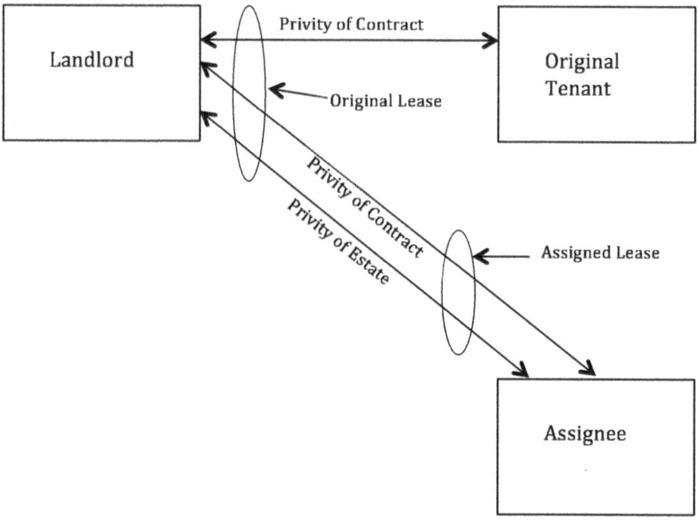

discussed there, whenever a contract is assigned, the person assigning the contracts essentially guarantees that the duties under the contract will be performed by the assignee. So, if the landlord does not receive rent payments on time from the assignee, the landlord can (1) go after the original tenant, (2) go after the assignee, and (3) start an eviction action against the assignee. This makes sense, because the landlord relied on the original tenant's reputation and creditworthiness when entering into the original lease. The original tenant chose the person to whom the lease was assigned, not the landlord. It only seems fair that the original tenant would be responsible for the promises made to the landlord.

You will also notice that the original tenant is no longer in privity of estate with the landlord. Thus, the original tenant no longer has any property rights under the lease. Among the rights the original tenant assigned to the assignee is the right to exclude others. This includes the right to exclude the original tenant. If the original tenant goes onto the property after it has been assigned, he is nothing more than a trespasser. He does not even have the right to go onto the property in an emergency, say, to repair a water leak that is flooding the basement. Under a sublet, however, the original tenant acts as landlord to the subtenant, so he would retain the right to enter the property in an emergency.

Another way for the tenant to pass leasehold rights to a new tenant is with a **release**. A release does just what the name suggests—it releases the tenant from any further duties under the lease. The release is between the landlord and the tenant and effectively terminates duties under the original lease. You will frequently see the term "assignment and release." This means that the original tenant assigns the lease to an assignee, and the landlord not only consents to the assignment but will no longer look to the original tenant as a guarantor of the assignee's performance.

Restrictions on Assignment or Subletting

You might ask if the landlord can prevent assignments or sublets. Actually, it's pretty common for landlords to do so. After all, the landlord is relying on the reputation and creditworthiness of the tenant when agreeing to a lease. Assignments and subletting can get messy for landlords, who frequently do not like them. The lease can simply state, "Tenant shall not assign or sublet this lease." That language works quite nicely. Note that assignments and sublets are different things. So, if the lease prohibits only assignments, it does not prohibit sublets, and vice versa. If the lease does not mention any restrictions on assignments or sublets, they are allowed. Or more simply, every lease can be assigned or sublet unless the lease specifically prohibits these things. You may see variations on the prohibition language in leases, for example, requiring the landlord's written consent to assignments or sublets.

Renewal

Contrary to what you may believe, leases do not automatically renew. If you lease an apartment for six months, the contract is an estate for years, and at the end of the six months you no longer have a right to be in the apartment. However, it is common for leases to include provisions to continue on some basis after the end of the term. Take a look at the sample lease in the appendix. You will see how this is handled in paragraph 15. If that provision was not there, the lease would expire at the end of its term. Another way for leases to continue is by the use of an **option to renew**. This gives the tenant the opportunity to renew the lease, either under the original terms or new terms that are described in the lease. Typically, the tenant must give the landlord some advance notice that the tenant intends to exercise the option to renew. If the tenant does not provide that notice, the lease will terminate on its ending date. That way, the landlord can start looking for a new tenant if the lease is not renewed.

Termination

A lease can terminate in many different ways:

- Perhaps the simplest is that the lease period has ended, with no renewal provisions in the lease.
- The landlord and tenant may agree to merely end the lease before the end of the lease term.
- The tenant could be evicted, either actually or constructively.[7]
- The leased premises are destroyed by something outside the control of the landlord and tenant, such as a fire, tornado, or flood.
- The lease could be assigned to a new tenant with a release from the landlord.
- The tenant could purchase the leased premises. As the purchaser now has both the rights of the tenant and the rights of the landlord, the lease merges into the purchase of the premises and is thus terminated.
- The tenant could abandon the premises by vacating with no intention to return. This would give the landlord the right to reenter the property, resume control over it, and seek a new tenant. Note that the landlord will have a duty to mitigate damages, as discussed earlier in this chapter.

Just because a lease terminates does not mean that any outstanding duties owed by the landlord or tenant are extinguished. For example, the tenant may still owe unpaid rent, and the landlord may hold a security deposit that might need to be refunded to the tenant.

Retaliatory Eviction

If a landlord attempts to evict a tenant because the tenant has taken some lawful action, this is called a **retaliatory eviction**. For example, a tenant complains to the local housing authority about unsafe conditions on the property and then the landlord attempts to evict the tenant for doing so. The fact that the eviction was in retaliation for taking a lawful action will be a defense to the eviction action. What's more, the tenant may be entitled to damages (and attorney's fees) caused by the attempted eviction. However, if the tenant is in default under the lease, perhaps behind in rent payment, the fact that the tenant complained about the condition of the property will not prevent the landlord from evicting the tenant for unpaid rent.

---

7. Constructive eviction is discussed later in this chapter.

Part Performance

As discussed in the chapter on contracts, some contracts must be in writing to be enforceable, including a lease of real property in excess of one year. What if the landlord and tenant don't get around to signing the lease document? Perhaps it has been passed back and forth several times and has simply been forgotten. Does this mean that the tenant has no right to be there and has been a trespasser? Probably not. As long as the tenant (1) was in possession of the premises, (2) paid rent (which was accepted by the landlord), and (3) made some improvements to the property, courts will enforce the lease without it being in writing. After all, if a landlord allows someone to be on the property, accepts rent payments, and allows improvements to be made to the property, it is extremely difficult for that landlord to claim that there was no lease. Otherwise, why did the landlord allow these things to happen?

Condition of Premises

What condition does the premises need to be in when leased, and what does the landlord have to do to keep it in that condition? In addition to the implied warranty of habitability discussed later in this chapter, there are a few other things to consider. One of these is the **covenant of quiet enjoyment**. Even though it is called "quiet" enjoyment, it has nothing to do with noise. Instead, it is an implied promise by the landlord that tenant will not be disturbed and can occupy the premises without interference by others. The landlord also has a duty to maintain the premises in compliance with building and housing codes. Note that these requirements are legal minimums, and the lease agreement can certainly require the landlord to do more.

Security Deposits

Nearly all landlords require tenants to deposit an amount of money, often equal to one month's rent, with the landlord as security to cover any damages caused by the tenant during the lease. In Ohio, if the amount of the security deposit is $50 or one month's rent (whichever is greater) and the tenant occupies the property for six months or more, the landlord must pay the tenant interest on the security deposit every year at the rate of 5 percent per year.[8] Within

---

8. Ohio Rev. Code § 5321.16.

30 days of the end of the lease, the landlord must provide an itemized list of deductions taken from the security deposit and pay the difference to the tenant. If the landlord wrongfully withholds the security deposit, the tenant can recover the amount wrongfully withheld plus damages equal to that amount and attorney's fees.[9] Of course, the tenant must provide the landlord with an address to send the refunded amount.

Depositing Rent in Court

Can a residential tenant withhold rent if the landlord does not fulfill obligations under the law or under the lease? The answer is simply, no. The tenant's obligation to pay rent is not conditioned on the landlord's obligations, so even if the landlord breaches some duty under the lease, the tenant must still pay rent. But that doesn't sound fair, does it? However, a remedy is available to the tenant. The tenant must first notify the landlord of the deficiencies in writing, and if the landlord does not remedy them in a reasonable time, the tenant may make all rent payments to the clerk of courts where the property is located. The landlord can receive these rental payments upon demonstrating to the court that the deficiencies have been corrected.[10] This is sometimes the best option where a so-called slum landlord allows the condition of the property to deteriorate, doesn't make needed repairs, doesn't maintain adequate smoke detectors, and so forth. Otherwise, the tenants wouldn't have any leverage to get the landlord to maintain the property. Evicting a tenant who is depositing rent in court would be a retaliatory eviction, as discussed earlier.

Implied Warranty of Habitability

Every residential lease includes a warranty by the landlord that the premises are fit for humans to live there. This is called the **implied warranty of habitability**. The toilets should work. The building should have heat in the winter. The property should not be overrun with rats. A breach of the implied warranty of habitability can result in a **constructive eviction**. A constructive eviction allows the tenant to terminate the lease and leave property that has become uninhabitable. The landlord, by failing to keep the property habitable, has in effect evicted the tenant. Now, this does not mean that you can get out of your

---

9. *Id.*
10. Ohio Rev. Code § 5321.07 *et. seq.*

apartment lease if the toilet gets stopped up; you must give the landlord the opportunity to correct the problem. But if not corrected, eventually the landlord
will have breached the implied warranty of habitability, and you can treat it as
a constructive eviction.

Commercial Leases

Commercial leases involve property that is used for a trade or business but
otherwise work very much the same way as residential leases. Commercial
leases *do not* include an implied warranty of habitability. After all, the premises are being leased for something other than a place for people to live. In addition, commercial leases frequently have different rental payment terms, as
discussed in the next section.

Gross and Net Leases

If you have rented an apartment, you probably had a **gross lease**. Under a
gross lease, the tenant pays rent and the landlord is responsible for property taxes,
maintenance, and insurance on the property (but not the contents). The landlord must make these payments, and the tenant has no obligation to make sure
they are paid. Under a **net lease**, the tenant pays some or all of these obligations.
So, a net lease could be one where the tenant pays rent to the landlord and must
maintain the property. If the tenant is responsible for taxes, maintenance, and
insurance, the lease is sometimes referred to as a **triple net lease**. Gross leases
are more common in residential leasing, and net leases are very common in commercial leases. This makes some sense. Suppose a landlord leases an empty commercial building to a tenant, who then makes modifications to the building for
the tenant's own purposes, such as remodeling a storefront to accommodate a particular business. These improvements may increase the tax value of the building, be more costly to insure, and require additional maintenance. Surely the
tenant should bear the burden of these additional expenses. In a residential lease,
the tenant leases living space and pretty much takes things as they are. It is quite
unlikely that a residential tenant would do the kinds of things that would increase the cost of taxes, maintenance, or insurance on the property.

A special form of net lease is a **ground lease**. In this situation, the tenant leases
vacant commercial land, with the expectation that the tenant will construct a
commercial building on the property. In essence, the tenant is only leasing a
spot on the planet and will own the structure that is built there. In order for

these leases to make economic sense, the lease term will be quite long, perhaps 30 or 40 years, the expected useful life of the building. Some ground leases require the tenant to leave the structure in place at the end of the lease; others require the tenant to **flat lot** the premises. With a flat lot, the tenant is required to remove the building and return the property to vacant land, perhaps planting grass. You might be surprised that a tenant would be willing to bulldoze a building at the end of the lease, but consider this—suppose the property was used for a gas station. Surely the tenant would not want to make it too easy for the next tenant to open up a competing business. Because the value of the building has depreciated to zero during the term of the lease, the tenant has no economic reason not to return the property to vacant land, other than the cost of demolition and repairs to the site.

Another common kind of commercial lease is a **percentage lease**. These are often found in retail leases and typically require the tenant to pay rent in the form of a fixed amount each month, together with a percentage of the gross retail sales. At first, this may seem a bit punitive toward the retail tenant, but I think on further reflection you will see the logic in this practice. Imagine that you are the owner of a small specialty retail store in a large mall. Surely certain portions of your sales come from people who are at the mall to shop at other stores. Some of these may even be impulse purchases from people who didn't even know your store existed.

Discussion Questions

1. Why is a lease considered a nonfreehold estate?
2. Explain the difference between an estate for years and an estate from year to year.
3. Describe the steps that a landlord needs to take to evict a tenant in Ohio.
4. Explain the difference between privity of estate and privity of contract. Why is the distinction important?
5. Explain the difference between subletting and assignment.
6. Describe a situation in which a tenant would want to deposit rent in court rather than pay the landlord directly.

Key Terms

Assignee
Assignment

Commercial lease
Constructive eviction
Conveyance
Covenant of quiet enjoyment
Estate for years
Estate from year-to-year
Eviction
Flat lot
Forcible entry and detainer
Gross lease
Ground lease
Holdover tenancy
Implied warranty of habitability
Mitigate damages
Net lease
Nonfreehold
Option to renew
Percentage lease
Periodic tenancy
Privity of contract
Privity of estate
Release
Rental agreement
Residential lease
Retaliatory eviction
Sublease
Subletting
Subtenant
Tenancy at sufferance
Tenancy at will
Term tenancy
Three-day notice
Transfer
Triple net lease
Writ

Chapter 8

Transfer of Real Property

One of the key features of property is that ownership of it can change over time. We can divide changes of ownership into two broad categories—*voluntary* and *involuntary*. A voluntary change in ownership occurs when an owner intends for ownership of the property to be transferred to another, such as when property is sold or given away. An involuntary change in ownership occurs when property is transferred from one owner to another, without the consent of the original owner. In this chapter, we will examine many of the ways that property ownership can move from one person to another.

Voluntary Transfer

Voluntary transfers occur when the original owner transfers ownership of property to another person when otherwise under no compunction to do so. By far, the most common voluntary transfer is a sale of real property.

Sale

You will recall from Chapter 1 that ownership of real property can be represented by a bundle of rights. The right to sell property to another is one of the most fundamental rights of ownership. In a sale, the original owner transfers **title** (ownership) to the property to the new ownership in exchange for payment of the purchase price. While payment of the purchase price is typically in the form of money, nothing would prevent a valid sale from being consummated by payment of the purchase price in another form—say, transferring ownership of land in exchange for a boat. So long as there is valid consideration, as discussed in Chapter 6 on contracts, there will be a valid sale.

But where did the ownership originate? If we trace real property back far enough, will we find an original owner in Ohio? For the most part, all of the land in Ohio was once owned by the federal government and was transferred to individuals. Frequently, the federal government gave the land to individuals who served the country in wars. For example, much of Clermont County (where the author resides) was granted to soldiers who served in the Revolutionary War. Lands were given as indicated in the following excerpted chart:[1]

Rank	Land grant
Colonel	5,000 acres
Major	4,000 acres
Captain	3,000 acres
Noncommissioned officers	400 acres
Soldier serving three years	200 acres

When personal property is sold, the transfer is documented with a **bill of sale**, or a receipt.[2] The new owner can hold out the bill of sale as proof of ownership. If any dispute arises over ownership, a bill of sale is strong evidence of the true owner of the personal property. However, with real property, a bill of sale does not suffice. We use a deed instead. Anyone who has played Monopoly has a basic understanding of the use of a deed as evidence of ownership of real property. We will examine deeds in more detail in Chapter 10.

Perhaps you remember the song line, "Signed, sealed, delivered, I'm yours."[3] This fairly summarizes how real property is transferred. The seller (grantor) signs the deed; the grantor's signature is sealed, or notarized; and finally the deed is actually delivered or given to the buyer (grantee) or someone acting on behalf of the grantee. If these steps are not done properly, the real property transfer will not work, and ownership of the real property does not pass.

In essentially all real property sales, some time elapses between the agreement to buy and sell and when money and the deed are exchanged (the **closing**). This agreement is documented by a contract—which consists of a promise to sell and a promise to purchase. In Chapter 6, we examined the essential elements of a real estate contract—capacity, offer, acceptance, and consideration. In addition, a contract for the conveyance of an interest in real property

---

1. W. E. Peters, *Ohio Lands and Their Subdivision*, 109 (The Messenger Printery Co. Press 1918).

2. In some cases, a **certificate of title** evidences ownership of personal property, as with an automobile. We will discuss this in more detail when we examine **registered land** in Chapter 9.

3. *Wonder, Stevie, Signed, Sealed, Delivered I'm Yours* (Signed Sealed Delivered, 1970).

must be in writing to satisfy the statute of frauds. Therefore, you can nearly always expect a written contract to document the deal and bind the parties to the sale transaction.[4] Appendix B includes a sample real estate purchase contract that you might want to examine in some detail to appreciate the sorts of things that typically are included in these contracts.

Land Contract

A **land contract**, sometimes called a **contract for deed**, is a form of sale. It is essentially a form of seller financing. The seller (referred to as a **vendor**) and the buyer (referred to as a **vendee**) enter into a contract where the vendee agrees to purchase real property from the vendor. The vendee makes regular payments to the vendor. The vendor retains ownership of the property until all of the payments have been made and all conditions under the contract have been fulfilled. At that time, the vendor executes and delivers a deed to the vendee, who then becomes the owner of the property. While making payments, the vendee has **equitable title** to the property, meaning the right to possess the property, and the vendor cannot sell the property to another.

If the vendee defaults on the contract, the vendor can sue in **contract forfeiture**. This will result in the vendee forfeiting, or giving up, all the money paid to the vendor and equitable title to the property.

So, in a land contract, the vendor remains the owner until all of the payments and other conditions have been satisfied, and only then does the vendee receive a deed. The vendee in a land contract runs the risk of default on the contract, resulting in not only losing the property but all of the payments made to the seller as well. The vendor in a land contract runs a risk because the entire purchase price is not received up front.

A land contract can help a buyer who could not otherwise qualify for a loan, due to bad credit, unwillingness of lenders to make a loan to purchase a particular piece of property, and so forth. A seller can benefit by being able to sell property that otherwise may not be saleable, and is protected by retaining ownership of the property until all payments have been made. The seller can frequently

---

4. I say "nearly all" because I can imagine a situation where a buyer shows up with a bundle of cash and the seller has a deed all ready to go even before the parties agree to the sale transaction. In this extremely unlikely situation, there would be no time lag between agreement and closing—and no real need for a written contract, as the agreement and closing would basically occur simultaneously. In my years of practicing real estate law, I have never seen this occur, but that doesn't mean that it would never happen. After all, law is all about *possibilities* and not *probabilities*. While this is not probable, it *is* possible.

require a large cash down payment for assurance that the buyer is serious and able to complete the transaction. Land contracts are more frequently used in commercial real estate transactions than in residential transactions.

Rent-to-Own Lease

A land contract is quite similar to a **rent-to-own** lease, but there are some differences. A rent-to-own lease includes a landlord–tenant relationship together with an option for the tenant to purchase the property at some later time for an agreed-upon price. The lease portion of the transaction is essentially the same as a traditional lease, with regular payments and a fixed term. The option portion of the transaction gives the tenant the right to purchase the property at the end of the lease term. The option component requires separate consideration, as it is essentially a contract with the landlord to keep open an offer to sell to the tenant for a period of time.

Often, a portion of the rental payments is placed in an escrow account and applied to the purchase price of the property if the tenant decides to exercise the option at the end of the lease. This way, the tenant is building equity toward the purchase while paying rent. If the tenant decides not to exercise the option and purchase the property, the money in escrow will either be refunded to the tenant or retained by the landlord, depending on the terms of the lease and option agreements. In any case, the consideration paid for the option is retained by the landlord, as it was payment for the landlord keeping open the offer to sell to the tenant during the lease term.

Gift

Real property can be given as a gift. We sometimes see newly married couples being given a house or a building site as a wedding present. Occasionally, gifts of real property are made to other friends and relatives. Finally, people frequently give a gift of real property to a charity, such as land on which to build a new school or park. Such transactions are not actually all that uncommon, and you will probably encounter real estate gifts at some point in your career.

Once again, to transfer ownership of the property by gift, a deed needs to be signed, sealed, and delivered. For example, suppose when Uncle Scrooge died, Donald found a deed to Scrooge's Money Bin Building in his desk drawer. The deed was filled out properly, Uncle Scrooge had signed it, and his signature was notarized. Is Donald now the owner of the money bin? No. Because Donald found the deed in Uncle Scrooge's desk drawer, it was never delivered to him, so Donald does not become the owner of the money bin by virtue of the undelivered deed. Sorry Donald. We would need to look at Uncle Scrooge's estate and how it is probated to determine if Donald becomes the owner of the money bin.

Perhaps surprisingly, a gift must also be accepted to complete the transaction. You might ask why anyone would not accept a gift of real property. After all, who wouldn't want a free house? But if you think about the myriad sorts of real property out there, surely you can imagine those that you would not agree to accept. For example, a badly polluted industrial site that would require serious remediation before it could be usable might not be appreciated. Likewise, a residential property with an uninhabitable dwelling that would need to be demolished and rebuilt could be seen as undesirable. Indeed, it is quite possible for real property to have a practical value of less than zero. I was involved in the transfer of a contaminated industrial property where the grantor transferred a deed to the property to the grantee, together with a payment of cash sufficient to remediate the environmental contamination. In essence, the grantor paid the grantee to take the property—this site had a negative value. Surely you would not want to accept it as a gift.

Involuntary Transfer

Sometimes, real property is transferred from one owner to another without the original owner directly consenting to the transfer. We refer to these as **involuntary transfers**.

Foreclosure

If you don't make your car payments, Repo Man will come in the middle of the night and take your car away. The bank[5] can do this because the car itself secures your loan; in other words, the car acts as **collateral** for the loan. The bank can take the car for nonpayment because you agreed to let it do so when you signed the pile of papers as you bought the car. What's more, in Ohio the bank retains the "pink slip," or *title* to the car, until the loan is paid.

Likewise, a real estate loan is usually secured by the real property itself, which serves as collateral for the loan. And, if you don't make the payments as they come due, the bank will effectively repossess the real property. In the

---

5. Throughout this section I will use the term *bank* to refer a lender—that lender could be a bank, a savings and loan, a credit union, a rich relative, or anyone else who loans money.

United States are two basic approaches to using real property as collateral for a loan—they are referred to as **title theory** and **lien theory**. The difference between these two lies in how the law looks at the bank's interest in the real estate as collateral. In states that use title theory, the bank actually obtains a partial ownership interest in the real property, and upon default of the loan, the bank's ownership interest becomes complete. Thus, the bank becomes the owner of the property, and that is pretty much that.

In a lien theory state, the bank has a lien on the property, and a default on the loan merely gives the bank the right to sue in foreclosure—not to take immediate possession of the property. Ohio is a lien theory state. The foreclosure lawsuit will ask the court to order the property to be sold at auction and the proceeds used to pay off any liens on the property.

How did the bank get the power to foreclose? In a way quite similar to the auto repossession situation discussed earlier, the owner of the property transferred that power to the bank when the owner signed the mortgage document. In effect, at the closing, one of the sticks in the bundle of rights was transferred to the bank—the right to start a foreclosure action upon default of the loan. We will examine real estate financing and foreclosure in greater detail in Chapter 12.

Eminent Domain

Eminent domain, which was discussed in Chapter 5, is certainly an involuntary transfer of real property, where the government forces a sale of the property to be used for public purposes.

Inverse Condemnation

Inverse condemnation is a concept closely related to eminent domain. Suppose the state widened a highway and exercised its powers of eminent domain over the property that was needed for the project. What if the eminent domain action took the entire parking lot of a retail business, but left the store building intact, resulting in the business's customers having no place to park? This would effectively shut down the business and be an example of an inverse condemnation. Here, the property owner would sue the government in eminent domain (rather than the other way around—hence *inverse* condemnation) to force the government to purchase the entire property. The argument would be that the government, by taking the parking lot, destroyed the entire commercial value of the property and should be required to pay just compensation for all of it, and not just the part that included the parking lot.

In deciding the case, the court would look at three factors: (1) the nature of the government action, (2) the economic impact of the action on the subject property, and (3) the extent to which the action interferes with the owner's reasonable, investment-backed expectations.[6] Now apply these factors to our hypothetical situation to see what the court would decide: (1) The nature of the governmental action is eminent domain, (2) the economic impact would be negative through the loss of customer parking, and (3) the owners probably reasonably expected that their customers could park in the adjoining lot and visit the store. I believe that our hypothetical situation would result in the government being forced to purchase the entire property.

Property owners have also used inverse condemnation when additional government regulations result in undue restrictions on the use of their property. For example, suppose a developer purchased a plot of land with the intention of constructing a high-rise office building on the site in a central business district of a major city. The developer likely paid a hefty premium for the plot because of the anticipated value of the location for a high-rise building. Then, what if the government passed a new zoning regulation for the area that restricted the building site to only single-story construction. In effect, the new zoning regulation might result in a successful action for inverse condemnation—at least for the diminution in value of the building site from a high-rise location to a single-story location.[7] The nature of the government action was a zoning change, the result was a reduction in value of the property as a building site, and the action interfered with the developer's reasonable investment expectations.

Adverse Possession

The concept of **adverse possession** can be traced back to at least the Code of Hammurabi—one of the oldest known written laws, dating from about 2250 BC. "If a chieftain or a man leave his house, garden, and field ... and some one else takes possession of his house, garden, and field and uses it for three years: if the first owner return and claims his house, garden, and field, it shall not be given to him, but he who has taken possession of it and used it shall continue to use it."[8]

---

6. This test is extrapolated from *Penn Central Transportation Co. v. New York City*, 438 U.S. 104 (1978). This case dealt with inverse taking based on overreaching regulations, but courts have used these factors in cases like the one described in the hypothetical.

7. This hypothetical is loosely based on the facts of the *Penn Central* case.

8. Code of Hammurabi, c. 1780 BCE, translated by L. W. King, http://www.fordham.edu/halsall/ancient/hamcode.html.

Essentially, if you are a trespasser long enough, you will become an owner. These days, obtaining property by adverse possession is a bit more complex. To become an owner of property by adverse possession, a person must meet all of the following:

1. The property must be **actually possessed**—used as a true owner would use it. Merely walking on the property is not enough. Maintaining the property, cutting and removing timber, constructing an improvement on the property, and the like will be required.
2. The use must be **hostile**—used without the permission of the true owner.
3. The use must be **open and notorious**—not hidden, but so apparent that the true owner would notice it if he or she bothered to look.
4. The use must be **exclusive**—used by the adverse possessor and not the true owner.
5. The use must be **continuous**—without any break in possession for the statutory period (21 years in Ohio).

As to the *continuous* requirement, it is not necessary that the same adverse possessor be using the property. Through the concept of **tacking**, possession can be passed to subsequent adverse possessors of the property, so long as the use, when added together, is at least as long as the statutory period.

In addition, the adverse possessor needs to bring a **quiet title action** to complete ownership of the property. A quiet title action is a lawsuit brought in court to establish ownership and title to the real property. An adverse possessor who is successful in a quiet title action becomes the true owner and can convey clear title to the property to another subsequent person.[9]

Partition

Suppose that Fred and George were brothers that owned real property together, either as tenants in common or by virtue of Ohio statutory survivorship. Fred wanted to develop the property by constructing a commercial building on the land, but George wanted to develop the property by constructing an apartment building. They have discussed, rediscussed, and fought about how to use the property many times over, yet have not been able to agree on what to do with it. Both Fred and George are unwilling to budge from their position on what to do, and neither is willing to compromise. What can be done? Are they simply stuck in this argument forever?

---

9. The same tests are used with respect to an easement by prescription (see Chapter 2).

There is a solution. Either Fred or George could file a **partition** action with the court of common pleas in the county where the property is located. The court will then resolve the dispute[10]— not by deciding if a commercial building or an apartment building should be constructed, but by (as the name suggests) partitioning the land. If the property is capable of being divided into two parcels, the court will do so in proportion to their ownership interests, and Fred will wind up as the sole owner of one parcel and George the sole owner of the other parcel. If the property cannot be divided (because, say there is already a building located on it), the court will order that it be sold and the proceeds divided between Fred and George in proportion to their ownership interest.

You may wonder why Fred and George don't simply divide the property or sell it themselves. They could easily do that if they both agreed as to how to work everything out. But, as is often the case, co-owners of property who cannot agree on how to use the property also cannot agree on how to sever the ownership interests. A partition action is a fairly drastic solution and is often used as a last resort when owners have reached an impasse. Sometimes, the mere act of starting a partition action can cause the owners to find common ground and reach an agreement, rather than have the property divided or sold.

Escheat

If an owner of real property in Ohio dies without any heirs, their property will be transferred to the State of Oho. This is referred to as **escheat**. This is a last resort, and the probate court will order an escheat only if no heir or relative of the owner can be found or if no one who is entitled to inherit the property wishes to receive it. Likewise, if the courts have deemed real property to be abandoned and the true owner cannot be found, it can escheat to the state.

Discussion Questions

1. Explain the difference between a land contract and rent to own. Describe situations in which each might be used.

2. Explain the difference between eminent domain and inverse condemnation.

3. Explain each of the elements in adverse possession.

4. Describe a situation that might result in a partition action.

---

10. *See,* Ohio Rev. Code § 5307.

5. Describe the elements of transferring ownership of real property by deed (Signed, sealed, and delivered).

Key Terms

Actual possession
Adverse possession
Bill of sale
Closing
Collateral
Continuous
Contract for deed
Contract forfeiture
Equitable title
Escheat
Exclusive
Hostile
Inverse condemnation
Involuntary transfer
Land contract
Lien theory
Open and notorious
Partition
Quiet title action
Rent to own
Tacking
Title
Title theory
Vendee
Vendor
Voluntary transfer

Chapter 9

Legal Descriptions of Property

Here's a question to ponder. How do you know which car is your car? I think we all recognize and know our own car by seeing it. But if several identical cars with the same make and model, the same color, and the same model year were parked in a parking lot, how would you know which one is yours? Perhaps you would recognize it by the license plate or by the items in the passenger compartment or by that dent on the left rear bumper. But what if it was a car you just bought new from the dealer and the temporary tags had blown off? How would you be able to identify your specific car? And how could you prove that it is your car?

Probably after even a short time thinking about this problem, you would remember that every car has a Vehicle Identification Number (VIN) that is unique to that particular car. The VIN would uniquely identify your car, and your bill of sale from the car dealer could be matched up to work out which one was your car.

Now, ponder the same kind of question about real property. Suppose you owned five acres of vacant land. How could you know which five acres belong to you? Real property has no license plate, VIN, or other distinctive attribute that would uniquely identify it as yours. What's more, how could you specifically determine where your land ends and your neighbor's land starts?

By now, surely you realize that the name of this chapter reveals the answer— by its **legal description**. A legal description is the method by which we can uniquely identify real property and its boundaries. Legal descriptions do just that, they describe the legal boundaries of real property. Every parcel of real property in Ohio has a legal description that distinctively identifies it and its location on the planet.

A legal description is an important part of a deed, just as a VIN is an important part of a car registration—it is a method of identifying a particular parcel of real property and is then linked to the owner of the property. Legal descriptions are closely related to **surveys**, which are used to plan, design, and establish real property boundaries. Every jurisdiction has its own peculiar system of surveying, and Ohio has survey systems galore.

The importance of legal descriptions cannot be overstated. In a deed only the land that is described in the legal description is actually transferred. If the legal description has even a tiny error, the buyer may not receive all of the land that was purchased. For this reason, legal descriptions are carefully proofread, perhaps multiple times. One proofreading technique for legal descriptions is to have one person read the legal description to another person, starting at the end and working toward the start of the description, one word at time. This way, it is less likely that an error would be overlooked, as can easily be the case when reading forward because our minds often fill in missing words.

History of Ohio Lands

Ohio was the first state formed out of lands owned by the **public domain**, or the people of the United States. Of course, Native Americans once held the land that now makes up Ohio. In parallel with the American Revolution, there was an armed struggle between settlers headed west (at the time, Ohio was part of the western frontier) and the Native Americans who were already there. At the time, Britain was backing the Native Americans, and fierce battles resulted in Britain ceding the trans-Appalachian west to the new United States of America in the Treaty of Paris in 1783. This conflict is only poorly known, and it is even more obscure how Britain had the power to cede the Native American lands to the United States.[1]

Earlier, in 1780, the Continental Congress resolved that western lands acquired by treaty with Britain "shall be disposed of for the common benefit of the United States and be settled and formed into distinct republican States, which shall become members of the Federal Union, and have the same rights of sovereignty, freedom, and independence, as the other States."[2] Thus, when Britain ceded the land that now includes Ohio, it became part of the United States and entered the public domain.

This is intended to be only a brief glimpse of how the United States came to hold the land that makes up Ohio. The important thing to understand is that after 1783, the United States owned all of Ohio lands. So, how did the land come to be held and owned by individuals? The United States used much

---

1. George W. Knepper, *The Official Ohio Lands Book* 4 (Auditor of the State of Ohio 2002).

2. http://famguardian.org/publications/propertyrights/westwast.html

of the land to compensate those who were involved in or harmed by the American Revolution. For example, much of the so-called Virginia military tracts was used to satisfy obligations of the United States to those who fought in the revolution. The Symmes purchase was used to repay loans made to the colonies to finance the war. Some lands were made available to invite settlement and homesteading. Other lands were used to reimburse colonials for their war losses, for United States military purposes, to provide endowments for universities and schools, and other such purposes. I think it is fair to say that the fledgling US government used Ohio lands as a kind of bank account to settle its debts and encourage westward expansion.

Ohio as a Laboratory for Developing Survey Systems

As these land transfers took place, real property descriptions were necessary so that the new owners could uniquely identify their land and the boundaries. All too often, the individual areas of land were surveyed using a system that was peculiar to that area. Later on, under the leadership of Thomas Jefferson, a standardized survey system was developed, but even that did not spring forth fully formed. It is almost as if Ohio was used as a laboratory to try out different survey systems to see which one would be adopted as the national standard. As a result, Ohio has more than 20 different survey systems. Perhaps surprisingly, all of these underling survey systems are still at the root of land descriptions in Ohio. The author lives in the Virginia Military Survey area, and its original survey book is located in the Clermont County Recorder's office. A photograph of one page of that survey book is shown in Figure 9-1.

One of the earliest legal descriptions of Ohio land reads as follows:

> 444 acres of land lying in Fayette County, on the south side of Sewell Mountain on the head waters of Little Meadow River joining a survey made for Matthew Arbuckle and a survey of 1,000 acres made for Andrew Hamilton, and bounded as follows, to-wit: Beginning at a gum and two maples near the Little Meadow River corner to Arbuckle and with S 50 E 145 poles[3] crossing the same to four chestnuts on a North hill side corner to Finney and with N 55 E 140 poles to

---

3. This is a direction and a distance. S 40 E 145 poles means "Face south, then turn 40° toward the east, next go in that direction 145 poles." A *pole* is an older measure of distance, which equals 16.5 feet. Thus, 145 poles would be 2,392.5 feet.

Figure 9-1 — Virginia Military Survey

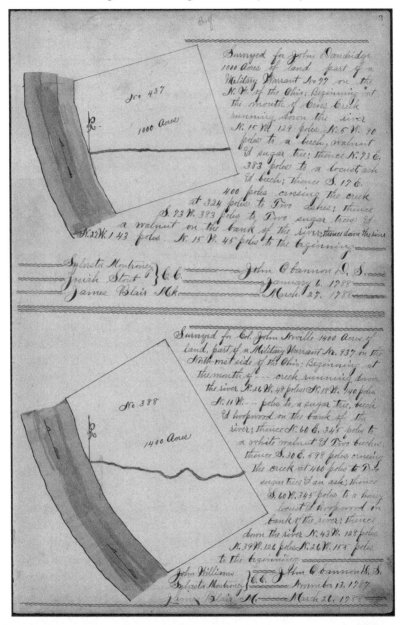

two Spanish oaks and hickory on the top of a ridge N 20 E 40 poles to a double chestnut N 55 E 100 poles to a large black oak N 75 E 80 poles to a large black oak on a flat corner to Finney and leaving N 58 W 320 poles to a chestnut corner to Hamilton and with S 25 W 300 poles to the beginning.[4]

Metes and Bounds Descriptions

Figure 9-2 is a sketch of the property described in the previous section. This method of describing real property is called **metes and bounds**. A *mete* is basically a straight line that describes the border of a parcel of land. A *bound* is a more general property description, perhaps land that is bordered by a river or a highway.

A metes and bounds property description starts at a **point of beginning** and continues around the border of a property, specifying a direction and a distance to a **corner** of the property. Then, the next border is described by a new direction and distance to the next corner of the property. This continues all the way around the property until returning to the point of beginning. As you can see in the metes and bounds property description in the previous section, it is necessary to describe how to get to the point of beginning. In the example, the following language is used to describe how to find the point of beginning:

> 444 acres of land lying in Fayette County, on the south side of Sewell Mountain on the head waters of Little Meadow River joining a survey made for Matthew Arbuckle and a survey of 1,000 acres made for Andrew Hamilton, and bounded as follows, to-wit: Beginning at a gum and two maples near the Little Meadow River corner to Arbuckle ...

The gum tree and two maple trees represent the point of beginning in this property description. Early metes and bounds property descriptions frequently relied on nearby physical objects to describe corners of the property boundaries. As you can imagine, the gum and maple trees that existed in the 18th century might well no longer be present. Surveyors today would have to act as historians and archeologists to determine just where the gum and maple trees once stood. In more recent times, metes and bounds surveys do not usually rely on physical objects, such as trees and rocks. Rather, property descriptions refer

---

4. W. E Peters, *Ohio Lands and Their Subdivision*, 20 (The Messenger Printery Co. 1918). The original property description has been corrected to make the point of beginning and the end point coincide. Modern surveying tools are more accurate than those used in the 18th century.

Figure 9-2—Sample Metes and Bounds Drawing

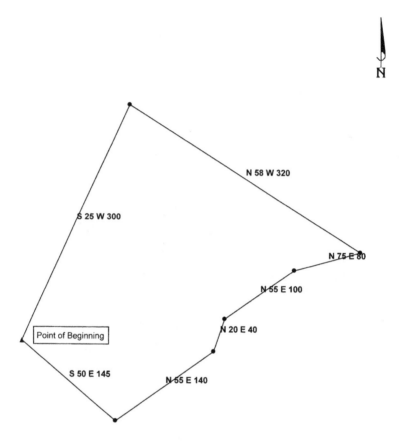

to points, such as "S 40 E 525 feet to a point." Modern surveys are generally more accurate than those that rely on trees and such. What part of the tree is the corner: the center of the tree, the nearest part, or the furthest part? What happens when the tree grows, or blows over in a storm? However, we can still find surveys that use physical objects as a corner. For example, Figure 9-3 is from a current Ohio survey that uses a rock as a property corner. As you can imagine, using physical objects can cause difficulty in precisely identifying property boundaries. It is a fairly common practice for surveyors to drive an iron pin into the ground, often using a piece of concrete reinforcement, called rebar, at the corners of the property as it is surveyed. Then, the end of the rebar can

Figure 9-3 — Survey with Rock as Corner

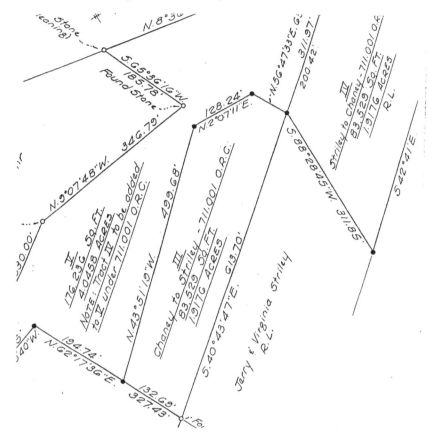

be dimpled with a hammer and punch to more precisely identify the property corner.

Metes and bounds survey systems are common in the southern part of Ohio and are still in general use today, with several variations. Many of the differences in the various metes and bounds survey systems involve how the point of beginning is determined for a particular parcel of land. Land in Ohio is divided into large areas called **townships** and **ranges**.[5] Remember, Ohio was a

---

5. To make things even more confusing, the terms *township* and *range* have completely different meanings in an area that uses metes and bounds property descriptions than they do in an area that uses the rectangular coordinate system.

laboratory for developing survey systems; thus, in some instances the township is the larger area, and in other instances the range is the larger area. To determine the point of beginning, we must start at a known location, then travel some distance to the point of beginning. From the point of beginning, we would then describe the property itself. For example, a survey might start, "Located in the State of Ohio, County of Brown, Clark Township." This would indicate a particular part of the state. Then the survey could continue, "Starting at a point at the intersection of the center line of Smith Road and the center line of Johnson Road." This would indicate a known point in Clark Township, which is in Brown County. Then the survey might continue, "thence South 60 degrees East a distance of 67 feet to the point of beginning." This would uniquely identify the point of beginning and the first corner in the metes and bounds survey, and the description of the property itself would then follow. Over time, **survey markers**, such as the one shown in Figure 9-4, are being used as the starting point for legal descriptions. A survey marker is typically set in concrete and represents a precise, known location. Using survey markers is a much better way to start a metes and bounds survey than trees, rocks, or road intersections.

Remembering that more than 20 different survey systems are used in Ohio, the actual method to find the point of beginning can vary widely across the state. It is not important to understand the particulars of any specific survey system. Rather, you should try to get a general feel for how metes and bounds property descriptions work. Appendix C contains instructions on how to sketch a diagram of a parcel of real property from a metes and bounds description.

Rectangular Coordinate System

By now, you may be thinking that the metes and bounds system is a bit awkward, to say the least. Suppose that you were to essentially overlay a sheet of graph paper on a map of real property. Then you could simply describe the location of real property by naming the squares on the graph paper that correspond to the property in question. In essence, that is exactly how the **rectangular coordinate system** works. If you have ever flown over the Midwest, you may have noticed areas that seem to be laid out in regular square-shaped regions. In all likelihood, you were looking at an area that was formed using the rectangular coordinate system.

Perhaps the most difficult part of understanding the rectangular coordinate system involves getting a firm grasp on the terminology that is used in this system. Let's look at the basics of this system. Surely you have seen a globe with the lines of longitude that run from the North Pole to the South Pole. These

Figure 9-4—Survey Marker

are the starting points in the rectangular coordinate system, except that they are referred to as **meridians**. For each survey system in a particular rectangular coordinate system, one north–south meridian, called a **principal meridian**, is used as a starting point. This meridian crosses an east–west line that is referred to as a **baseline** (see Figure 9-5). So in any particular area, exactly one principal meridian and one baseline are used. What's more, each principal meridian is given a unique name, which identifies the survey area. For example, two of the principal meridians in Ohio are the First Principal Meridian[6] and the Michigan Meridian.

---

6. It shouldn't be a surprise that the First Principal Meridian lies on the western border of Ohio. After all, Ohio was the "laboratory" for the development of survey systems in the United States.

Figure 9-5 — Principal Meridian and Baseline

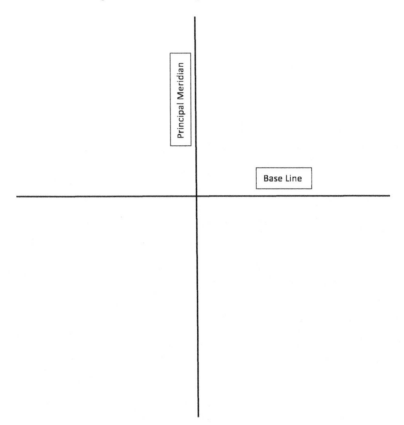

Next, starting at the intersection of the principal meridian and the baseline, the area is divided into a grid of squares, which are 6 miles on each side, referred to as **townships**. These townships are identified by a pair of numbers, which show their location in relation to the principal meridian and baseline. For example, the shaded area in Part A of Figure 9-6 is Township 3 South, Range 3 East (abbreviated T3S, R3E or simply 3S3E). This area, like all townships in the rectangular coordinate system, is 6 miles on each side and contains an area of 36 square miles. The townships are first numbered north and south from the baseline, then east and west from the principal meridian. Other townships in Figure 9-6 have been numbered to show this identity.

Figure 9-6—Rectangular Coordinate System

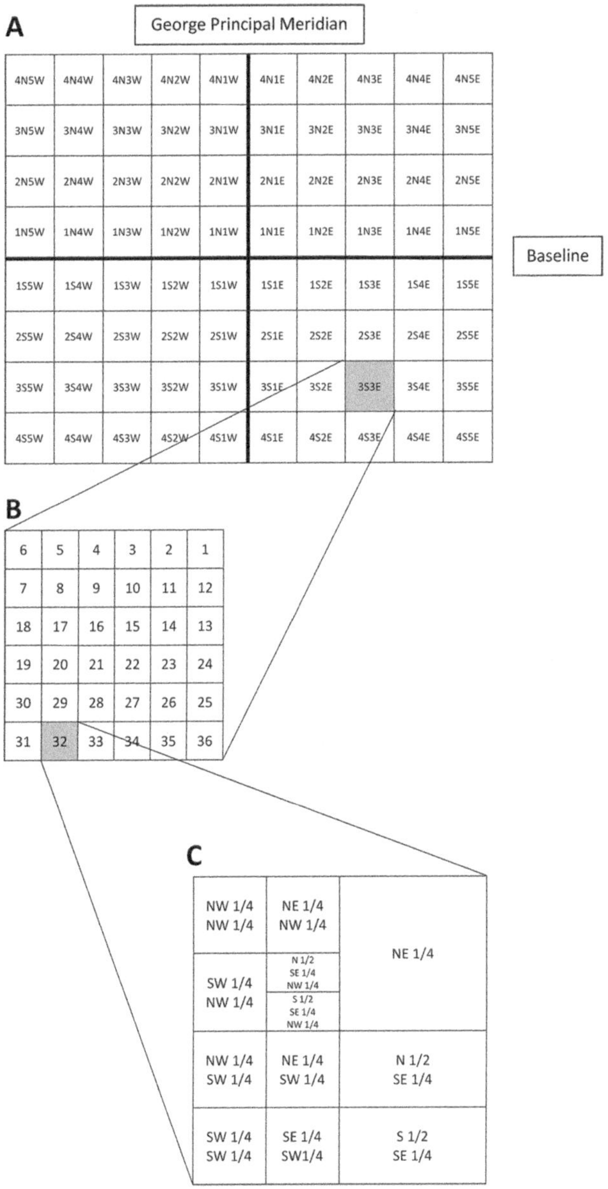

A

George Principal Meridian

4N5W	4N4W	4N3W	4N2W	4N1W	4N1E	4N2E	4N3E	4N4E	4N5E
3N5W	3N4W	3N3W	3N2W	3N1W	3N1E	3N2E	3N3E	3N4E	3N5E
2N5W	2N4W	2N3W	2N2W	2N1W	2N1E	2N2E	2N3E	2N4E	2N5E
1N5W	1N4W	1N3W	1N2W	1N1W	1N1E	1N2E	1N3E	1N4E	1N5E
1S5W	1S4W	1S3W	1S2W	1S1W	1S1E	1S2E	1S3E	1S4E	1S5E
2S5W	2S4W	2S3W	2S2W	2S1W	2S1E	2S2E	2S3E	2S4E	2S5E
3S5W	3S4W	3S3W	3S2W	3S1W	3S1E	3S2E	3S3E	3S4E	3S5E
4S5W	4S4W	4S3W	4S2W	4S1W	4S1E	4S2E	4S3E	4S4E	4S5E

Baseline

B

6	5	4	3	2	1
7	8	9	10	11	12
18	17	16	15	14	13
19	20	21	22	23	24
30	29	28	27	26	25
31	32	33	34	35	36

C

NW 1/4 NW 1/4	NE 1/4 NW 1/4	NE 1/4
SW 1/4 NW 1/4	N 1/2 SE 1/4 NW 1/4 / S 1/2 SE 1/4 NW 1/4	
NW 1/4 SW 1/4	NE 1/4 SW 1/4	N 1/2 SE 1/4
SW 1/4 SW 1/4	SE 1/4 SW1/4	S 1/2 SE 1/4

But 36 square miles is a mighty large area. So, each township is further divided into 1-mile by 1-mile **sections**, which of course contains 1 square mile, which happens to be 640 acres. These sections are numbered in a rather odd way. Starting in the upper right corner (the section in the far northeast of the township), the sections are numbered *right to left* from 1 to 6. Then, the next row down is numbered from 7 to 12 going from *left to right*. You can think of this as being similar to how a field is plowed. First from right to left, then down a row and back from left to right, down a row, and so forth. Part B of Figure 9-6 shows how a township is divided and numbered into sections. In this example, township 32 has been highlighted.

Each section is further divided into fractional parts. Part C of Figure 9-6 shows examples of how several fractional areas would be described. For example, the area in the upper right of Part C is the North East 1/4. Normally, we put north at the top and east on the right. Since the area in the upper right of Part C is one-fourth of the section and it is in the northeast corner of the section, it is simply called the North East 1/4. Assuming that the property survey was in an area that is described using, say, the George Meridian,[7] a complete description of this area of land would be,

> The North East Quarter of Section 32 of Township 3 South Range 3
> East of the George Meridian.

When reading a rectangular coordinate system real property description, you always start with the parcel of land, describe its fractional part of the section, then the section number, followed by the township and range, and then the principal meridian for that area. By the way, since an entire section is 640 acres, this quarter section is one-fourth of 640, or 160 acres.

Looking at the area in the lower right of Part C of Figure 9-6, you will notice that it is the southern half of the southwest quarter of the section and contains half of a quarter of 640 acres, or 80 acres. The complete description of this parcel is as follows:

> The South Half of the South East Quarter of Section 32 of Township
> 3 South Range 3 East of the George Meridian.

---

7. The name George Meridian has been simply made up for this illustration. Each area of land in the rectangular coordinate system is associated with a particular principal meridian. As stated earlier, two of the principal meridians used in Ohio are the First Principal Meridian and the Michigan Meridian. I chose not to use either of those principal meridians because not all of the land in Ohio is described using the normal rectangular coordinate system designations. (See "Special Considerations for Ohio Real Property Descriptions" in this chapter.)

Take some time to examine several of the fractional areas so that you can become familiar with how they are identified. By the way, sections do not have to be divided into the particular fractional areas shown in Part C of Figure 9-6. But, they are always divided into fractional areas, then further subdivided into smaller fractional areas, until the particular property has been identified. Also remember that a section contains 640 acres, so you can calculate the number of acres in a parcel by multiplying the accumulated fractional parts by 640. For example, the North East 1/4 of the North West 1/4 would contain 40 acres (1/4 of 1/4 of 640 acres).

You may realize that the rectangular coordinate system works well in theory, but only if the earth were flat. Since the earth is curved, the north–south lines separating ranges should not be parallel and start to converge as we move northward. If you have trouble picturing this, look at a globe, where the lines of longitude meet at the North and South Poles. In the rectangular coordinate system, the errors due to the curvature of the earth are accumulated in each township, and the far northern and western sections are adjusted to account for this. Thus, sections 1, 2, 3, 4, 5, 6, 7, 18, 19, 30, and 31 will be slightly less than the ideal 640 acres, with the more northerly sections being adjusted more than the southern sections.

Finally, in the official rectangular coordinate system, section 16 is designated for school purposes. The goal was to ensure that local schools would be centrally located and that there would be land available for them. Unfortunately, this good intention has been more frequently ignored and altered than it has been recognized and honored.

Plat Maps

You may be thinking that the metes and bounds system and the rectangular coordinate system work just fine for large areas of land, such as a farm or some other parcel of several acres. And they are quite useful in that context. But what about land in a subdivision, where each lot is perhaps only a fraction of an acre? Isn't there a better way? After all, in the rectangular coordinate system, a single acre is less than half of a quarter of a quarter of a quarter of a quarter of a section. That would be cumbersome indeed. The solution lies in the use of a **plat map**.

When a subdivision is created, it is surveyed and a plat map is created. A developer will hire a surveyor to prepare a plat map and submit it for approval by the county authorities, such as the county planning commission, engineer, and board of trustees. It is next recorded in the county recorder's office and can then be used to uniquely identify a parcel of land.

Figure 9-7 Plat Map

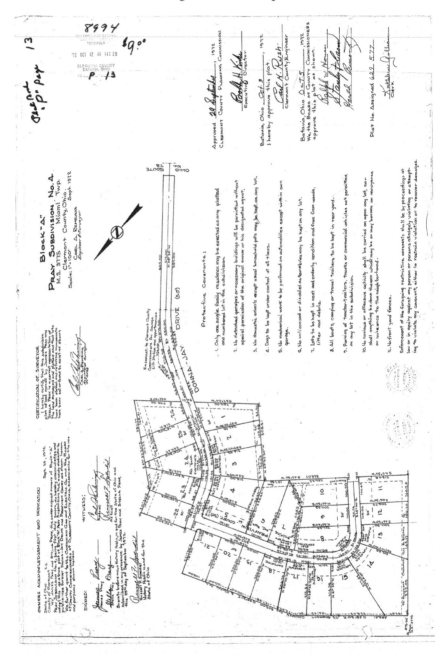

A plat map indicates the name of the subdivision, a drawing of the individual lots contained in it, any easements, the names of streets, building setbacks, and so forth. An example of a plat map is shown in Figure 9-7. Frequently, land-use restrictions will be contained on the plat map, such as the restriction numbered 11 in Figure 9-7, "No front yard fences." The boundaries of each lot are indicated by means of metes and bounds or rectangular coordinates. The example in Figure 9-7 uses the metes and bounds method. Each parcel is given a lot number, which is clearly indicated on the plat map. The plat map in Figure 9-7 contains 26 numbered lots.

An individual lot can now be specifically identified quite easily. For example, the lot numbered 21 in Figure 9-7 would have the following legal description:

> Lot 21 of Pray Subdivision #4, Block A, as recorded in Plat Book P, page 13 of the Plat Records of Clermont County, Ohio.

You can pretty easily understand the source of all this information. Lot 21 is located at the corner of Donna Jay Drive and Prayview Court on the plat map. The name of the subdivision is found in the caption at the top of the page, and the plat book and page number are located just below that. (The county recorder's office maintains books of all recorded documents, and each recorded document is identified by a reference to the book and page number.)

Any other lot in this subdivision would have the same legal description, with only the lot number being changed. You will likely see plat maps used for single-family homes, apartment buildings, condominiums, commercial developments, and industrial parks.

Registered Land—Torrens System in Ohio

The **Torrens system** is yet another alternative. Sir Robert Torrens of Australia invented this system in 1852, which is sometimes referred to as **registered land**. This system was adopted in Ohio by the Torrens Act of 1913. The Torrens system makes ownership of land certain, without the need for a title search each time land is transferred to a new owner. Ownership of registered land is indicated on a **certificate of title**, which operates very much like a title to an automobile. Any liens or other claims against the property must be shown on the certificate of title, or they simply do not exist.

Creating registered land is a rather involved process that is undertaken by a **registered land agent**, who carefully researches title to the property, arranges for a survey, and files a case with the local court of common pleas. When the application for registered land is approved, the boundaries of the property are

Figure 9-8—Alternative Section Numbering

36	30	24	18	12	6
35	29	23	17	11	5
34	28	22	16	10	4
33	27	21	15	9	3
32	26	20	14	8	2
31	25	19	13	7	1

guaranteed to be correct by the State of Ohio. What's more, registered land can never be acquired through the process of adverse possession, and the certificate of title is proof positive of the marketability of the title to the property, so title searches are not necessary. Involuntary liens (such as a judgment lien) against the property require special notice to the property owner. In short, after property has been officially designated as registered land, state law protects the ownership of the property.

This system is rather labor and time intensive, and it is falling into disuse. Many counties have simply abolished it, but it is still used in several counties in Ohio. For example, Hamilton County, where it is fairly widely used, contains more registered land than any other county in Ohio.

Special Considerations for Ohio Real Property Descriptions

As discussed earlier, Ohio served as a laboratory for trying out different real property survey systems and real property descriptions. As a result, more than 20 different survey systems are still in use today. The survey systems described in this chapter—metes and bounds, rectangular coordinate system, and plat maps—provide the underpinnings for all of the real property descriptions in Ohio. These survey systems were described in this text in the way that they are most often used, not only in Ohio but throughout the United States.

However, various parts of Ohio have a few rather distinct differences. Some areas of Ohio number sections in the rectangular coordinate system in a very different way. For example, Figure 9-8 shows one alternative section numbering system. Figure 9-9 shows a completely different rectangular coordinate system, which is used in some areas in Ohio and includes the oddly named

Figure 9-9—Fractional Ranges Near Center

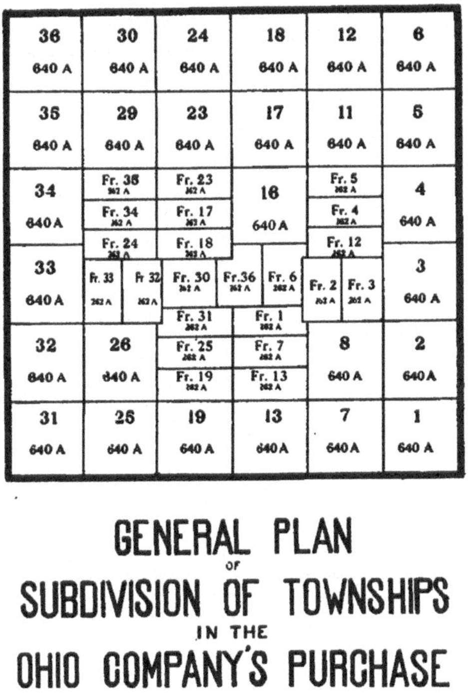

"fractional ranges," found near the center. Finally, Figure 9-10 shows the Between the Miami Rivers Survey, which has yet another numbering system and also contains fractional ranges, which are bounded by the Ohio River. Many other variations are in use in other parts of Ohio, as well.

The important takeaway from this section is that you may find an odd real property description system used in the area where you are practicing. You should become familiar with the particulars of that survey system and the corresponding real property descriptions used there. Just because it doesn't match up with the ones described in this chapter does not mean that the survey or property description is in error. You may need to look more closely at the details of the system being used in that particular part of Ohio.

Figure 9-10—Between the Miami Rivers

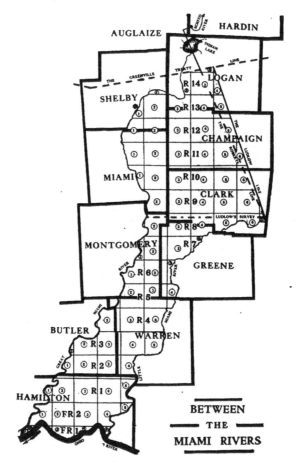

Discussion Questions

1. Explain why legal descriptions are important and necessary.

2. Explain what "S 40 E 250 poles" means in a metes and bounds description.

3. Describe how a survey reaches the point of beginning in a metes and bounds description.

4. How many acres would be in the following parcel?

The South West 1/4 of the South East Quarter of Section 24 of Township 3 North Range 4 East of the George Meridian.

5. Explain what a plat map is and how it makes real property descriptions simpler. Identify some of the information that can be found on a plat map.

6. Explain the advantages and disadvantages of registered land.

Key Terms

Baseline
Corner
Legal description
Meridian
Metes and bounds
Plat map
Point of beginning
Principal meridian
Public domain
Range
Rectangular coordinate system
Section
Survey
Survey marker
Township

Chapter 10

Deeds

Deeds

I think we all have a pretty good idea of what a deed is. After all, how often have we seen deeds referenced in melodramas—"If you don't give me the deed to the ranch, I'll tie you to the railroad track." Surely the deed is an important document, or why would the evildoer take such drastic action?

A **deed** is an official document used to transfer ownership of real property. The process of signing, sealing (notarizing), and delivering the deed actually accomplishes the transfer. A deed contains the name of the **grantor** (the person transferring the property), the **grantee** (the person receiving the property), and a legal description of the property. Some states, including Ohio, have other specific requirements, which are addressed later in this chapter. It is important to understand that the deed itself does not represent ownership, but that the process of signing, sealing, and delivering the deed is what actually transfers the property to its new owner. Remember from Chapter 8 where Donald happened to find a signed, notarized deed in his rich Uncle Scrooge's top desk drawer *after Scrooge died*? You will recall that because Scrooge never delivered the deed, Donald is not the owner merely because the deed is in his name. To reiterate, a deed is used to transfer ownership and is not proof of ownership itself. Sorry, the money bin is not Donald's. Perhaps Scrooge named Donald in his will.

Types of Deeds

Ohio recognizes four types of deed—general warranty, limited warranty, quitclaim, and fiduciary. Each of these can be used to transfer real property, but the difference is in the warranties, or guaranties that are included with the deeds. The grantor makes these warranties to the grantee. The warranties are primarily concerned with the quality of title to the property, and range from a full guarantee to no guarantee at all.

In Chapter 8, we described **title** as being roughly equivalent to ownership. In the most basic sense this is true. But as we will see in Chapter 11, title can be defective in a number of ways. For example, suppose you own your house but have a mortgage loan on it. You are indeed the owner, but you probably do not have clear title to the property, because the bank will most likely have lien on the property. You would need to pay off the loan on the property to have clear title. The fact that the lien exists would be considered a **title defect**. In other words, there is some claim against the property other than your ownership. We will look at each of the deed types and examine the various warranties that are made with each one.

General Warranty

In essence, a **general warranty deed** says that the title is perfect—if any defects are later found, the grantor guarantees that he or she will do what is necessary to remove the defects or be liable for damages caused by the title defects. A general warranty deed is considered the best deed possible and is the deed that is usually used in real property transfers. Some states require that the warranties be stated explicitly in the deed itself, but in Ohio, it is quite easy to create these general warranties. By statute in Ohio, the following language will create a general warranty deed[1]:

> Grantor (marital status), of ABC County, for valuable consideration paid, grants, *with general warranty covenants*, to Grantee, whose tax-mailing address is (address), the following real property. (Emphasis added.)

A general warranty deed contains six warranties, as described below.

---

1. Ohio Rev. Code § 5302.05.

Warranty	Meaning	Present or Future
Seisin	Grantor has good title to the property being conveyed.	Present
Right to Convey	Grantor has the right to convey the property.	
No Encumbrances	No encumbrances are on the property, other than those that have been previously disclosed.	
Quiet Enjoyment*	Grantor will forever guarantee that the grantee, heirs, and assigns will be able to possess the property without interference from someone claiming superior title.	Future
Warranty*	Grantor will forever defend the title in the grantee, heirs, and assigns.	
Further Assurances (Not recognized in Ohio)	Grantor will forever do whatever is reasonably necessary to fix title problems that may arise later.	

* For all practical purposes, the warranty of Quiet Enjoyment and the oddly named Warranty of Warranty are essentially the same thing. Since they are traditionally broken out separately, I have done so here. In Ohio, you can simply lump them together.

You have no doubt noticed that some of the warranties are designated as "present" and some are designated as "future." The present warranties are effective at the time of conveyance and do not extend beyond that time. If you think about this for a moment, it will make sense. For example, the warranty of Seisin effectively guarantees that the grantor is the current owner and has good title to the real property. As soon as the property is conveyed to the grantee, the grantor is no longer the owner and the warranty does not carry forward in time. However, if it turns out that the grantor *did not* have good title to the property at the time of the conveyance, the grantee could make a claim against the warranty of Seisin. What's more, the present warranties only are given from the grantor to the grantee.

The future warranties essentially last forever and protect not only the grantee but also *any* owner of the real property from the grantee forward. The term "heirs and assigns" is frequently used in the law to mean the present owner and any subsequent owner, forever. *Heirs* is easily understood as being anyone to whom the grantee leaves the real property upon his or her death. *Assigns* means anyone to whom the grantee might sell, give away, or otherwise transfer ownership of the property in the future, as well as anyone to whom that person might sell, give away, or otherwise transfer that property, and so on. Since these warranties apply to events that occur after the conveyance, they are clearly future warranties.

You may be wondering about the value of these warranties. After all, if a person sells his or her house to another, the proceeds of the sale (if any) are frequently almost immediately used to purchase another home. So, even if a grantee (or future owner) has a warranty claim, the grantor may not be able to correct the problem or pay damages. And you would be right. But, if the grantor is "on the hook" for the warranties, he or she is certainly motivated to pay off a lien or prove that it had been paid, by producing a canceled check or other documentation. However, as we will see in Chapter 11, this is where title insurance kicks in and becomes responsible for correcting these problems.

Limited Warranty

A **limited warranty deed** (sometimes known as a **special warranty deed**) is very much like a general warranty deed. It has the same warranties both present and future, but with one major difference—the warranties apply only to things that the grantor has done. A general warranty deed guarantees against *any* problems with title to the property, but a limited warranty deed guarantees against problems that the *grantor* has created. Any problems with title that existed before the grantor owned the real property are not covered by a limited warranty deed, and the grantee assumes the risk for things occurring before the grantor owned the property.

In some states, creating a limited warranty deed requires all of the warranties and conditions to be spelled out explicitly on the deed itself. As you can imagine, this can create a rather lengthy and cumbersome document. In Ohio, however, it is rather easy to create a limited warranty deed. By statute in Ohio, the following language will create a general warranty deed[2]:

> Grantor (marital status), of ABC County, for valuable consideration paid, grants, *with limited warranty covenants*, to Grantee, whose tax-mailing address is (address), the following real property. (Emphasis added.)

I suspect that you might be wondering why any grantee would accept a limited warranty deed. In some circumstances they are entirely appropriate, and they are frequently used in commercial real estate transactions. For example, imagine that you have inherited an abandoned factory building, and a large corporation wants to purchase it from you. You had no interest in the prop-

---

2. Ohio Rev. Code § 5302.07.

erty before you inherited it, so you probably would not want to transfer ownership to the corporation on a general warranty deed and be responsible for any title defects that occurred before you owned it. What's more, between you and the large corporation, the corporation is in a better position to assume this risk, and would likely purchase title insurance to protect its interest in the factory building.

Here's a real example. My client had sold a large commercial manufacturing facility to another company and gave a general warranty deed. Several years later, my client agreed to purchase the property back from the other company. Thus, my client was already responsible for any title problems that occurred before the property was sold to the other company. My client's concern was that the other company hadn't somehow messed up title to the property. Hence, a limited warranty deed was appropriate.

As I mentioned, limited warranty deeds are frequently used in commercial real estate transactions. But that does not mean that they are always used or that buyers are automatically willing to accept a limited warranty deed. The type of deed to be used to transfer ownership of the property is frequently the topic of lengthy negotiations. As you might imagine, a buyer who insists on a general warranty deed might expect to pay more for the property than it would if it were to receive a limited warranty deed. These negotiations can require a lot of give and take between the parties before a deal is reached.

Quitclaim Deed

A **quitclaim deed,** or quit claim deed (sometimes erroneously called a "quick claim" deed) is one that contains no warranties or guarantees at all. It simply ends (quits) any claim that the grantor may have in the property. In essence a quitclaim deed says, "Whatever I have, which may be nothing, I transfer to you." I sometimes joke in class that in exchange for $1000, I will be willing to sign a valid quitclaim deed transferring all of my interest in Paul Brown Stadium (where the Cincinnati Bengals play, and frequently lose) to you. Of course I have no interest in Paul Brown Stadium, but that would not make the deed any less valid. I will have given you absolutely nothing in exchange for your $1000. By the way, I think this transaction would contain enough consideration to constitute a valid contract. You were under no prior obligation to pay me $1000, and I was under no prior obligation to sign a quitclaim deed.

You might wonder why a quitclaim deed has any purpose at all since it contains no warranties and might be transferring exactly nothing. Actually, these characteristics of quitclaim deeds are what make them so useful. Perhaps a couple of real examples may help. Suppose that Fred and Wilma own a house

Figure 10-1 — Gertrude Family

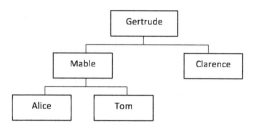

together as tenants in common, having bought the house from Barney and Betty and receiving a general warranty deed in that transaction. Now, several years later, Fred and Wilma get a divorce, and Wilma receives the house as part of a property settlement. A quitclaim deed from Fred to Wilma would be entirely appropriate here. Fred would just be giving up any claim he has to the property and not guaranteeing anything about the title. After all, Wilma received a general warranty deed from Barney and Betty, which protects her against title defects, and any subsequent title problem would have occurred when she and Fred were owners. And Fred is probably in no mood to give Wilma anything more than the minimum required.

Quitclaim deeds are also frequently used to resolve title and ownership issues that may have occurred in the past. Here is a real example from my practice, with minor fact and name changes to protect client confidentiality. This involves Gertrude and her family (see Figure 10-1). Gertrude had two children, Mable and Clarence. Mable and her husband had two children, Alice and Tom, who are now my clients. Gertrude gave a general warranty deed for her house to her daughter, Mable. Mable, who had a house of her own, accepted the deed, promptly put it in her safe, and did not record it.[3] Mable then died, leaving everything to her husband, who continued living in the house with Alice and Tom and did not know about the deed in the safe. Sometime later, Gertrude died, and her son Clarence inherited everything under Gertrude's will. Because no one knew about the deed to the house, it was transferred to Clarence as part of the probate process. Then, some 25 years later, Alice and Tom's father died and left everything to Alice and Tom. In the process of clean-

---

3. We will discuss recording deeds and the importance of doing so later in this chapter. This example will illustrate the kinds of problems that can occur when deeds are not recorded. This is an example of what is known as a *wild deed*.

ing out their father's house, they found the deed of Gertrude's house to Mable in the safe. Since they are now the heirs to everything, they might have some ownership interest to Gertrude's house. My clients, Alice and Tom, have always considered that Gertrude's house belonged to their uncle Clarence, since he had lived there for almost 30 years, but the deed in the safe called that into question. They did not want to dispute their uncle's ownership of the property. How can they clear up the title to Clarence? Surely they can't give a general or a limited warranty deed because they may not have any title to transfer to Clarence. Quitclaim deeds from Alice and Tom to Clarence clear the cloud on title to Gertrude's house. There is no need to go to probate court or try to work out just who has what interest in that house. Surely you can see that quitclaim deeds from Alice and Tom solve this mess rather neatly.

Fiduciary Deed

The final kind of deed used in Ohio is a **fiduciary deed**, which is used when someone other than an owner of real property (a fiduciary) transfers ownership to another person. Two common situations that call for a fiduciary deed are property that is sold by an executor of an estate while in probate, and a sale by the sheriff of property in foreclosure. Neither the executor nor the sheriff is an owner of the property, but they have the power to transfer ownership of it. A general warranty, a limited warranty, and a quitclaim deed will not work, because these transfer ownership of property held by the person making the deed.

A fiduciary deed does, however, have warranties attached to it. In Ohio, the person making a fiduciary deed guarantees that the fiduciary –

1. was duly appointed;
2. was acting in the fiduciary capacity and not in their own interest;
3. was authorized to make the sale; and
4. has complied with all applicable laws.[4]

A fiduciary deed, then, is the best deed that can be given when property is sold by the executor or administrator of an estate, the sheriff, a guardian on behalf of an incompetent person, a trustee of a trust, a receiver in a bankruptcy-like matter, or someone else acting in a similar capacity.

---

4. Ohio Rev. Code § 5302.09.

Which Deed to Use?

Transactions where the grantor is also the owner of the property usually have some tension between the grantor and grantee. Ideally, a grantor would want to give only a quitclaim deed, and a grantee would want to receive a general warranty deed for rather obvious reasons. So, which one to use? There is no simple answer. If a bank is involved in the transaction by loaning money to the buyer to purchase the property, it will almost always insist that a general warranty deed be used. In commercial transactions, as pointed out earlier, the deed type is often the subject of serious negotiations. In some instances, only a quitclaim deed makes sense. Finally, if someone other than the owner is making the deed, a fiduciary deed is appropriate.

Like almost all legal questions, the correct answer to which deed to use is "it depends." That rather flip statement is true, but only the first half of the answer. The "depends" part is where all the action is and where real estate professionals earn their fees.

Here is a quick summary of the deed types and the warranties that each provides to the grantee:

Deed Type	Guarantee
General warranty	Title is perfect.
Limited warranty	I didn't mess up title.
Quitclaim	Whatever I have is yours.
Fiduciary	I have the right to do this and I have done everything properly.

Recording Deeds

How does someone who owns real property let the rest of the world know that they are the owner? The simple answer is that the deed is **recorded** at the county recorder's office in the county where the property is located. A small filing fee is charged to record a deed, but the importance of doing so cannot be overstated.

You remember back to the problem with Gertrude's house and how Mable was given a deed that she securely placed in her safe before dying. Although it is a good idea to place important papers in a secure location, Mable should have taken the next step and had the deed recorded. That way, the whole world would be on notice that she is the owner. Then, when Gertrude died and left everything to Clarence, the executor of Gertrude's estate would know that Mable already owned the house and therefore it was not a probate item.

Three basic types of recording systems are used in the United States, with different states having adopted different systems. The recording systems can be broken down into **race** statutes, **notice** statutes, and **race-notice** statutes. To provide a consistent example with which to understand the differences between these three types of statutes, we will consider a particular transaction.

Imagine a crooked real property owner named Darth, who wanted to pull a real property sales scam. One day, he sold his house to Luke and gave a general warranty deed. The very next day he sold the same house to Leia and gave her a general warranty deed. Darth promptly vanished and cannot be located, so the guarantees in the general warranty deeds are effectively impossible to enforce. Both Luke and Leia paid money to Darth for the property.

Leia promptly took her deed to the county recorder's office and had it recorded. Luke also took his deed to be recorded a few days later. Here is the question—between Luke and Leia, who has the better claim to the house? The answer depends on the type of recording statute in use in the state where the property is located.

Race Statute

A **race statute** is probably the easiest to understand, and its name suggests exactly how it works. In a race statute state, whoever gets to the recorder's office first is the winner. Imagine a foot race between Luke and Leia, each trying to be the first to record. In our example, since Leia was the first to record, her title to the house is superior to that of Luke. Leia would win in a race statute jurisdiction even if she knew that Darth had previously sold the house to Luke. Now, that doesn't mean Luke is completely out of luck. All he has to do is find Darth, sue him, win, and collect damages. Right.

Notice Statute

In a **notice statute** jurisdiction, a subsequent purchaser who does not know about a previous sale[5] will prevail. So, if Leia did not know about Darth's sale of the house to Luke, she would prevail. If Leia knew about the previous sale to Luke, Luke would win. The "notice" element of a notice statue is all about the subsequent purchaser's knowledge of other sales. As you can imagine, this

---

5. This is known as a "bona fide purchase for value without notice."

situation can give rise to significant litigation as to what Leia knew and when she knew it. If Luke had recorded his deed before Darth sold the house to Leia, she would be on notice that Luke was the owner therefore she would not be a "bona fide purchaser for value *without notice*." In that situation, Luke would win. The recording of the deed puts the entire world on notice of ownership, so that Leia would be held to know about the sale to Luke even if she didn't bother to check the county recorder's office.

Race-Notice Statute

As its name suggests, the **race-notice** recording statute has elements of both the race and the notice systems. In a race-notice jurisdiction, the first person to record, without knowledge of another sale, wins. This differs from the race statute, where knowledge about other sales is irrelevant. In a race-notice jurisdiction, the first bona fide purchaser for value to record, without notice of a previous sale, will prevail. So, in our example, if Leia knew about the sale to Luke, and Luke did not know about the sale to Leia, Luke would prevail, because he would be the first to record without knowledge of another sale. Ohio is a race-notice jurisdiction.[6]

Required Elements of Recorded Deeds in Ohio

Ohio requires that deeds conform to certain requirements before a county recorder will accept them to be recorded. These are summarized below:

1. The grantor must be identified.
2. The grantor's marital status must be stated to alert the grantee to possible dower interests held by the grantor's spouse.
3. The grantee must be identified.
4. The grantee's tax mailing address must be identified, so that real estate property tax bill can be sent to the right place.
5. The deed must include a statement that consideration was given. This concept is similar to how *consideration* is used in contracts, but with a bit of a difference. You will recall that in contracts, consideration means legal detriment. It's what is given up as part of the contract. For a sale of prop-

---

6. Ohio Rev. Code § 5301.25(A). "Until so recorded or filed for record, [deeds are invalid] insofar as they relate to a subsequent bona fide purchaser having, at the time of purchase, no knowledge of the existence of that former deed, land contract, or instrument."

erty, the consideration is ownership of the property in exchange for purchase money. "Love and affection" is valid consideration for a deed, but not for a contract, because nothing is given up.

6. The deed must clearly indicate that the grantor intends to convey the property. This can be as simple as "grantor hereby grants to grantee."
7. The deed must contain a legal description of the property being transferred.
8. The grantor must sign the deed.
9. The deed must be notarized.
10. For deeds signed before February 1, 2002, the grantor had to sign in the presence of two witnesses, who also had to sign the deed.
11. The prior deed reference (book and page) must be identified. When deeds are recorded, a copy is placed in large books at the recorder's office. These books are numbered sequentially, and each page is numbered. So, for instance, a reference to "Book 234 Page 123" will specifically identify where a person can find a particular deed. More recently, deeds are recorded electronically, and some jurisdictions no longer have paper deed books. But recorded deeds are still referenced by book and page number.
12. The person preparing the deed (usually an attorney) must be identified.

A sample Ohio deed appears in Appendix D. You will notice that this is a quitclaim deed and transfers property in Ohio statutory survivorship form. Take a few minutes and compare this deed to the requirements for a recorded deed in Ohio.

Some counties may impose additional requirements to record a deed. For example, you may be required to leave a specific amount of blank space on the face of the first page of the deed for the county recorder to stamp the book and page number of the deed. It is always a good idea to check the county recorder's website for any special requirements for recorded deeds in that county.

Transfer Tax

Two things are considered certain—death and taxes—and in many ways, taxes are more certain than death. Counties in Ohio collect a tax on each real property transfer, which is based on the value of the property being transferred. This is sometimes referred to as a **conveyance tax**. This usually includes a minimal fixed tax (often $0.50) plus an additional amount of $2.00–$3.00 per thousand dollars in value. Thus, a sale of real property for $100,000 might incur a transfer tax of $300.50. This amount is calculated as $3.00 per thousand dollars in value plus a minimal fee of $0.50.

Several transactions are not subject to transfer tax in Ohio. The form used to claim these exemptions is found in Appendix E. Rather than listing the exceptions here, you are encouraged to look at the form in Appendix E to get a feel for the transactions that are exempt from transfer taxes.

Release of Spouses' Interest

As discussed in Chapter 4, married people in Ohio have dower rights in all Ohio real property held by the other spouse at any time during the marriage. If these dower rights are not released, they continue to exist, even after the property has been sold to another person. For instance, suppose Bob owned 200 acres of vacant land before he and Kristyn were married, and then he sold the land to Della during the marriage. Kristyn would have dower rights in the land, because Bob held it during the marriage. If Kristyn did not release her dower rights, she would have a one-third life estate in the property held by Della if Bob dies during the marriage. I'm sure that Della would not be at all pleased to learn, perhaps several years later, that Kristyn has a claim on the land. For this reason, standard deed forms in Ohio include a dower release provision. This can be as simple as, "I hereby release my dower interest in the subject property," followed by Kristyn's signature on the deed itself.

Sometimes spouses first discover the existence of their dower rights as a real estate transaction is under way. This can give rise to some marital friction, as the non-owner spouse might seek some compensation from the owner spouse in exchange for releasing his or her dower interest. "If you want me to sign the dower release, honey, then you will do such-and-such for me." As you might imagine, this can cause friction between the spouses and can delay or mess up a real estate transaction.

Reservations and Exceptions

When property is conveyed from a grantor to a grantee, sometimes the grantor will transfer fewer than all of the "sticks" in the bundle of rights. In these cases, the grantor is said to have made a **reservation** of rights and therefore retains these rights. Suppose a grantor believes that there is a deposit of oil, coal, uranium, or some other valuable resource underneath the property and wants to sell the land but retain the mineral rights. Language such as "grantor reserves to himself (or herself) all mineral rights associated with the property" would cause the mineral rights to be retained by the grantor, even after the sale. What's more, the grantor could later sell the mineral rights to someone else. Remember that we can always split up the bundle of rights and transfer only part of them to a new owner. Grantors frequently use reservations to retain easements across property that has been sold. Remember the example from Figure 2-1 in Chapter 2, where the landowner split his property into two parcels and granted an easement to the new owner. The owner could have decided to keep the right parcel and sell the left parcel. In this case, the grantor would deed the left parcel to the new owner and reserve a driveway easement. That way, the new owner would take the left parcel subject to the easement in favor of the right parcel.

Similarly, sometimes an owner of real property does not own the entire bundle of rights associated with the property. Indeed, things like easements, tax liens, and the like are very common in Ohio. For instance, my house sits on a parcel of land that is subject to several easements for water lines, sewer lines, and underground electrical and cable wires. All of these easements are recorded in the county recorder's office, so if I were to sell my property, I would include an **exception** for them such as, "grantor excepts from this transfer any easements and tax liens of record." Try as I might, I simply cannot sell more than I own, and I certainly do not own unfettered rights to my property, as it is encumbered by these easements and tax lien. In Ohio, property is subject to a lien in connection with the county real property tax. Real estate taxes are paid in arrears (typically twice a year, around midsummer and near the end of the year, but this varies by county). The summer payment covers taxes for the period from January 1 to the payment date, and the end-of-year payment covers taxes for the balance of the year.[7] The county tax lien, however, automatically attaches to the property on January 1, so in effect, the tax lien never goes away. Therefore, you cannot transfer property not subject to the tax lien. This is why an adjustment is made at closing for county property taxes. We will discuss this in more detail in Chapter 13.

Deed Restrictions

In the previous chapter, we looked at platted property, and the example in Figure 9-7 included some restrictions on the use of the property. Take a look at that figure now and you will notice the restrictions, which include one single-family house on each lot, only domestic pets, and others. These are re-

---

7. This assumes that the taxes are paid six months in arrears. In some Ohio counties, taxes are paid a year in arrears.

ferred to as **deed restrictions**. In this example, the restrictions appear on a plat, but they could just as easily be placed on a deed itself. For example, a grantor may sell an adjoining parcel of land and include a deed restriction on the sold parcel requiring any building on that property to be at least a certain distance from the border with grantor's existing land. Only the imagination and negotiation skills limit restrictions that can be placed on realty by way of deed restrictions.

Deed restrictions "run with the land"; that is, they are binding on future owners of the land. However, deed restrictions are not necessarily permanent. The passage of time, change in how surrounding land is used, lack of enforcement of the restrictions, and such things can cause deed restrictions to become lost. For example, in the restriction described in the previous paragraph, suppose that on the property sold by grantor a building was constructed that was closer than allowed distance. If the original grantor did not enforce the restriction, over time it would lose effect. The old adage applies—if you don't protect your rights, you will lose them.

Some deed restrictions are simply void from the beginning or become void over time for public policy reasons. For example, any deed restriction that prohibited sale or lease of the property to another person based on race, color, national origin, religion, or gender would simply not be enforceable. Public policy exceptions to deed restrictions evolve as society changes over time. At one time, it was not too uncommon to find deed restrictions banning sale of certain parcels to others based on race. These deed restrictions are now simply void.

Discussion Questions

1. Give an example where each of the following deeds would be appropriate:
    a. General warranty deed
    b. Limited warranty deed
    c. Quitclaim deed
    d. Fiduciary deed
2. Explain the difference between the present warranties and the future warranties in a general warranty deed.
3. Explain the difference between the following:
    a. Race recording statute
    b. Notice recording statute
    c. Race-notice recording statute
4. Explain why a deed to be recorded in Ohio must identify the marital status of the grantor.

5. Explain the difference between a deed reservation and a deed exception.

Key Terms

Conveyance tax
Deed
Deed restriction
Exception
Fiduciary deed
General warranty deed
Grantee
Grantor
Limited warranty deed
Notice statute
Quitclaim deed
Race statute
Race-notice statute
Recording deeds
Reservation
Special warranty deed
Title
Title defect

Chapter 11

Title Searching

Why Is a Title Search Necessary?

Suppose you wanted to buy a new car. How would you know that the person from whom you are buying the car is actually the owner? How would you know that the car is fully paid for and not subject to a lien? For automobiles, it's actually pretty easy—you would want to see a so-called clean certificate of title. An official certificate of title from the clerk will indicate the current owner as well as any liens on it. In fact, banks (or other lenders) normally hold the original certificate of title until any loans are paid off, and in this case the owner is instead issued a "memorandum certificate of title." So, if a seller has only a memorandum certificate of title, the car is not fully paid for and you should not purchase it until the seller can provide an official clean certificate of title.

With real property, things are not quite so simple. As you recall from the previous chapter, just because someone has a deed to the property does not necessarily mean that the person is the actual owner. Except for registered land, which is issued a certificate of title similar to one of automobiles, no official document is produced by any government entity that indicates the owner of real property and any liens that may be attached to it. Instead, deeds and any liens are recorded by the county recorder's office, and a buyer would need to look there to verify the identity of the owner and any liens or other recorded defects that may be associated with the real property.

What Is a Title Search?

As you might guess, a **title search**, sometimes called a **title examination**, is the process of searching the *public* records of the various offices in the county (and in some cases outside of the county) where the property is located to determine the owner and if the property has any liens or other defects. This is a rather involved process and is usually undertaken by **title examiners**, although since the recorder's office records are public information, anyone can walk in and look things up. However, unless a person is quite familiar with how documents are recorded and the procedure for searching them, it is probably a job best left to those who do it professionally. Many graduates of paralegal and other programs go on to become title examiners themselves. If you enjoy research and detailed work, you might find this an apt career choice. A title search involves examining all of the public records associated with a piece of real property to determine who the present owner is and to see if the property has any liens or other recorded defects. It is not at all uncommon to uncover problems with title that need to be corrected before a prudent buyer would be willing to purchase the property. As a very simple and common example, the property might be subject to a mortgage that would need to be satisfied before the purchase is completed.

Title Examination in General

Basically, the title search process involves starting with the current owner, examining the deed or other document that was used to transfer ownership to that person, and then working backward. As you will recall from the chapter on deeds, one of the requirements of a recorded deed is a reference to the prior document. The title examiner would then look at the previous deed to make sure that it was in proper form. From that deed, the prior deed would be examined, and so forth, going back several years to a time well beyond the statute of limitations.[1] Any problems that might exist before then would be too old for someone to successfully make a claim.

After following the chain of title through the recorded deeds, the title examiner would then use the **grantee index** to match up the chain of title. We will look at this in more detail later in this chapter, but it is enough to understand that it is simply a list of transactions that show the grantee and grantor for each transaction. The grantee index lists the grantees in a sort of alphabetical

---

1. In Ohio, the statute of limitations for claims involving real property is 21 years. However, title searches typically go back at least 40 years to a deed with an unbroken chain of title to the current owner. This is the minimum required by the Ohio Marketable Title Act (Ohio Rev. Code § 5301.47 et. seq.). There may be reasons to look back beyond 40 years, but a discussion of that is beyond the scope of this text.

order by year. Next to the grantee will be the name of the grantor, the date of transfer, and a book and page number where the deed or other transfer was recorded. Next, the title examiner would look up the grantor in the grantee index to see how that person received title to the property. The grantor in the last transaction would become the grantee in the previous transaction. Then the process would be repeated, again going back several years beyond the statute of limitations. By doing this, the title examiner is able to produce a timeline of each previous owner and how they obtained title to the property.

Next, the title examiner would start with the oldest owner that was found in the chain of title and use the **grantor index** to move forward from that time. Each transfer or lien or other recorded defect will be listed in the grantor index, so the title examiner will be able to see not only the chain of title from the oldest owner being looked at, but also each lien and other recorded defect (such as an easement) that was placed on the property by or against each owner. First, the chain of title backward and the chain of title forward should match up. If they do not, the title examiner would need to determine why. Second, any mortgages, liens, or other recorded defects will turn up, and the title examiner would want to look at those to make sure that they had been released and satisfied. Surely a buyer of real property would not be too happy to learn after the purchase that a lien placed on the property 15 years ago by a previous owner is still in place.

Finally, the title examiner will look at court and other public records to see if the property was involved in any lawsuits or other actions. As a quick example, property may have been awarded to one spouse in a divorce, but the other spouse never signed over a quitclaim deed. Or, perhaps an *in rem* **action** (a form of lawsuit where the property itself is named as a party to the suit) currently exists or remains unsatisfied. Real property is frequently involved in probate matters, where it is willed or otherwise transferred to an heir. Maybe a former owner lost a lawsuit, and a judgment lien was placed on the property. All of these court and public records would need to be inspected to see how they might affect the property. Indeed, title to some property may be so messed up that it is impractical for it to be sold. A parcel of land may have so many claims and title defects that it is simply too costly to correct them. A potential buyer would be better off looking for another piece of real estate to purchase.

At the end of these processes, the title examiner would prepare a **title report**, which will detail everything that the search found. This report will give the buyer, the buyer's real estate agent, the title company, and perhaps the buyer's attorney information about the current state of title to the property and any defects that need to be addressed before a sale.

Grantee and Grantor Indexes

As mentioned earlier in this chapter, two of the key tools used by a title examiner are the grantee and grantor indexes. These are merely lists of transactions that are arranged in order by either grantee, in the case of the grantee index, or grantor, in the case of the grantor index. These are perhaps best understood by looking at samples of each of them.

Figures 11-1 and 11-2 contain excerpts of a grantee index and a grantor index.[2] By looking at the grantee index, we can see from whom each grantee received an interest in real property, including mortgages and other encumbrances. For example, on February 26, 1986, Patrick Star entered into a mortgage with James Savings and Loan. You could find a copy of the recorded mortgage in book 234, page 217, of the mortgage records. Likewise, Mary Jones obtained property from Steve Dayton on March 7, 1986, by warranty deed, which has been recorded in book 236, page 435.

Take a look at the explanations on Figures 11-1 and 11-2 to help understand how these indexes can be used to trace ownership of property back in time to a point well beyond the statute of limitations and then forward from that point to the current time. Along the way the title examiner should be able to uncover all recorded encumbrances on the property.

Ohio recorders' offices now keep up with recorded documents and indexes by computer. This makes title searching much easier, but these records frequently do not go back far enough (certainly not 40 years), so using paper indexes and recorded documents is still a necessary part of title examination.

Tract Indexes

Some recorder's offices in Ohio maintain a **tract index**, sometimes called a **property index**. This index lists all recorded documents related to a particular tract of land on a single page. If the local recorder's office has a tract index, this may be a good place to start a title examination. However, a complete title search should use all of the information available, so a prudent title examiner will also look to the grantee and grantor indexes to make sure that nothing has been missed.

---

2. The sample grantee and grantor indexes have been simplified a bit. Real indexes often contain additional information, such as a brief description of the property, such as "1.04 acres." Such brief descriptions do not rise to the level of a full legal description but contain enough information to help identify the particular property. What's more, indexes created before recorders' offices started maintaining records by computer were frequently handwritten, which can create legibility and other problems.

Figure 11-1 — Sample Grantee Index Excerpt

Sample Grantee index excerpt

Grantee	Grantor	Date	Document	Book	Page
Johnson, Madeline	Lyons, Patricia	2/7/86	Quitclaim Deed	233	314
Johnston, Nathan	Williams, Mark	2/18/86	Warranty Deed	233	421
James Savings and Loan	Star, Patrick	2/26/86	Mortgage	234	217
Jones, Mark	Smith, Paul	3/7/86	Warranty Deed	234	654
Jones, Mary	Dayton, Steve	3/12/86	Warranty Deed	236	435
Jacobs, Mitch	Calvert, Loretta	5/29/86	Limited Warranty Deed	237	143
Jacoby, Nancy	Martin, Della	6/14/86	Warranty Deed	237	152

You will notice a few things about this sample grantee index. First, all of the transactions took place in 1986. Transactions are recorded in chronological order and, when the recorders' offices did things on paper, a new physical index book would be started each year. Each page in the index will contain similar names, in this case, those whose last name starts with J and first name starts with M or N. There is always a method to figure out which page in the index contains which names. Frequently, there is a chart at the bottom of each page that indicates which page number corresponds to which set of names.

Let's look at the entry for Mary Jones. You will see that she received property from Steve Dayton on March 12, 1986 by warranty deed, which was recorded in book 236 on page 435. If we were doing a title examination of this property, we would inspect the deed in deed book 236 on page 435. Next, we would look at the grantee index page that included last name starting with D and first names that included S to find how Steve Dayton obtained title to the property and inspect his deed. This process will be repeated backwards until we reach a point in time well beyond the statute of limitations. Then, we would turn to the grantor index, which looks very much the same as the grantee index, except that it is arranged in order by grantor, rather than by grantee.

Other Considerations

The title examiner should also take note of any deed restrictions, easements, rights of way, and other things that cause the current owner of real property to own fewer than all of the sticks in the bundle. These should be called to the attention of a potential buyer so that no surprises come up later on. Real property in Ohio commonly has such things attached to the property. For example, utility easements for water, sewer, power, cable television, and the like,

Figure 11-2—Sample Grantor Index Excerpt

Sample Grantor index excerpt

Grantor	Grantee	Date	Document	Book	Page
Dennis, Thomas	Reeves, Phoebe	2/8/86	Warranty Deed	233	327
Davidson, Samuel	Krome, Fred	2/15/86	Limited Warranty Deed	233	418
Demarco, Todd	Herman, Deborah	2/24/86	Warranty Deed	234	213
Diego, Shannon	Loving, Greg	3/9/86	Quitclaim Deed	235	152
Dayton, Steve	Jones, Mary	3/12/86	Warranty Deed	236	435
Drummond, Tiffany	Johnson, Raymond	5/14/86	Warranty Deed	237	67
Dunn, Sven	Bauer, Jeff	6/22/86	Limited Warranty Deed	237	238

As was the case with the grantee index, you will notice a few things about this sample grantor index. First, all of the transactions took place in 1986. Transactions are recorded in chronological order and, when the recorders' offices did things on paper, a new physical index book would be started each year. Each page in the index will contain similar names, in this case, those whose last name starts with D and first name starts with S or T. There is always a method to figure out which page in the index contains which names. Frequently, there is a chart at the bottom of each page that indicates which page number corresponds to which set of names.

Let's look at the entry for Steve Dayton. You will see that he transferred property to Mary Jones on March 12, 1986 by warranty deed, which was recorded in book 236 on page 435. This is the same transaction we looked at earlier in the grantee index. Each transaction is recorded twice, once in the grantee index and again in the grantor index.

If you think about how these indices work, you will realize that a title examiner can use the grantee index to work backwards in time from owner to previous owner and thereby create a chain of ownership for the property, going back to a point well beyond the statute of limitations. Then, using the grantor index, the title examiner can go forwards in time from that point forward. As the title examiner works forward in time, all voluntary and involuntary liens and other encumbrances on the property should show up, and each encumbrance should be examined to see if it had been subsequently released, or if it is still in effect.

while technically reductions in the bundle of rights, actually can make the property more valuable, as they provide important services to the parcel.

As mentioned earlier, in Ohio, property tax and tax liens always exist on realty. A thorough title examination will look at current tax payments and note any delinquent real property taxes. Surely a new owner would not want to find out later that several years of back taxes have not been paid. Because the tax liability on real property is secured by a county tax lien, the new owner would have little recourse but to pay the back taxes and try to extract reimbursement from the former owner (assuming that the owner can be found) by a lawsuit. It would be far better to know this up front.

Probate court records also need to be examined to see if a transfer of real property out of an estate was not recorded in the county recorder's office. Grandmother could have left the family farm to Mom, who then left it to Daughter, all of whom lived there their entire lives. I think you can see how recording the transfer of ownership out of Grandmother and Mom's estates could be overlooked—after all, isn't that a "mere formality"? A title search using the grantee and grantor indexes might well discover the transfer of the property to Grandmother (and probably Grandfather), but the chain could end there.

Likewise, the records of the county court clerk would need to be examined. Perhaps the property itself was the subject of a lawsuit in an *in rem* action. Maybe someone obtained the realty by adverse possession and a quiet title lawsuit was brought, but that decision was never recorded in the county recorder's office. Or a prior owner might have lost a lawsuit and obtained a verdict, which was converted into a judgment lien against the property, which remained unrecorded.

Any of these situations, and many others, could create a **cloud on the title** to the property, or some doubt as to the identity of the true owner. A careful title examiner is rather like a detective who tracks down clues and tries to work out exactly what happened in the past. The resulting title report should identify all of the problems

Correcting Errors in Chain of Title

As you can imagine from the discussion so far, it is not uncommon to find problems in the chain of title. Most of these problems can be corrected fairly easily. Some common things that come up include a mortgage or other lien that was paid off but never released—this may have been simply overlooked by the lender who failed to send the lien release to the recorder's office. The lender can usually be convinced to correct this (assuming the lender still exists) or the borrower can produce a "paid in full" receipt.

A married couple may have been divorced and the realty awarded to one of them, but that fact was never indicated in the recorder's office. A quitclaim deed can usually solve this. Sometimes, a quitclaim deed was indeed signed, sealed, and delivered but never recorded. The property owner might find the quitclaim deed among the divorce papers that were simply filed away.

As discussed in the chapter on deeds, someone may have some potential ownership interest in the property but not be aware of it or even concerned about it. Once again, a quitclaim deed can solve this problem—you may remember that this is how the problem was solved with the property that was once owned by Gertrude in the example in that chapter.

Sometimes, an **affidavit**, a signed, sworn statement, may correct a title problem. Suppose that a property owner had some work done on the house, say a roofing repair. The roofer may have placed a mechanic's lien on the property to help guarantee payment. That roofer may no longer be in business, or may otherwise be unavailable. An affidavit from the owner swearing that the roofer was paid, perhaps with a copy of a canceled check, might clear up this problem.

Not all title problems, however, can be easily fixed. Indeed, some problems may be so serious as to make the property unsalable. For example, suppose a property owner lost a lawsuit with a judgment amount in excess of the value of the property. The defendant could have recorded a judgment lien on the property, which wouldn't be released without full payment of the judgment amount. If the property owner has no asset other than the realty, it may be impossible to satisfy the judgment creditor and release the lien.

Buyer Title Protection

How then can a buyer of realty be assured that he or she is receiving good title to the property? A title search might turn up some problems. Those problems might be solved by a lien release, quitclaim deed, affidavit, or other document. But, what can the buyer receive to quell any discomfort about the quality of title? Several methods can be used, and some are better than others. As you might expect, the better methods are increasingly more expensive. We will look at several of these in this section.

Owner Affidavit

Perhaps the cheapest and least valuable title assurance is an **owner affidavit**. This is merely a guarantee made by the seller that title to the property is good. If a title problem is found in the future, the seller promises to correct the problem. You will recall that a general warranty deed contains several guarantees or covenants. An owner affidavit is similar but is sworn under oath. If a problem arises in the future, the new owner could sue the seller under one or more of these guarantees. However, an owner affidavit is only as good as the person who makes it. A seller who now has no assets may be "judgment proof," and even though the buyer might obtain a favorable outcome suing on an owner affidavit, extracting relief may be fruitless. Of course an owner affidavit from a wealthy person, sas Bill Gates, may have some value.

Title Abstract

A **title abstract** is simply a report that shows the chain of title to the property, typically going back many, many years. In Ohio, a title abstract may go back all the way to the original land grant from the United States in the late 1700s. The title abstract would then show every transfer of the property from owner to owner up to the current owner of the property. In essence, it is a listing of all of the transfers in the grantee and grantor indexes going far back in time. While this is good and interesting historical reading, it does little to guarantee that the title is presently good. Wild deeds, unrecorded transfers, unrecorded easements, and such will not show up on a title abstract.

Attorney Opinion Letters

The next best form of title assurance is an **attorney's opinion letter**, which states that, in the opinion of the attorney, there are no title problems on the property. The attorney will have had a title search performed, perhaps examined a title abstract, and concluded that title to the subject property is marketable and has no defects. The value of the attorney's opinion letter is that, if a title problem turns up later, the attorney can be sued on the opinion and the buyer can look to the attorney's malpractice insurance for a recovery. This is clearly a better option than suing the former property owner under a deed covenant. But once again, the value of this form of title assurance is only as good as the attorney and his or her malpractice coverage.

Title Guarantees

Title guarantees are sometimes used in northwest Ohio. After conducting a title examination, an attorney or a title company guarantees the accuracy of the title search. This is a better form of title protection than an attorney opinion letter, because the property owner need only prove that the title search has errors. In contrast, suing on an attorney opinion letter requires proof that the attorney committed malpractice in addition to proving that the title opinion was in error.

A title guarantee only guarantees the accuracy of the title search; it does not cover title defects that are not in the public record. Therefore, unrecorded easements, wild deeds, forged documents, and the like are not covered. What's more, a title guarantee will pay off only up to the face value of the guarantee, which is usually the purchase price of the property. If a defect in the title search is later discovered that is more expensive than the face value of the guarantee, that extra amount is simply not covered.

Title Insurance

Title insurance is the best form of title protection and, surprisingly enough, is exactly what it says. It is an insurance policy written by a title insurance company that insures that title to the real property is good. If a problem with title turns out later, the insurance company promises to do whatever is necessary to correct the problem or otherwise make the policyholder whole. Of course, the company will have carefully examined the current state of title before issuing a title insurance policy. When the title company is satisfied that title is good, it will issue a **commitment for title insurance**, which basically says that if the insurance premium is paid, the company will issue a title insurance policy.

Since insurance companies are in business to make money, not pay claims, it will not issue a commitment for title insurance unless it is satisfied that no problems exist with the title. Some buyers mistakenly think that if a title insurance company is willing to issue a commitment for title insurance, this means that title to the property is perfect and therefore they do not need to pay for title insurance. This assumption is not true. Such problems as wild deeds, forged deeds, invalid divorces, unrecorded easements, errors in recording, fraud, and other such problems will not show up in a title examination but may be covered by title insurance. Purchasing real estate is a major financial transaction, and the relatively small cost of title insurance seems to be a worthwhile investment to protect the larger expense associated with the purchase.

Owner's Fee Policy v. Lender's Policy

Two kinds of title insurance policies are commonly issued—**owner's fee policy** and **lender's policy**. As the names suggest, the two policy types protect different things. An owner's policy protects the owner of the property, and a lender's policy protects the interest of the bank or other lender who financed the purchase transaction. In Ohio, the cost of title insurance premiums are set by statute, so any title insurance company that a buyer uses will charge the same premium. As of the time of writing, an owner's fee policy covering real estate purchased for $150,000 will cost $862, and a lender's policy covering a mortgage loan for the same amount will cost $600. Both of these costs are typically borne by the buyer and can be included in the amount borrowed to purchase the realty, and thus the cost is spread out over the life of the loan.

A mortgage lender is very likely to require that the buyer pay for a lender's policy of title insurance as a condition of making the loan. Some buyers wrongly assume that purchasing a lender's policy of title insurance protects their title to the property. This assumption is incorrect. The lender's policy of title insurance protects the lender and not the owner. What's more, it is a **declining value policy**. This means that the coverage protects only the lender up to the amount that remains unpaid on the mortgage loan. Suppose, for example, that 20 years into a 21-year mortgage loan, a fraudulent deed is discovered in the chain of title, and the true owner sues to recover the real property. An owner's fee policy of title insurance would step in and do whatever is necessary to make the owner whole, which could include purchasing the property from the true owner, refunding the purchase price to the policyholder, or taking some other action that would clear up the problem. If only a lender's policy is on the property, the title insurance company would be obligated only to make the lender whole. In this particular circumstance, the title insurance company may simply pay the lender the balance of the principal of the loan. As 20 years of mortgage payments have already been made, it would be on the hook for only the principal balance in the final year, which would be a rather inconsequential amount. In the meantime, the purchaser may well lose the property with no recourse.

Standard Exceptions

Title insurance policies do not cover all potential title problems. A few exceptions are typically not covered. These include rights of parties in possession (this exception would include, for example, the rights of a current tenant), encroachments, boundary issues and other matters that an accurate survey would disclose, and construction liens.

Often the title company will delete these exceptions if it feels adequately protected otherwise. For example, an affidavit from the current owner stating that no other person has any right of possession can be used to delete the exception dealing with parties in possession. Likewise, a survey could be conducted to remove the survey exception. In addition, the title insurance company may be willing to delete other exceptions in the form of additional endorsements to the title insurance policy, for an additional premium fee.

Transferability of Title Insurance

An owner's fee policy of title insurance protects only the purchaser of the policy and is not transferrable to a new owner. So if the property was subsequently sold to a new owner, that owner would need to obtain his or her own owner's fee policy of title insurance to have coverage. In some instances the title company may "re-issue" a new policy to a subsequent purchaser at a discount if that company already has coverage in place. This can be a significant benefit and cost savings to a buyer.

The lender's policy of title insurance protects the lender, whomever that may be now or in the future. So if the underlying loan is sold or transferred to a new holder, that new holder will be covered by the lender's policy of title insurance. Perhaps it is best to think of a lender's policy of title insurance as protecting the loan and not any particular person or entity. As we will see in Chapter 12, mortgage loans are commonly sold or otherwise transferred. However, if the owner refinances the property or otherwise takes out a subsequent loan on the property, a new lender's policy of title insurance would be required to protect that new lender. In some instances the title company may re-issue a new policy to a subsequent lender at a discount if there is proof that a lender's policy for title insurance is already in place. This can be a significant benefit and cost savings to a buyer as well.

Discussion Questions

1. Explain the difference between a grantee index, a grantor index, and a tract index.

2. What is a wild deed?

3. Why would a title examiner need to look at probate court records to complete a title search?

4. Explain the difference between the following:
    a. Owner affidavit
    b. Title abstract
    c. Attorney opinion letter
    d. Title guarantees
    e. Title insurance
Which provides the best protection for a buyer?
Which provides the least protection for a buyer?

5. Explain the difference between an owner's fee policy of title insurance and a lender's policy of title insurance.

6. If a buyer pays for a lender's policy of title insurance, why would they want to also purchase an owner's fee policy of title insurance?

Key Terms

Affidavit
Attorney opinion letter
Cloud on the title
Commitment for title insurance
Declining value policy
Grantee index
Grantor index
In rem action
Lender's policy
Owner affidavit
Owner's fee policy
Property index
Title abstract
Title examination
Title examiner
Title guarantee
Title insurance
Title report
Title search
Tract index

Chapter 12

Finance, Liens, and Foreclosure

These days, almost every purchase of real property deals with some kind of financing. Very few people, or indeed companies, have the ready cash available to purchase realty without borrowing money to purchase real estate. As you might imagine, a bank[1] will want to be protected against default should the borrower not be able to make the loan payments when they come due. So, much of the legal aspects of real estate finance involve protections for the lender. In my real estate law class I frequently say that there are two rules about real estate finance. Rule one: the bank never loses. Rule two: if the bank loses, see rule one. What I mean by this is that banks are often protected in multiple ways against losing money if a borrower defaults on a real estate loan. In this chapter, we will look at several of these protections.

Some basic terminology is useful at the onset so that we can use those terms throughout this chapter. As discussed in the footnote on this page, I use the term *bank* to mean the **lender**, which is sometimes called the **creditor**. The person borrowing the money is, naturally enough, called the **borrower** or **debtor**. The bank's primary line of protection against default by the borrower is through a **mortgage**, which is basically a transfer of one of the sticks in the bundle of rights to the bank—which is the right to foreclose on the realty if the loan goes into default. The borrower, who signs the mortgage, is sometimes referred to as the **mortgagor** and the bank is sometimes called the **mortgagee**. The "or" does the acting, and the "ee" is acted upon. The designation of mortgagor and mortgagee may seem to operate in the opposite way. After all, isn't the bank making the loan and thus doing the acting? This confused me for quite some time until I realized that the bor-

---

1. Throughout this chapter I use the term *bank* to refer to the lender. Although a bank is not always the entity that lends money to finance a real estate transaction, that term is used here to include banks, savings and loans, credit unions, private mortgage lenders, and sometimes even parents.

rower is doing the acting by transferring one of the sticks in the bundle of rights to the bank. This act makes the borrower the mortgagor and the bank the mortgagee.

Loan Commitment

When a potential borrower obtains a real estate loan, they are essentially entering into a contract with the bank. The borrower fills out a loan application, on which it offers to make payments to the bank in exchange, and the bank accepts by agreeing to lend the funds. If the bank approves the loan, it will issue a **loan commitment**, in which it agrees to lend the money upon certain conditions, such as the borrower signing a note, a mortgage, providing a lender's policy of title insurance, maintaining casualty insurance on the property, and so forth. The loan commitment is typically valid only for a very few days and locks in an interest rate if the transaction is completed during that time. If the borrower does not go through with the loan, the bank will frequently simply keep the loan application fee. On the other hand, if the bank reneges on the loan commitment during the time it is in effect, the borrower may have a claim for damages. The most likely reason that the bank would renege on a loan commitment is that interest rates have gone up substantially during the time the loan commitment is in effect and it no longer wants to make the loan at the lower interest rate. However, the borrower whose loan commitment wasn't honored may have a claim for breach of the loan commitment if the borrower has to pay a higher interest rate or additional fees to obtain financing.

Promissory Note and Mortgage

A real estate financing is usually documented with two items—a **promissory note** and a mortgage.[2] The promissory note represents the loan itself. It is a contract between the borrower and the bank in which the borrower promises to make regular payments to the bank in exchange for the bank making a loan. The mortgage, on the other hand, is a real property interest that is transferred to the bank by the borrower. Think of it as one of the sticks in the bundle of rights—the right of the bank to foreclose on the property if the borrower

---

2. A sample promissory note appears in Appendix F, and a sample mortgage appears in Appendix G.

defaults on the promissory note. The promissory note and the mortgage are thus tied together—a default under the promissory note triggers the bank's right to exercise its rights under the mortgage and foreclose on the property. It is common for a promissory note to include an **acceleration clause**—which causes the entire balance of the loan to become immediately due in the event of a default. Otherwise, a lender would have to sue each month for that month's missed payment. With an acceleration clause, a default allows the bank to immediately sue to foreclose and recover the entire amount then due.

It is quite common for people to refer to the loan as a "mortgage," but that is inaccurate. Statements like, "I need to make the mortgage payment," and, "I will pay off my mortgage in only two more years," are effectively equating the mortgage to the promissory note, but they are two separate things. I even fall into this misuse of nomenclature. But please understand that the loan, evidenced by the promissory note, and the right to foreclose, evidenced by the mortgage, are two separate things.

Mortgages come in two basic forms—sometimes called **title theory** and **lien theory**. These operate very differently and vary from state to state. In a title theory state, the bank holds title to the property in the name of the borrower in the form of a **deed of trust**. If the borrower defaults on the underlying loan in a title theory state, title to the property passes to the bank through a nonjudicial proceeding. In essence, upon default of the loan, the bank becomes the owner. In a lien theory state, if the borrower defaults on the loan, it triggers a right for the bank to sue in a judicial proceeding.

As you might guess, it is much easier for the bank to recover in a title theory state than in a lien theory state. Ohio is a lien theory state. The lien theory judicial proceeding is referred to as **foreclosure**. Foreclosures in Ohio are discussed in an upcoming section of this chapter.

Perfecting Security Interests

A mortgage is said to secure performance of the borrower under the note. This is an example of a **secured transaction**, where the borrower provides **collateral** for a loan. You may already be aware of another kind of secured transaction—an automobile loan. We all understand that if the borrower stops making payments, the car may very well be repossessed in the middle of the night. In Ohio, automobile loans are secured by the lender physically holding the title document. The borrower gets a document that can be used to register, but not sell, the vehicle. In other states, vehicle titles have liens noted on the title itself. In either case, the lender's security interest is said to be per-

fected. Perfection is the process by which the lender obtains the power to seize the collateral if the loan defaults.

With real estate in Ohio, recording the mortgage with the county recorder perfects the bank's security interest. That puts the entire world on notice that there is a lien on the property, which will turn up in a title examination. A person who his interested in purchasing the property thus has the ability to know that the seller does not have clear title to the property and can make sure that the lien is released at closing.

Other liens, as discussed later in this chapter, are also recorded in a similar way and can be discovered in a title examination. As pointed out earlier, a particular property may be so encumbered that it simply cannot be sold. If the total amount of the recorded liens far exceeds the market value of the property, the owner may be unable to raise enough money, through the proceeds of selling the property and otherwise, to pay off all the liens. Recording these liens will perfect them as well.

Mortgage Insurance

Remember the two rules about banks? Rule one: the bank never loses. Rule two: if the bank loses, see rule one. Mortgage insurance is one of the ways that banks make sure that they never lose. If a borrower's down payment is less than a certain percentage of the value of the realty (typically 20 percent), the bank may require that the borrower purchase **mortgage insurance**. The bank is the beneficiary of the insurance, and the borrower pays the premiums.

If the borrower defaults on the loan, after the bank exercises all of the other rights it may have, including foreclosure, it can make a claim against the mortgage insurance policy to cover any shortfall. So, at the end of the day, the bank can be made whole.

It may seem strange that the mortgage insurance premiums are paid by the borrower to protect the bank. Some borrowers mistakenly think that the mortgage insurance they are buying protects them in case they cannot make payments, perhaps due to illness or job loss. They can be unpleasantly surprised to learn that they are paying to protect the bank. You may ask how banks can get away with requiring mortgage insurance. The answer is actually pretty simple—because they can. Most mortgage loans are structured in such a way that they can be sold to other lenders in what is known as the **secondary market**. A secondary market participant buys the loan and mortgage rights from the original lender and goes on to collect the payments. Secondary markets are part of what makes real estate lending possible for residential properties. You may have heard of Fanny Mae and Freddy Mac, which are both quasi-governmental agencies that set mortgage lending standards. Most participants in the secondary mortgage market will insist that loans they purchase comply with Fanny Mae and Freddy Mac standards, both of which require mortgage insurance for loans where the borrower makes a down payment of less than 20 percent of the purchase price.

There are other lending programs, such as FHA guaranteed loans. These loan programs commonly require mortgage insurance or something quite similar. Borrowers can escape from purchasing mortgage insurance by making a down payment hefty enough to purchase the property. This makes some sense, because if a 20 percent down payment is made, the value of the property would have to decline that much before the bank's mortgage interest would be even partially at risk of loss.

Foreclosure Legal Proceedings in Ohio

You will recall that real estate loans consist of two parts—a promissory note and a mortgage. The promissory note is the document that creates the debt and the obligation to make payments on it, and the mortgage gives the lender the power to foreclose on the property in case of default under the note.

If a debtor defaults, the lender can file a lawsuit in the court of common pleas where the property is located. The complaint for foreclosure is actually pretty simple. It first states that the lender loaned the borrower money as evidenced by a promissory note, which is attached as an exhibit. Next, the complaint states that payment under the promissory note was secured by a mortgage on the property, which is also attached as an exhibit. Then the complaint will allege that the borrower has defaulted on the loan and give specifics of the default. Finally, the complaint will ask the court to foreclose on the property. The complaint must be served on all interested parties, which include the debtor as well as all other lien holders.

The debtor has 28 days to file an answer, but it can be difficult if not impossible to successfully deny the allegations in the complaint; therefore, debtors often don't file an answer at all, resulting in a default judgment in favor of the lender. If the defendant loses, and that is almost always the case, the court then orders that the property be sold at auction.

The county sheriff then obtains an appraisal for the property and announces the sale. The auction is literally held on the steps of the courthouse. The minimum amount that the sheriff can agree to accept is two-thirds of the value in the appraisal obtained by the sheriff. If no bid is at least that amount, the sheriff then orders another appraisal. This seems to make sense, because if no one is willing to pay at least two-thirds of the appraised value, the appraised value is likely too high. Not surprisingly, often the lender initiating the foreclosure shows up at the auction and bids exactly two-thirds of the appraised value.

Next, the sheriff goes to the common pleas court to have the sale confirmed. Basically, the court examines all of the records associated with the foreclosure to make sure that everything was done properly. Assuming all is well, the court will bang the gavel and confirm the sale. This discharges all of the liens against the property. The buyer will receive a fiduciary deed, which, as you recall, contains no warranties other than that the sheriff is authorized to conduct the sale and has complied with everything necessary to complete the sale. The successful bidder must pay the sales price in a very short time, using what are known as **immediately available funds**, typically a cashier's check. The proceeds of the sale are distributed in order of priority of the security interests, as described in the next section.

In Ohio, the mortgagor has one last chance to rescue the property from the foreclosure process, called the **equity of redemption**. This allows the mortgagor to pay the full amount of the unpaid debts on the property at any time up until the court bangs the gavel confirming the sale. You may wonder how a property owner could manage to do this. Sometimes, the reality of losing one's home causes property owners to get very creative in finding money. Friends, family, and even some high-interest lenders may step up and help out. Occasionally, the borrower can renegotiate the terms of the loan between the time the complaint is filed and the court orders the foreclosure sale. For example, the borrower may have had personal circumstances, such as a job loss or illness, that made it difficult to make payments on the loan. If those circumstances have now changed, the lender may be willing to add the missed payments to the end of the loan and accept an immediate payment in exchange for this concession. Think offer, acceptance, and consideration. A borrower who is lucky enough to negotiate such a deal with the lender is almost certainly unable to try the same thing with the same lender later.

But remember that the mortgage holder can still sue under the promissory note. Recall that a real estate loan transaction consists of two parts: the promissory note, which creates the debt, and the mortgage, which secures payment. After a creditor receives whatever may be available from the proceeds of a foreclosure, the balance can still be sought from the debtor under the promissory note. This is all good in theory, but in practice, if someone has defaulted on a real estate loan, the likelihood of recovering anything in a legal action under the promissory is very slim. There is a big difference between winning a judgment and collecting under it.

Priority of Security Interests and Liens

You may have heard about first and second mortgages, and sometimes additional ones. What's the deal with these? How does a mortgage get to be first, and how is that important? The answer is surprisingly simple. A first mortgage is recorded in the county recorder's office first, a second mortgage next, and so on. Basically, all of the mortgages and liens have priority in the order that they were recorded.

A lender may be willing to lend money only up to a certain amount on a first mortgage, due to the creditworthiness of the buyer, the appraised value of the property, the type of loan program being offered, and other reasons. The buyer may then seek another lender to borrow from to complete the financing. The second lender then has a second mortgage. As a second priority, the second lender can command a higher interest rate or other concession for accepting a greater risk than the first mortgagee. Always remember, the greater the risk to the lender, the greater the cost of the loan to the borrower.

In the event that a property is sold in a foreclosure, the proceeds of the sale are paid to the lien holders in the order that they are recorded. Keep in mind that in Ohio, the county tax lien never goes away and is essentially the first claim on the proceeds. So, the county taxes are paid first (if the property goes into foreclosure, the taxes are almost always unpaid). Then, whatever money is left is used to pay the first lien. If anything is left, it goes to the second lien, and so forth. What happens if the money is enough to pay the taxes and the first mortgage, but not enough to pay off the second mortgage? Simply put, the second mortgage holder gets whatever is left and that's that.

So, basically, the priority of security interests is merely the order that they are recorded in the county recorder's office. When a sale or financing is closed, the lenders instruct the person recording the liens on the order in which to file them. Then, when the mortgages and other liens are taken to the recorder's office, the clerk is told which to file first, second, and so on.

A judgment debtor who files a lien against the property may find himself or herself far down the line in the order of payments. It is usually a good idea to look at the county recorder's office before filing a lien on real estate to see how many others already have priority.

Sometimes, however, creditors may agree to allow another lender to take priority in an order other than the order of recording. An illustration might help. Suppose a person buys a house and obtains a first and a second mortgage. The first mortgage will be recorded, followed by the second mortgage. Now, suppose that interest rates have significantly dropped on first mortgages, and the owner wants to refinance the first mortgage. The owner applies for a new loan with a lender, and the proceeds from that loan pay off the older first mortgage. But, if this new mortgage is simply recorded at the county recorder, it will be in line behind the original second mortgage.

The solution to this problem is that the second mortgage lender can agree to allow the new first mortgage lender to have first priority. This is accomplished by means of an **intercreditor agreement**, which is sometimes called a **subordination agreement**.[3] This is an agreement made between the two creditors setting the priority of the security interests in some other sequence than simply the order of recording. You may wonder why the original second lender would agree to this. There may be several reasons. As examples, a lower interest rate on the first mortgage may make it easier for the borrower to make payments on both loans; proceeds from the new loan may be used to improve the property and thus increase the value of the secured asset. Intercreditor agreements and subordination agreements are especially common in commercial real estate lending.

Other Liens

In addition to the first, second, and perhaps other mortgages on the property, other liens may be placed against the property. Liens can be classified as voluntary or involuntary. A voluntary lien is one that is placed on the property with the owner's consent, but an involuntary lien attaches without the owner's consent. An example of a voluntary lien would be a mortgage associated with a promissory note, and an involuntary lien would include a judgment lien. We have already discussed mortgages in some detail, and the other various types of liens are discussed below. All of these various liens give the right to initiate a foreclosure on the property. However, this is only occasionally done, because (except for the auditor's tax lien) the lien is likely to be well down the line in priority. Thus, the proceeds of the foreclosure would be used to pay off the higher priority liens first, often leaving little or nothing remaining. The liens do have some coercive value in that the property cannot be successfully sold and clear title given to a purchaser without first paying off all of the various liens.

Auditor's Tax Lien

As observed earlier, all real property is subject to a tax collected by the county auditor. To secure payment of this tax, an automatic lien is on every

---

3. Actually, there are some technical differences between an intercreditor agreement and a subordination agreement, but these differences are beyond the scope of this book.

parcel of realty in Ohio. This lien always exists and takes priority over all other liens. A first mortgage may be first in line for repayment, but it is first after the auditor's tax lien. As we will see in Chapter 13 on closings, the purchaser of realty will be required to pay the real estate taxes when they become due. Since part of the real estate taxes will probably cover periods when the seller owned the property, an adjustment is made at closing, such that the buyer is paid an amount to cover the seller's share of the property taxes when they come due.

Mechanics' Liens

In Ohio, if a contractor is doing work on realty or supplying materials for the work, a mechanic's lien can be placed on the property. This lien creates a claim against the improved real estate to secure payment for the construction work and materials.

Federal and State Tax Liens

When a property owner fails to pay federal and state taxes when they are due, the taxing authority can place a lien on the property to secure payment for the unpaid taxes. This usually occurs only after serious efforts have been made to collect the amount due.

Judgment Liens

A person who has received a monetary court judgment against a real property owner has the right to place a judgment lien against the property. In Ohio, this is accomplished by obtaining a certified judgment from the clerk of the court and recording it with the county recorder where the property is located.[4]

Lis Pendens

When a lawsuit has been filed concerning real estate, the plaintiff can file a *lis pendens*, which is Latin for "suit pending" against the property with the county recorder.[5] This will alert a potential purchaser that the title to the property is being challenged. A *lis pendens* serves as constructive notice of the un-

---

4. Ohio Rev. Code §2329.02.
5. Ohio Rev. Code §2703.26.

derlying lawsuit. This can effectively prevent the property from being sold until the matter is resolved because lenders are extremely unlikely to loan money to a borrower to purchase the property and title insurance companies will not insure title. If the owner does manage to sell the property to a buyer, say in an all-cash deal without title insurance, the buyer of the property takes it subject to the *lis pendens* and may indeed lose the property without any recourse if the underlying lawsuit vests title in someone else.

Forced Sales of Property Other Than Foreclosure

A foreclosure action is not the only way that real property can be transferred by a **forced sale**. A forced sale is one in which the owner of the property does not necessarily want the property to be sold, but it is sold anyway.

Eminent Domain

As discussed in Chapter 5, the master stick gives governmental entities the right to exercise their powers of eminent domain and force a property owner to sell their realty. So long as the sale is for a "public purpose," which has been broadly defined by the US Supreme Court, but somewhat more limited in Ohio, the only real argument the property owner has is about the value of the property.

Partition

In Chapter 8, we discussed the concept of partition. In a partition action, co-owners of realty who cannot resolve differences about the property can have a court resolve the problem. If the property can be divided, the court will do so. This usually is done only when it is possible for the court to divide the property into parcels that reflect the ownership interests of the co-owners. If this is not possible, the court can order the property sold and the net proceeds divided among the co-owners.

Bankruptcy

A thorough discussion of bankruptcy is well beyond the scope of this text and is best discussed in a separate course on the subject. Indeed, the topic of bankruptcy could easily fill another book by itself. However, one possible outcome in a bankruptcy proceeding is that the bankruptcy court can order real property held by the debtor to be sold and the proceeds used to pay debts. Exceptions and exemptions may apply to a debtor's primary place of residence in Ohio.

Discussion Questions

1. Explain the difference between a promissory note and a mortgage. Why are both necessary to protect the lender?

2. Explain what "perfecting" a security interest means.

3. Explain what mortgage insurance is and who is protected by it.

4. Explain why it is difficult for a borrower to file a meaningful answer to a complaint for foreclosure.

5. Explain the equity of redemption.

6. Explain the difference between a first mortgage and a second mortgage and what differentiates them.

Key Terms

Acceleration clause
Borrower
Collateral
Creditor
Debtor
Deed of trust
Equity of redemption
Foreclosure
Immediately available funds
Intercreditor agreement
Lender
Lien theory
Lis pendens
Loan commitment
Mortgage
Mortgage insurance
Mortgagee
Mortgagor
Perfection
Promissory note

Secondary market
Secured transaction
Subordination agreement
Title theory

Chapter 13

Closing Real Estate Transactions

Perhaps no process in the purchase and sale of real estate is more stressful than the **closing**—the process by which the transaction is consummated, documents are signed, and money changes hands.[1] For many people, buying a personal residence represents the single largest investment they may make in their lifetime, and payments on the real estate loan often are their single largest monthly obligation. Closings may entail a bewildering mountain of papers to sign, payments to be made, documents notarized, and puzzling disclosure forms. It can be helpful to understand that, usually, everybody wants the same thing—to finish up the transaction and hand title over to the new owner.

---

1. Closings are sometimes called **settlements**.

I think it is helpful to look at what each party involved in the closing wants to occur. Let's look at the goals of each participant:

Participant	Goal
Buyer	• Receive clear title to the property, with seller's loan paid off and all liens released • Receive a valid deed, with any dower rights released • Receive credit for taxes they may have to pay (at a later date) for the time the property was occupied by the seller • Receive proof that seller has made (and paid for) any agreed repairs • Receive all of the required financial disclosures • Receive the keys, security code, garage door opener "clicker" • Have the deed recorded
Seller	• Receive payment for the property • Have the balance of seller's loan paid off • Receive all of the required financial disclosures • Be released from further obligations regarding the property
Buyer's bank	• Obtain buyer's signature on loan documents—note and mortgage • Receive assurance that seller's loan has been paid and all liens released • Receive any up-front money owed by buyer • Receive proof of casualty insurance on the property • Receive lender's policy of title insurance • Have the mortgage recorded
Seller's bank	• Receive payoff of seller's loan
Title company	• All of the above, plus • Receive payment for title insurance • Receive payments for filing and other services associated with the closing
Buyer's real estate agent	• Receive commissions for the transaction
Seller's real estate agent	• Receive commissions for the transaction

As you can see, a lot of things must be accomplished at the closing. What's more, some of these are dependent on each other, sometimes in a logical circle. For example, the seller's bank won't release any liens until they are paid, but the buyer's bank won't release any funds until the liens are released. At first this may look like a stalemate, but that is the entire reason for the closing. Each party brings the necessary documents and other things to the closing, and when everyone is satisfied that everything is proper, the documents and things are exchanged. In essence, everything happens at the same time. The seller's bank gets paid and releases the liens, the buyer's bank transfers the funds, the deed is delivered, and so forth.

One thing to notice is that the buyer's and seller's real estate agents are at the closing simply for the purpose of collecting their respective commissions. Often times, the real estate agents develop relationships with the buyer and seller as they wind their way through the process of negotiating a price and a contract, arranging for financing, organizing for inspections and walk-throughs, and so forth. But after the deal is struck and the fine points are resolved, the closing is typically turned over to a title company or an attorney to finalize the documents and oversee the closing. Many real estate agents do show up for the closing to offer moral support for their clients, but they have no real obligations to perform at the closing, other than possibly to make sure it doesn't go off the rails.

Types of Closings—Formal v. Escrow

Real estate closings can be conducted either of two basic ways—**formal** (sometimes called **round table**) or **escrow**. The difference between the two types is when people show up for the closing. For a formal closing, all of the participants or their representatives are present at the same time in the same place, often a conference room at a law office or a title company. An agent from the title company or an attorney typically conducts the closing.

In an escrow closing, all of the documents and other things are delivered to a neutral third person, called an **escrow agent**, to be held in trust until everything is in place. The escrow agent is effectively an agent for all parties involved and owes a fiduciary duty to them. Together with the documents, **escrow instructions** are delivered as well.

The escrow instructions tell the escrow agent what to do with the documents. For example, escrow instructions from the buyer's bank will instruct the escrow agent to make sure that all of the necessary lien releases are in place, that there is proof of casualty insurance on the property, that the lender's policy of title insurance is present, that any up-front payment from the buyer has been received by the escrow agent, and so forth. Then the buyer's escrow instructions will tell the escrow agent to release the funds and distribute them as agreed, record the deed, and then record any mortgages in the proper order. The seller's escrow instructions will contain similar things.

The actual escrow closing occurs when the escrow agent is satisfied that everything needed to consummate the transaction is in place. At that time, the escrow agent undertakes to follow the various escrow instructions and deliver documents, pay various parties, and record deeds and mortgages at the county recorder's office.

Each type of closing has distinct advantages and disadvantages. Which type to use usually depends on the custom in a particular area. Here is a summary of some of the advantages and disadvantages of each:

Closing type	Advantages	Disadvantages
Formal (round table)	• Because everyone is present, any last-minute snags can be immediately re-solved. • Likewise, any additional documents that need to be signed can be accom-modated.	• It may be difficult to schedule everyone to be present at the same time. • If major problems arise, the closing may have to be rescheduled, which can re-sult in a significant delay. • Doctrine of relation back (see next section) does not apply.
Escrow	• Everyone does not need to be present at the same time, so scheduling can be easier and parties can even be out of the country at the time of the actual closing. • Participants are able to show up to sign and bring documents at more con-venient times. Fewer people may need to be present, which can reduce costs. • Doctrine of relation back (see next section) applies.	• Any snags may require participants to show up more than once to sign or bring documents. • The buyer and seller may not be able to meet in per-son (this can sometimes be an advantage, if the trans-action was contentious).

Doctrine of Relation Back

As you will recall, the act of delivering a deed is what actually transfers own-ership of property. The delivery has to be made to the buyer *or someone act-ing on behalf of the buyer.* In an escrow closing, the escrow agent is that person acting on behalf of the buyer. Thus, if the seller delivers a deed to the escrow agent and subsequently dies, goes insane, or otherwise loses capacity, the trans-action can still close because of the **doctrine of relation back.** So long as the seller's deed and necessary documents, payments, and other things were given to the escrow agent, they are considered delivered when received by the escrow agent. The delivery of the deed relates back to the time it was delivered to the escrow agent, even though the closing may actually take place a few days or weeks later. If the seller gets married between delivery of the deed to the escrow agent and the actual closing, the seller's new spouse will not have dower rights in the property.

Likewise, if the buyer delivers all of the documents, payments, and other things that are required to be given by the buyer to the escrow agent before dying, the transaction can still close and the property then becomes part of the buyer's estate.

The doctrine of relation back applies only to escrow closings, which can be a major advantage. It does not apply to formal closings, because parties or their representatives must all actually be present at the same time, and delivery cannot occur until that time.

Walk-Through

If you are purchasing real property, surely you want to take one last look to make sure that things are in the condition expected and that everything being purchased is still there. This is pretty common and is accomplished by a **walk-through**. Typically a walk-through occurs before the closing, perhaps even on the morning of an afternoon closing. The buyer's agent usually arranges for the agent and the buyer to have access to the property for the purpose of inspecting it. During the walk-through, the buyer can be satisfied that about the condition of the property.

The walk-through is not a home inspection, which should be conducted by a professional home inspector. If the property is vacant, it is perhaps even more important to do a walk-through, as vacant property can be a target for vandalism and inadvertent damage. If the electricity and water has been turned off, it may be a wise idea to have it turned on for the walk-through to make sure that all of the appliances and other items are working.

Most real estate contracts have specific language requiring the seller to deliver the property in substantially the same condition as it was when the offer was accepted and that repairs have been made as agreed.

A prudent buyer will bring a copy of the purchase agreement for referral to make sure that everything that was agreed to remain on the property is still there and that the water, electrical, and other systems are functioning. Also, the walk-through can be used to verify that things that were to be removed are no longer present.

Sometimes, floors and walls may have been damaged as a result of the seller removing personal items or moving furniture. This really can't be discovered earlier than the walk-through and may need to be addressed at the closing.

Most real estate contracts have specific language requiring the seller to deliver the property in substantially the same condition it was in when the offer was accepted and that repairs have been made as agreed. A walk-through is the final chance for the buyer to determine if the seller has kept this agreement.

Prorations

Prorations are used to apportion future costs fairly between the buyer and seller. Prorations are used with taxes, homeowners' association fees, and other ongoing expenses associated with owning real property in Ohio.

In Ohio, real estate taxes are paid in arrears. Some Ohio counties bill six months in arrears, and others bill one year in arrears. While the tax lien attaches on January 1 of each year, the taxes are not actually due to be paid until 6 or 12 months later. This means that the buyer will owe taxes for a period that seller was occupying the property. The taxes are prorated to credit the buyer for the seller's share of the taxes that buyer will have to eventually pay. The calculation method varies from location to location within Ohio, but the following is a quick example that shows the essence of the calculation.

Suppose that property taxes are $3,650 per year. This means that property taxes are $10 per day ($3,650 divided by 365). If the seller is responsible for 50 days' worth of taxes, the buyer will receive a credit of $500 ($10 times 50) at closing. This is usually done in the form of a reduction in the amount the buyer will need to pay at closing.[2]

Buyers sometimes get irate when the tax bill arrives and they realize that they are paying taxes for a period of time when they did not own the property. However, the taxes were prorated at closing, so they have been made whole when they pay the full amount. The buyer may need some explanation to understand that they have already been reimbursed for this expense.

Likewise, homeowners' association fees and other such things are prorated at closing so that the proper person winds up paying the proper amount. Whoever is managing the closing is responsible to calculate the proration and disclose it at closing. We will look at closing disclosures later in this chapter.

---

2. Some places in Ohio make proration calculations on the basis of a 360-day year (12 equal months of 30 days). The method used is basically set by local custom.

Closing Protection Insurance

Ohio now requires that **closing protection insurance** be offered by title insurance companies to all parties closing a real estate transaction—buyers, sellers, and lenders. This insurance protects against "theft, misappropriation, fraud, or other failure to properly disburse settlement, closing, or escrow funds" by the escrow agent. No one is required to purchase this insurance, and some have likened it as being akin to a "protection racket" offered by the mafia. However, the cost of closing protection insurance is small in relation to the size of a typical real estate transaction, certainly less than $100, and perhaps as little as $20 for a buyer. Should closing protection insurance be purchased? This is indeed a question for each individual to answer, but it seems to me that the miniscule cost may be justified, because a several hundred thousand dollar transaction may be at stake.

Disclosures Connected with Residential Closings

Borrowing money to purchase one's home is a large investment and often involves many confusing details. While commercial buyers may be more familiar and comfortable with the process, homebuyers purchase realty less frequently and are more apt to be bewildered by everything that occurs. Congress has enacted some procedural safeguards to help homebuyers better understand what is happening.

Until October 2015, there was one set of disclosures, which was required under **RESPA**, the Real Estate Settlement Procedures Act. As of October 2015, a different set of disclosures was mandated under the **Dodd–Frank Act**. The next sections will examine the two acts and the differences that have resulted.

RESPA

RESPA was put in place to provide disclosures to residential real property purchasers. The entire loan and closing process can be very confusing to the average buyer, so the act was designed to provide information in a standardized format. Basically, RESPA required three documents to be delivered to the purchaser—a **Good Faith Estimate**, a **Truth in Lending** form, and a **HUD-1** closing statement.

The Good Faith Estimate (Figure 13-1) and the Truth in Lending (Figure 13-2) forms provide information about mortgage loans, so that a borrower could (at least in theory) compare real estate loan offerings from different lenders. The Truth in Lending form is primarily concerned with interest rates, and the Good Faith Estimate discloses details about a particular loan offering. When a buyer made a loan application, the lender had three days to send these forms to ap-

Figure 13-1 — Good Faith Estimate

OMB Approval No. 2502-0265

 Good Faith Estimate (GFE)

Name of Originator	Borrower
Originator Address	Property Address
Originator Phone Number	
Originator Email	Date of GFE

Purpose

This GFE gives you an estimate of your settlement charges and loan terms if you are approved for this loan. For more information, see HUD's *Special Information Booklet* on settlement charges, your *Truth-in-Lending Disclosures*, and other consumer information at www.hud.gov/respa. If you decide you would like to proceed with this loan, contact us.

Shopping for your loan

Only you can shop for the best loan for you. Compare this GFE with other loan offers, so you can find the best loan. Use the shopping chart on page 3 to compare all the offers you receive.

Important dates

1. The interest rate for this GFE is available through [　　　　　　　]. After this time, the interest rate, some of your loan Origination Charges, and the monthly payment shown below can change until you lock your interest rate.

2. This estimate for all other settlement charges is available through [　　　　　　　].

3. After you lock your interest rate, you must go to settlement within [　] days (your rate lock period) to receive the locked interest rate.

4. You must lock the interest rate at least [　] days before settlement.

Summary of your loan

Your initial loan amount is	$
Your loan term is	years
Your initial interest rate is	%
Your initial monthly amount owed for principal, interest, and any mortgage insurance is	$ per month
Can your interest rate rise?	☐ No ☐ Yes, it can rise to a maximum of %. The first change will be in
Even if you make payments on time, can your loan balance rise?	☐ No ☐ Yes, it can rise to a maximum of $
Even if you make payments on time, can your monthly amount owed for principal, interest, and any mortgage insurance rise?	☐ No ☐ Yes, the first increase can be in and the monthly amount owed can rise to $. The maximum it can ever rise to is $
Does your loan have a prepayment penalty?	☐ No ☐ Yes, your maximum prepayment penalty is $
Does your loan have a balloon payment?	☐ No ☐ Yes, you have a balloon payment of $ due in years.

Escrow account information

Some lenders require an escrow account to hold funds for paying property taxes or other property-related charges in addition to your monthly amount owed of $ [　　　　].

Do we require you to have an escrow account for your loan?

☐ No, you do not have an escrow account. You must pay these charges directly when due.

☐ Yes, you have an escrow account. It may or may not cover all of these charges. Ask us.

Summary of your settlement charges

A	Your Adjusted Origination Charges *(See page 2.)*	$
B	Your Charges for All Other Settlement Services *(See page 2.)*	$
A + B	Total Estimated Settlement Charges	$

Figure 13-1—Good Faith Estimate, *continued*

Understanding
your estimated
settlement charges

Your Adjusted Origination Charges	
1. Our origination charge This charge is for getting this loan for you.	
2. Your credit or charge (points) for the specific interest rate chosen ☐ The credit or charge for the interest rate of [_____] % is included in "Our origination charge." (See item 1 above.) ☐ You receive a credit of $[_____] for this interest rate of [_____] %. This credit **reduces** your settlement charges. ☐ You pay a charge of $[_____] for this interest rate of [_____] %. This charge (points) **increases** your total settlement charges. The tradeoff table on page 3 shows that you can change your total settlement charges by choosing a different interest rate for this loan.	
A Your Adjusted Origination Charges	$

Your Charges for All Other Settlement Services	
3. Required services that we select These charges are for services we require to complete your settlement. We will choose the providers of these services. *Service* *Charge*	
4. Title services and lender's title insurance This charge includes the services of a title or settlement agent, for example, and title insurance to protect the lender, if required.	
5. Owner's title insurance You may purchase an owner's title insurance policy to protect your interest in the property.	
6. Required services that you can shop for These charges are for other services that are required to complete your settlement. We can identify providers of these services or you can shop for them yourself. Our estimates for providing these services are below. *Service* *Charge*	
7. Government recording charges These charges are for state and local fees to record your loan and title documents.	
8. Transfer taxes These charges are for state and local fees on mortgages and home sales.	
9. Initial deposit for your escrow account This charge is held in an escrow account to pay future recurring charges on your property and includes ☐ all property taxes, ☐ all insurance, and ☐ other [_____].	
10. Daily interest charges This charge is for the daily interest on your loan from the day of your settlement until the first day of the next month or the first day of your normal mortgage payment cycle. This amount is $[_____] per day for [____] days (if your settlement is [_____]).	
11. Homeowner's insurance This charge is for the insurance you must buy for the property to protect from a loss, such as fire. *Policy* *Charge*	

B Your Charges for All Other Settlement Services	$
A + B Total Estimated Settlement Charges	$

Some of these charges can change at settlement. See the top of page 3 for more information.

 Good Faith Estimate (HUD-GFE) 2

Figure 13-1—Good Faith Estimate, *continued*

Instructions

Understanding which charges can change at settlement

This GFE estimates your settlement charges. At your settlement, you will receive a HUD-1, a form that lists your actual costs. Compare the charges on the HUD-1 with the charges on this GFE. Charges can change if you select your own provider and do not use the companies we identify. (See below for details.)

These charges **cannot increase** at settlement:	The total of these charges **can increase up to 10%** at settlement:	These charges **can change** at settlement:
■ Our origination charge ■ Your credit or charge (points) for the specific interest rate chosen (after you lock in your interest rate) ■ Your adjusted origination charges (after you lock in your interest rate) ■ Transfer taxes	■ Required services that we select ■ Title services and lender's title insurance (if we select them or you use companies we identify) ■ Owner's title insurance (if you use companies we identify) ■ Required services that you can shop for (if you use companies we identify) ■ Government recording charges	■ Required services that you can shop for (if you do not use companies we identify) ■ Title services and lender's title insurance (if you do not use companies we identify) ■ Owner's title insurance (if you do not use companies we identify) ■ Initial deposit for your escrow account ■ Daily interest charges ■ Homeowner's insurance

Using the tradeoff table

In this GFE, we offered you this loan with a particular interest rate and estimated settlement charges. However:

■ If you want to choose this same loan with **lower settlement charges**, then you will have a **higher interest rate**.
■ If you want to choose this same loan with a **lower interest rate**, then you will have **higher settlement charges**.

If you would like to choose an available option, you must ask us for a new GFE.

Loan originators have the option to complete this table. Please ask for additional information if the table is not completed.

	The loan in this GFE	The same loan with lower settlement charges	The same loan with a lower interest rate
Your initial loan amount	$	$	$
Your initial interest rate[1]	%	%	%
Your initial monthly amount owed	$	$	$
Change in the monthly amount owed from this GFE	No change	You will pay $ **more** every month	You will pay $ **less** every month
Change in the amount you will pay at settlement with this interest rate	No change	Your settlement charges will be **reduced** by $	Your settlement charges will **increase** by $
How much your total estimated settlement charges will be	$	$	$

[1] For an adjustable rate loan, the comparisons above are for the initial interest rate before adjustments are made.

Using the shopping chart

Use this chart to compare GFEs from different loan originators. Fill in the information by using a different column for each GFE you receive. By comparing loan offers, you can shop for the best loan.

	This loan	Loan 2	Loan 3	Loan 4
Loan originator name				
Initial loan amount				
Loan term				
Initial interest rate				
Initial monthly amount owed				
Rate lock period				
Can interest rate rise?				
Can loan balance rise?				
Can monthly amount owed rise?				
Prepayment penalty?				
Balloon payment?				
Total Estimated Settlement Charges				

If your loan is sold in the future

Some lenders may sell your loan after settlement. Any fees lenders receive in the future cannot change the loan you receive or the charges you paid at settlement.

 Good Faith Estimate (HUD-GFE) 3

Figure 13-2—Truth in Lending Form

Form RD 1940-41
(Rev. 07-05)

UNITED STATES DEPARTMENT OF AGRICULTURE
RURAL HOUSING SERVICE

Form Approved
OMB No. 0575-0172

TRUTH IN LENDING STATEMENT

☐ Loan
☐ Assumption
☐ Credit/REO Sale
    subject to:
☐ RESPA
☐ Right to Cancel

To: _____

Lender: USDA _____

_____

Loan Type _____

_____

Date _____

ANNUAL PERCENTAGE RATE* The cost of your credit as a yearly rate.	Amount Financed The amount of credit provided to you or on your behalf.	Total of Payments The amount you will have paid after you have made all payments scheduled.	FINANCE CHARGE The dollar amount the credit will cost you.	Total Sale Price The total cost of your purchase on credit, including your down payment of $ _____
%	$	$	$	$ _____ (Credit Sales)

*The annual percentage rate does not take into account any deposit you may have been required to make by USDA.

You have a right at this time to receive an itemization of the Amount Financed.
☐ I want an itemization   ☐ I do not want an itemization

Your payment schedule will be:

Number of payments	Amount of each payment	When payments are due

Insurance: You may obtain insurance against loss or damage to property, or against liability arising out of ownership or use of the property, if required, from any recognized insurer you want.

Security: You are giving a security interest in: ☐ the property being purchased

☐ _____
(brief description of other property)

Late Charge: If a payment is late, you will be charged _____ % of the payment.
Prepayment: If you pay off early, you will not have to pay a penalty.

Assumption: Someone buying your house ☐ may, subject to conditions ☐ may not assume the remainder of the mortgage on the original terms.

See your loan documents (mortgage of deed of trust, promissory note, payment assistance, subsidy repayment agreement) for additional information about prepayments, default, and any required repayment in full before the scheduled date.

(NOTE: The above disclosures do not take into account any subsidy which may be granted, subject to conditions, in the form of payment assistance.)

I acknowledge receipt of the above disclosures. I received an original of this statement prior to becoming legally obligated to the lender. I understand that numerical amounts shown on this form are estimates only and that this is not notice of loan approval.

_____   _____
(Applicant)   (Applicant)

According to the Paperwork Reduction Act of 1995, no persons are required to respond to a collection of information unless it displays a valid OMB control number. The valid OMB control number for this information collection is 0575-0172. The time required to complete this information collection is estimated to average 5 minutes per response, including the time for reviewing instructions, searching existing data sources, gathering and maintaining the data needed, and completing and reviewing the collection of information.

Figure 13-2—Truth in Lending Form, *continued*

Itemization of the Amount Financed of $ ____________________

$ ____________________ Amount given to you directly.

$ ____________________ Amount paid on your account,

Amount paid to other on your behalf:

$ ____________________ to (public officials) (credit bureau).

$ ____________________ to (name of other creditor).

$ ____________________ to (other).

$ ____________________ Prepaid finance charge.

Page 2 - RD 1940-41

plicant. At the time, the three-day rule merely required that the forms be dropped in the mail three days after a residential loan application was submitted. The borrower might have received it some time later, due to delays in mailing. As you can see, the Good Faith Estimate contains information about the amount borrowed, the interest rate, how soon the loan needs to be closed to keep that interest rate, prepayment penalties, balloon payments, and various fees associated with the loan. Since this was only an estimate, some of the disclosed amounts could change before the loan was closed. What's more, the Good Faith Estimate was valid for only a relatively short time, perhaps 10 to 14 days. If the transaction was not closed within that time, a new Good Faith Estimate would be required. Because interest rates fluctuate, lenders are not willing to keep a loan offer open for very long.

At the closing, a different form was required, the HUD-1 (Figure 13-3). This document basically showed all of the sources of money for the closing, where it went, and how it was spent. Looking at the *second* page of the HUD-1 form *first* can be helpful, as it shows line-by-line where money goes, such as payment of taxes; mortgage, title, and homeowner's insurance; recording fees; daily interest charges; and similar things. These amounts are then summarized on the first page, which starts with the contract price for the home and then adds or subtracts various amounts to arrive at the amount due from the buyer and to the seller at the closing.

You might want to look at lines 211 and 511 on page 1 of the HUD-1. This is where county real property taxes are prorated between the buyer and seller. In the previous example was a proration of $500 for unpaid county taxes owed by the seller, which will eventually be paid by the buyer. On the HUD-1 form, lines 211 and 511 would each contain $500. The amount the buyer owes at closing is reduced by $500, and the amount the seller receives from the transaction is likewise reduced by $500. Thus, the buyer will have been paid for the seller's portion of the real estate taxes when they come due, in the form of a reduction on the amount the buyer pays at closing.

It was not uncommon for the HUD-1 form to be available to the buyer and seller on the day of closing. This could make for mad scrambles to the bank for the buyer to arrange for a cashier's check for the down payment due, or sometimes even for the seller, if the seller needed to bring money to the closing (as is sometimes the case when the seller owes more than the proceeds of the sale). Some closing agents would make the HUD-1 form available a couple of days before the closing, but it was not required.

Figure 13-3—HUD-1

OMB Approval No. 2502-0265

 A. **Settlement Statement (HUD-1)**

B. Type of Loan						

1. ☐ FHA 2. ☐ RHS 3. ☐ Conv. Unins.	6. File Number:	7. Loan Number:	8. Mortgage Insurance Case Number:
4. ☐ VA 5. ☐ Conv. Ins.			

C. Note: This form is furnished to give you a statement of actual settlement costs. Amounts paid to and by the settlement agent are shown. Items marked "(p.o.c.)" were paid outside the closing; they are shown here for informational purposes and are not included in the totals.

D. Name & Address of Borrower:	E. Name & Address of Seller:	F. Name & Address of Lender:

G. Property Location:	H. Settlement Agent:	I. Settlement Date:
	Place of Settlement:	

J. Summary of Borrower's Transaction		K. Summary of Seller's Transaction	
100. Gross Amount Due from Borrower		**400. Gross Amount Due to Seller**	
101. Contract sales price		401. Contract sales price	
102. Personal property		402. Personal property	
103. Settlement charges to borrower (line 1400)		403.	
104.		404.	
105.		405.	
Adjustment for items paid by seller in advance		**Adjustment for items paid by seller in advance**	
106. City/town taxes to		406. City/town taxes to	
107. County taxes to		407. County taxes to	
108. Assessments to		408. Assessments to	
109.		409.	
110.		410.	
111.		411.	
112.		412.	
120. Gross Amount Due from Borrower		**420. Gross Amount Due to Seller**	
200. Amount Paid by or in Behalf of Borrower		**500. Reductions In Amount Due to seller**	
201. Deposit or earnest money		501. Excess deposit (see instructions)	
202. Principal amount of new loan(s)		502. Settlement charges to seller (line 1400)	
203. Existing loan(s) taken subject to		503. Existing loan(s) taken subject to	
204.		504. Payoff of first mortgage loan	
205.		505. Payoff of second mortgage loan	
206.		506.	
207.		507.	
208.		508.	
209.		509.	
Adjustments for items unpaid by seller		**Adjustments for items unpaid by seller**	
210. City/town taxes to		510. City/town taxes to	
211. County taxes to		511. County taxes to	
212. Assessments to		512. Assessments to	
213.		513.	
214.		514.	
215.		515.	
216.		516.	
217.		517.	
218.		518.	
219.		519.	
220. Total Paid by/for Borrower		**520. Total Reduction Amount Due Seller**	
300. Cash at Settlement from/to Borrower		**600. Cash at Settlement to/from Seller**	
301. Gross amount due from borrower (line 120)		601. Gross amount due to seller (line 420)	
302. Less amounts paid by/for borrower (line 220)	( )	602. Less reductions in amounts due seller (line 520)	( )
303. Cash ☐ From ☐ To Borrower		**603. Cash** ☐ To ☐ From Seller	

The Public Reporting Burden for this collection of information is estimated at 35 minutes per response for collecting, reviewing, and reporting the data. This agency may not collect this information, and you are not required to complete this form, unless it displays a currently valid OMB control number. No confidentiality is assured; this disclosure is mandatory. This is designed to provide the parties to a RESPA covered transaction with information during the settlement process.

Figure 13-3—HUD-1, *continued*

L. Settlement Charges			
700. Total Real Estate Broker Fees		Paid From Borrower's Funds at Settlement	Paid From Seller's Funds at Settlement
Division of commission (line 700) as follows :			
701. $ to			
702. $ to			
703. Commission paid at settlement			
704.			
800. Items Payable in Connection with Loan			
801. Our origination charge	$ (from GFE #1)		
802. Your credit or charge (points) for the specific interest rate chosen	$ (from GFE #2)		
803. Your adjusted origination charges	(from GFE #A)		
804. Appraisal fee to	(from GFE #3)		
805. Credit report to	(from GFE #3)		
806. Tax service to	(from GFE #3)		
807. Flood certification to	(from GFE #3)		
808.			
809.			
810.			
811.			
900. Items Required by Lender to be Paid in Advance			
901. Daily interest charges from to @ $ /day	(from GFE #10)		
902. Mortgage insurance premium for months to	(from GFE #3)		
903. Homeowner's insurance for years to	(from GFE #11)		
904.			
1000. Reserves Deposited with Lender			
1001. Initial deposit for your escrow account	(from GFE #9)		
1002. Homeowner's insurance months @ $ per month $			
1003. Mortgage insurance months @ $ per month $			
1004. Property Taxes months @ $ per month $			
1005. months @ $ per month $			
1006. months @ $ per month $			
1007. Aggregate Adjustment -$			
1100. Title Charges			
1101. Title services and lender's title insurance	(from GFE #4)		
1102. Settlement or closing fee	$		
1103. Owner's title insurance	(from GFE #5)		
1104. Lender's title insurance	$		
1105. Lender's title policy limit $			
1106. Owner's title policy limit $			
1107. Agent's portion of the total title insurance premium to	$		
1108. Underwriter's portion of the total title insurance premium to	$		
1109.			
1110.			
1111.			
1200. Government Recording and Transfer Charges			
1201. Government recording charges	(from GFE #7)		
1202. Deed $ Mortgage $ Release $			
1203. Transfer taxes	(from GFE #8)		
1204. City/County tax/stamps Deed $ Mortgage $			
1205. State tax/stamps Deed $ Mortgage $			
1206.			
1300. Additional Settlement Charges			
1301. Required services that you can shop for	(from GFE #6)		
1302. $			
1303. $			
1304.			
1305.			
1400. Total Settlement Charges (enter on lines 103, Section J and 502, Section K)			

Figure 13-3—HUD-1, *continued*

Comparison of Good Faith Estimate (GFE) and HUD-1 Charrges		Good Faith Estimate	HUD-1
Charges That Cannot Increase	HUD-1 Line Number		
Our origination charge	# 801		
Your credit or charge (points) for the specific interest rate chosen	# 802		
Your adjusted origination charges	# 803		
Transfer taxes	# 1203		

Charges That In Total Cannot Increase More Than 10%		Good Faith Estimate	HUD-1
Government recording charges	# 1201		
	#		
	#		
	#		
	#		
	#		
	#		
	#		
	Total		
	Increase between GFE and HUD-1 Charges	$ or	%

Charges That Can Change		Good Faith Estimate	HUD-1
Initial deposit for your escrow account	# 1001		
Daily interest charges $ /day	# 901		
Homeowner's insurance	# 903		
	#		
	#		
	#		

Loan Terms

Your initial loan amount is	$
Your loan term is	years
Your initial interest rate is	%
Your initial monthly amount owed for principal, interest, and any mortgage insurance is	$ includes ☐ Principal ☐ Interest ☐ Mortgage Insurance
Can your interest rate rise?	☐ No ☐ Yes, it can rise to a maximum of %. The first change will be on and can change again every after . Every change date, your interest rate can increase or decrease by %. Over the life of the loan, your interest rate is guaranteed to never be **lower** than % or **higher** than %.
Even if you make payments on time, can your loan balance rise?	☐ No ☐ Yes, it can rise to a maximum of $
Even if you make payments on time, can your monthly amount owed for principal, interest, and mortgage insurance rise?	☐ No ☐ Yes, the first increase can be on and the monthly amount owed can rise to $. The maximum it can ever rise to is $
Does your loan have a prepayment penalty?	☐ No ☐ Yes, your maximum prepayment penalty is $
Does your loan have a balloon payment?	☐ No ☐ Yes, you have a balloon payment of $ due in years on
Total monthly amount owed including escrow account payments	☐ You do not have a monthly escrow payment for items, such as property taxes and homeowner's insurance. You must pay these items directly yourself. ☐ You have an additional monthly escrow payment of $ that results in a total initial monthly amount owed of $. This includes principal, interest, any mortgage insurance and any items checked below: ☐ Property taxes ☐ Homeowner's insurance ☐ Flood insurance ☐ ☐ ☐

Note: If you have any questions about the Settlement Charges and Loan Terms listed on this form, please contact your lender.

Mortgage Crisis of 2008

A few lenders took advantage of various timings under RESPA to make loans that were partly the cause of the recent mortgage crisis of 2008. For example, a borrower who might otherwise not qualify for a mortgage loan would be encouraged to apply for a first mortgage that contemplated a substantial down payment, and the down payment to be made by a second mortgage loan. The lender would process the first mortgage application, fund the loan, and then wait until closing (or immediately before) to submit the loan application for the second mortgage (which would be used to make the down payment). Since the borrower had already been approved for a first mortgage that had been funded, the automated loan approval system would approve the second mortgage.

This meant that a purchaser could buy a house without putting any money down, and wind up with a first and second mortgage on the property. Because second mortgages are more risky to the lender than first mortgages, their interest rates are typically substantially higher, resulting in larger monthly payments. As a result, borrowers might wind up with loans that they could not afford to pay. This scheme was only one of many tricks that some unscrupulous loan officers used. Since the loan officers were typically paid a commission on loans they originated, it was in their personal best interest to make as many loans as possible.

With homeowners in mortgages they could not afford, many borrowers wound up defaulting on their loans, with property going into foreclosure. As the number of foreclosures increased, many more homes went onto the market, resulting in an oversupply of available houses. Simple supply and demand then dictated that housing prices would fall. This caused some homeowners to owe more on their personal residence than it was worth. Such homeowners are said to be **underwater**. This sequence of events became a vicious cycle, and things spiraled somewhat out of control.

Recent Changes in Residential Real Estate Closings

The Dodd–Frank Act was enacted to put controls on residential real estate lending. Its stated purpose is to "assure that consumers are offered and receive residential mortgage loans on terms that reasonably reflect their ability to repay the loans and that are understandable and not unfair, deceptive or abusive."[3] If you have applied for a home mortgage loan or refinanced an existing loan

---

3. 15 USC 1639b.

in the past few years, you certainly will have felt the effect of some of these changes. Lenders are far more cautious, often requiring documentation of seemingly mundane things. For example, when the author recently refinanced his residence, the lender wanted written documentation as to why he received a reimbursement for travel to a scholarly conference. This was required because it showed up as an out-of-the-ordinary deposit to his checking account. In short, many lenders became hypervigilant and perhaps even a little gun-shy when it came to making residential mortgage loans.

Another part of the Dodd–Frank Act went into effect at the beginning of October 2015.[4] The new provisions added two new disclosure forms that replaced the Good Faith Estimate and the HUD-1 closing statement, together with new timing required for the disclosures. These new rules make it more difficult on mortgage lenders and closing agents, as information gets locked down earlier in the process.

A different form now replaces the Good Faith Estimate and the Truth in Lending forms. It is called a **Loan Estimate** (Figure 13-4). The Loan Estimate contains much of the same information as previous forms but is designed to be more readable, as it is in plain English. You will see, for example, that amounts that can change after closing, prepayment penalties, and balloon payments are more clearly indicated than on the Good Faith Estimate. The Loan Estimate must be sent to the potential borrower no later than the third business day after the lender receives a loan application. Again, dropping the Loan Estimate in the mail on the third business day after the loan application will suffice.

The **Closing Disclosure** (Figure 13-5) essentially replaces the old HUD-1 form. As you can see, the Closing Disclosure mirrors the Loan Estimate in many ways, making it easier for the borrower to compare the actual costs to the costs estimated shortly after the loan application. It is designed to be easier to read than the HUD-1 form and is intended to more clearly show exactly where money comes from and where it goes at the closing.

The biggest difference is when the Closing Disclosure must be delivered to the borrower, and the extent to which it can change before the actual closing. The Closing Disclosure must be *actually received* by the borrower at least three days *before* the closing. Delivery can be in person, by courier, by postal mail, or electronically. However, if the Closing Disclosure is sent by postal mail, an

---

4. This portion of Dodd–Frank was originally scheduled to go into effect August 2015 but was delayed until October 2015 to allow lenders and closing agents more time to implement its requirements.

Figure 13-4—Loan Estimate

FICUS BANK
4321 Random Boulevard · Somecity, ST 12340

Save this Loan Estimate to compare with your Closing Disclosure.

Loan Estimate

DATE ISSUED	2/15/2013
APPLICANTS	Michael Jones and Mary Stone
	123 Anywhere Street
	Anytown, ST 12345
PROPERTY	456 Somewhere Avenue
	Anytown, ST 12345
SALE PRICE	$180,000

LOAN TERM	30 years
PURPOSE	Purchase
PRODUCT	Fixed Rate
LOAN TYPE	☒ Conventional ☐ FHA ☐ VA ☐ _____
LOAN ID #	123456789
RATE LOCK	☐ NO ☒ YES, until 4/16/2013 at 5:00 p.m. EDT

*Before closing, your interest rate, points, and lender credits can change unless you lock the interest rate. All other estimated closing costs expire on **3/4/2013** at 5:00 p.m. EDT*

Loan Terms

		Can this amount increase after closing?
Loan Amount	$162,000	NO
Interest Rate	3.875%	NO
Monthly Principal & Interest *See Projected Payments below for your Estimated Total Monthly Payment*	$761.78	NO
		Does the loan have these features?
Prepayment Penalty		YES · **As high as $3,240** if you pay off the loan during the first 2 years
Balloon Payment		NO

Projected Payments

Payment Calculation	Years 1-7	Years 8-30
Principal & Interest	$761.78	$761.78
Mortgage Insurance	+ 82	+ —
Estimated Escrow *Amount can increase over time*	+ 206	+ 206
Estimated Total Monthly Payment	$1,050	$968

		This estimate includes	In escrow?
Estimated Taxes, Insurance & Assessments *Amount can increase over time*	$206 a month	☒ Property Taxes ☒ Homeowner's Insurance ☐ Other:	YES YES
		See Section G on page 2 for escrowed property costs. You must pay for other property costs separately.	

Costs at Closing

Estimated Closing Costs	$8,054	Includes $5,672 in Loan Costs + $2,382 in Other Costs – $0 in Lender Credits. *See page 2 for details.*
Estimated Cash to Close	$16,054	Includes Closing Costs. *See Calculating Cash to Close on page 2 for details.*

Visit **www.consumerfinance.gov/mortgage-estimate** for general information and tools.

Figure 13-4—Loan Estimate, *continued*

Closing Cost Details

Loan Costs	
A. Origination Charges	**$1,802**
.25 % of Loan Amount (Points)	$405
Application Fee	$300
Underwriting Fee	$1,097

B. Services You Cannot Shop For	$672
Appraisal Fee	$405
Credit Report Fee	$30
Flood Determination Fee	$20
Flood Monitoring Fee	$32
Tax Monitoring Fee	$75
Tax Status Research Fee	$110

C. Services You Can Shop For	$3,198
Pest Inspection Fee	$135
Survey Fee	$65
Title – Insurance Binder	$700
Title – Lender's Title Policy	$535
Title – Settlement Agent Fee	$502
Title – Title Search	$1,261

D. TOTAL LOAN COSTS (A + B + C)	$5,672

Other Costs	
E. Taxes and Other Government Fees	**$85**
Recording Fees and Other Taxes	$85
Transfer Taxes	
F. Prepaids	**$867**
Homeowner's Insurance Premium (6 months)	$605
Mortgage Insurance Premium (months)	
Prepaid Interest ($17.44 per day for 15 days @ 3.875%)	$262
Property Taxes (months)	

G. Initial Escrow Payment at Closing	$413
Homeowner's Insurance $100.83 per month for 2 mo.	$202
Mortgage Insurance per month for mo.	
Property Taxes $105.30 per month for 2 mo.	$211

H. Other	$1,017
Title – Owner's Title Policy (optional)	$1,017

I. TOTAL OTHER COSTS (E + F + G + H)	$2,382

J. TOTAL CLOSING COSTS	$8,054
D + I	$8,054
Lender Credits	

Calculating Cash to Close	
Total Closing Costs (J)	$8,054
Closing Costs Financed (Paid from your Loan Amount)	$0
Down Payment/Funds from Borrower	$18,000
Deposit	– $10,000
Funds for Borrower	$0
Seller Credits	$0
Adjustments and Other Credits	$0
Estimated Cash to Close	**$16,054**

Figure 13-4—Loan Estimate, *continued*

Additional Information About This Loan

LENDER	Ficus Bank	**MORTGAGE BROKER**
NMLS/__ LICENSE ID		**NMLS/__ LICENSE ID**
LOAN OFFICER	Joe Smith	**LOAN OFFICER**
NMLS/__ LICENSE ID	12345	**NMLS/__ LICENSE ID**
EMAIL	joesmith@ficusbank.com	**EMAIL**
PHONE	123-456-7890	**PHONE**

Comparisons — Use these measures to compare this loan with other loans.

In 5 Years	$56,582	Total you will have paid in principal, interest, mortgage insurance, and loan costs.
	$15,773	Principal you will have paid off.
Annual Percentage Rate (APR)	4.274%	Your costs over the loan term expressed as a rate. This is not your interest rate.
Total Interest Percentage (TIP)	69.45%	The total amount of interest that you will pay over the loan term as a percentage of your loan amount.

Other Considerations

Appraisal	We may order an appraisal to determine the property's value and charge you for this appraisal. We will promptly give you a copy of any appraisal, even if your loan does not close. You can pay for an additional appraisal for your own use at your own cost.
Assumption	If you sell or transfer this property to another person, we ☐ will allow, under certain conditions, this person to assume this loan on the original terms. ☒ will not allow assumption of this loan on the original terms.
Homeowner's Insurance	This loan requires homeowner's insurance on the property, which you may obtain from a company of your choice that we find acceptable.
Late Payment	If your payment is more than *15* days late, we will charge a late fee of *5% of the monthly principal and interest payment.*
Refinance	Refinancing this loan will depend on your future financial situation, the property value, and market conditions. You may not be able to refinance this loan.
Servicing	We intend ☐ to service your loan. If so, you will make your payments to us. ☒ to transfer servicing of your loan.

Confirm Receipt

By signing, you are only confirming that you have received this form. You do not have to accept this loan because you have signed or received this form.

_____   _____   _____   _____
Applicant Signature   Date   Co-Applicant Signature   Date

LOAN ESTIMATE   PAGE 3 OF 3 · LOAN ID #123456789

Figure 13-5 — Closing Disclosure

Closing Disclosure

This form is a statement of final loan terms and closing costs. Compare this document with your Loan Estimate.

Closing Information		Transaction Information		Loan Information	
Date Issued	4/15/2013	**Borrower**	Michael Jones and Mary Stone	**Loan Term**	30 years
Closing Date	4/15/2013		123 Anywhere Street	**Purpose**	Purchase
Disbursement Date	4/15/2013		Anytown, ST 12345	**Product**	Fixed Rate
Settlement Agent	Epsilon Title Co.	**Seller**	Steve Cole and Amy Doe		
File #	12-3456		321 Somewhere Drive	**Loan Type**	☒ Conventional ☐ FHA
Property	456 Somewhere Ave		Anytown, ST 12345		☐ VA ☐ _____
	Anytown, ST 12345	**Lender**	Ficus Bank	**Loan ID #**	123456789
Sale Price	$180,000			**MIC #**	000654321

Loan Terms

		Can this amount increase after closing?
Loan Amount	$162,000	**NO**
Interest Rate	3.875%	**NO**
Monthly Principal & Interest *See Projected Payments below for your Estimated Total Monthly Payment*	$761.78	**NO**

		Does the loan have these features?
Prepayment Penalty		**YES** • **As high as $3,240** if you pay off the loan during the first 2 years
Balloon Payment		**NO**

Projected Payments

Payment Calculation	Years 1-7	Years 8-30
Principal & Interest	$761.78	$761.78
Mortgage Insurance	+ 82.35	+ —
Estimated Escrow *Amount can increase over time*	+ 206.13	+ 206.13
Estimated Total Monthly Payment	$1,050.26	$967.91

		This estimate includes	In escrow?
Estimated Taxes, Insurance & Assessments *Amount can increase over time* *See page 4 for details*	$356.13 a month	☒ Property Taxes ☒ Homeowner's Insurance ☒ Other: Homeowner's Association Dues *See Escrow Account on page 4 for details. You must pay for other property costs separately.*	YES YES NO

Costs at Closing

Closing Costs	$9,712.10	Includes $4,694.05 in Loan Costs + $5,018.05 in Other Costs – $0 in Lender Credits. *See page 2 for details.*
Cash to Close	$14,147.26	Includes Closing Costs. *See Calculating Cash to Close on page 3 for details.*

Figure 13-5—Closing Disclosure, *continued*

Closing Cost Details

Loan Costs		Borrower-Paid		Seller-Paid		Paid by Others
		At Closing	Before Closing	At Closing	Before Closing	
A. Origination Charges		**$1,802.00**				
01 0.25 % of Loan Amount (Points)		$405.00				
02 Application Fee		$300.00				
03 Underwriting Fee		$1,097.00				
04						
05						
06						
07						
08						
B. Services Borrower Did Not Shop For		**$236.55**				
01 Appraisal Fee	to John Smith Appraisers Inc.					$405.00
02 Credit Report Fee	to Information Inc.		$29.80			
03 Flood Determination Fee	to Info Co.	$20.00				
04 Flood Monitoring Fee	to Info Co.	$31.75				
05 Tax Monitoring Fee	to Info Co.	$75.00				
06 Tax Status Research Fee	to Info Co.	$80.00				
07						
08						
09						
10						
C. Services Borrower Did Shop For		**$2,655.50**				
01 Pest Inspection Fee	to Pests Co.	$120.50				
02 Survey Fee	to Surveys Co.	$85.00				
03 Title – Insurance Binder	to Epsilon Title Co.	$650.00				
04 Title – Lender's Title Insurance	to Epsilon Title Co.	$500.00				
05 Title – Settlement Agent Fee	to Epsilon Title Co.	$500.00				
06 Title – Title Search	to Epsilon Title Co.	$800.00				
07						
08						
D. TOTAL LOAN COSTS (Borrower-Paid)		**$4,694.05**				
Loan Costs Subtotals (A + B + C)		$4,664.25	$29.80			

Other Costs						
E. Taxes and Other Government Fees		**$85.00**				
01 Recording Fees	Deed: $40.00 Mortgage: $45.00	$85.00				
02 Transfer Tax	to Any State			$950.00		
F. Prepaids		**$2,120.80**				
01 Homeowner's Insurance Premium (12 mo.) to Insurance Co.		$1,209.96				
02 Mortgage Insurance Premium (mo.)						
03 Prepaid Interest ($17.44 per day from 4/15/13 to 5/1/13)		$279.04				
04 Property Taxes (6 mo.) to Any County USA		$631.80				
05						
G. Initial Escrow Payment at Closing		**$412.25**				
01 Homeowner's Insurance $100.83 per month for 2 mo.		$201.66				
02 Mortgage Insurance per month for mo.						
03 Property Taxes $105.30 per month for 2 mo.		$210.60				
04						
05						
06						
07						
08 Aggregate Adjustment		– 0.01				
H. Other		**$2,400.00**				
01 HOA Capital Contribution	to HOA Acre Inc.	$500.00				
02 HOA Processing Fee	to HOA Acre Inc.	$150.00				
03 Home Inspection Fee	to Engineers Inc.	$750.00			$750.00	
04 Home Warranty Fee	to XYZ Warranty Inc.			$450.00		
05 Real Estate Commission	to Alpha Real Estate Broker			$5,700.00		
06 Real Estate Commission	to Omega Real Estate Broker			$5,700.00		
07 Title – Owner's Title Insurance (optional) to Epsilon Title Co.		$1,000.00				
08						
I. TOTAL OTHER COSTS (Borrower-Paid)		**$5,018.05**				
Other Costs Subtotals (E + F + G + H)		$5,018.05				

J. TOTAL CLOSING COSTS (Borrower-Paid)		$9,712.10				
Closing Costs Subtotals (D + I)		$9,682.30	$29.80	$12,800.00	$750.00	$405.00
Lender Credits						

Figure 13-5—Closing Disclosure, *continued*

Calculating Cash to Close	Use this table to see what has changed from your Loan Estimate.			
	Loan Estimate	**Final**	**Did this change?**	
Total Closing Costs (J)	$8,054.00	$9,712.10	**YES**	· See **Total Loan Costs (D)** and **Total Other Costs (I)**
Closing Costs Paid Before Closing	$0	– $29.80	**YES**	· You paid these Closing Costs **before closing**
Closing Costs Financed (Paid from your Loan Amount)	$0	$0	**NO**	
Down Payment/Funds from Borrower	$18,000.00	$18,000.00	**NO**	
Deposit	– $10,000.00	– $10,000.00	**NO**	
Funds for Borrower	$0	$0	**NO**	
Seller Credits	$0	– $2,500.00	**YES**	· See Seller Credits in **Section L**
Adjustments and Other Credits	$0	– $1,035.04	**YES**	· See details in **Sections K and L**
Cash to Close	$16,054.00	$14,147.26		

Summaries of Transactions	Use this table to see a summary of your transaction.

BORROWER'S TRANSACTION

K. Due from Borrower at Closing	$189,762.30
01 Sale Price of Property	$180,000.00
02 Sale Price of Any Personal Property Included in Sale	
03 Closing Costs Paid at Closing (J)	$9,682.30
04	
Adjustments	
05	
06	
07	
Adjustments for Items Paid by Seller in Advance	
08 City/Town Taxes to	
09 County Taxes to	
10 Assessments to	
11 HOA Dues 4/15/13 to 4/30/13	$80.00
12	
13	
14	
15	

L. Paid Already by or on Behalf of Borrower at Closing	$175,615.04
01 Deposit	$10,000.00
02 Loan Amount	$162,000.00
03 Existing Loan(s) Assumed or Taken Subject to	
04	
05 Seller Credit	$2,500.00
Other Credits	
06 Rebate from Epsilon Title Co.	$750.00
07	
Adjustments	
08	
09	
10	
11	
Adjustments for Items Unpaid by Seller	
12 City/Town Taxes 1/1/13 to 4/14/13	$365.04
13 County Taxes to	
14 Assessments to	
15	
16	
17	

CALCULATION	
Total Due from Borrower at Closing (K)	$189,762.30
Total Paid Already by or on Behalf of Borrower at Closing (L)	– $175,615.04
Cash to Close ☒ From ☐ To Borrower	**$14,147.26**

SELLER'S TRANSACTION

M. Due to Seller at Closing	$180,080.00
01 Sale Price of Property	$180,000.00
02 Sale Price of Any Personal Property Included in Sale	
03	
04	
05	
06	
07	
08	
Adjustments for Items Paid by Seller in Advance	
09 City/Town Taxes to	
10 County Taxes to	
11 Assessments to	
12 HOA Dues 4/15/13 to 4/30/13	$80.00
13	
14	
15	
16	

N. Due from Seller at Closing	$115,665.04
01 Excess Deposit	
02 Closing Costs Paid at Closing (J)	$12,800.00
03 Existing Loan(s) Assumed or Taken Subject to	
04 Payoff of First Mortgage Loan	$100,000.00
05 Payoff of Second Mortgage Loan	
06	
07	
08 Seller Credit	$2,500.00
09	
10	
11	
12	
13	
Adjustments for Items Unpaid by Seller	
14 City/Town Taxes 1/1/13 to 4/14/13	$365.04
15 County Taxes to	
16 Assessments to	
17	
18	
19	

CALCULATION	
Total Due to Seller at Closing (M)	$180,080.00
Total Due from Seller at Closing (N)	– $115,665.04
Cash ☐ From ☒ To Seller	**$64,414.96**

Figure 13-5—Closing Disclosure, *continued*

Additional Information About This Loan

Loan Disclosures

Assumption

If you sell or transfer this property to another person, your lender

☐ will allow, under certain conditions, this person to assume this loan on the original terms.

☒ will not allow assumption of this loan on the original terms.

Demand Feature

Your loan

☐ has a demand feature, which permits your lender to require early repayment of the loan. You should review your note for details.

☒ does not have a demand feature.

Late Payment

If your payment is more than *15* days late, your lender will charge a late fee of *5% of the monthly principal and interest payment.*

Negative Amortization (Increase in Loan Amount)

Under your loan terms, you

☐ are scheduled to make monthly payments that do not pay all of the interest due that month. As a result, your loan amount will increase (negatively amortize), and your loan amount will likely become larger than your original loan amount. Increases in your loan amount lower the equity you have in this property.

☐ may have monthly payments that do not pay all of the interest due that month. If you do, your loan amount will increase (negatively amortize), and, as a result, your loan amount may become larger than your original loan amount. Increases in your loan amount lower the equity you have in this property.

☒ do not have a negative amortization feature.

Partial Payments

Your lender

☒ may accept payments that are less than the full amount due (partial payments) and apply them to your loan.

☐ may hold them in a separate account until you pay the rest of the payment, and then apply the full payment to your loan.

☐ does not accept any partial payments.

If this loan is sold, your new lender may have a different policy.

Security Interest

You are granting a security interest in

456 Somewhere Ave., Anytown, ST 12345

You may lose this property if you do not make your payments or satisfy other obligations for this loan.

Escrow Account

For now, your loan

☒ will have an escrow account (also called an "impound" or "trust" account) to pay the property costs listed below. Without an escrow account, you would pay them directly, possibly in one or two large payments a year. Your lender may be liable for penalties and interest for failing to make a payment.

Escrow		
Escrowed Property Costs over Year 1	$2,473.56	Estimated total amount over year 1 for your escrowed property costs: *Homeowner's Insurance Property Taxes*
Non-Escrowed Property Costs over Year 1	$1,800.00	Estimated total amount over year 1 for your non-escrowed property costs: *Homeowner's Association Dues*
		You may have other property costs.
Initial Escrow Payment	$412.25	A cushion for the escrow account you pay at closing. See Section G on page 2.
Monthly Escrow Payment	$206.13	The amount included in your total monthly payment.

☐ will not have an escrow account because ☐ you declined it ☐ your lender does not offer one. You must directly pay your property costs, such as taxes and homeowner's insurance. Contact your lender to ask if your loan can have an escrow account.

No Escrow	
Estimated Property Costs over Year 1	Estimated total amount over year 1. You must pay these costs directly, possibly in one or two large payments a year.
Escrow Waiver Fee	

In the future,

Your property costs may change and, as a result, your escrow payment may change. You may be able to cancel your escrow account, but if you do, you must pay your property costs directly. If you fail to pay your property taxes, your state or local government may (1) impose fines and penalties or (2) place a tax lien on this property. If you fail to pay any of your property costs, your lender may (1) add the amounts to your loan balance, (2) add an escrow account to your loan, or (3) require you to pay for property insurance that the lender buys on your behalf, which likely would cost more and provide fewer benefits than what you could buy on your own.

Figure 13-5—Closing Disclosure, *continued*

Loan Calculations

Total of Payments. Total you will have paid after you make all payments of principal, interest, mortgage insurance, and loan costs, as scheduled.	$285,803.36
Finance Charge. The dollar amount the loan will cost you.	$118,830.27
Amount Financed. The loan amount available after paying your upfront finance charge.	$162,000.00
Annual Percentage Rate (APR). Your costs over the loan term expressed as a rate. This is not your interest rate.	4.174%
Total Interest Percentage (TIP). The total amount of interest that you will pay over the loan term as a percentage of your loan amount.	69.46%

Questions? If you have questions about the loan terms or costs on this form, use the contact information below. To get more information or make a complaint, contact the Consumer Financial Protection Bureau at **www.consumerfinance.gov/mortgage-closing**

Other Disclosures

Appraisal
If the property was appraised for your loan, your lender is required to give you a copy at no additional cost at least 3 days before closing. If you have not yet received it, please contact your lender at the information listed below.

Contract Details
See your note and security instrument for information about
• what happens if you fail to make your payments,
• what is a default on the loan,
• situations in which your lender can require early repayment of the loan, and
• the rules for making payments before they are due.

Liability after Foreclosure
If your lender forecloses on this property and the foreclosure does not cover the amount of unpaid balance on this loan,
☒ state law may protect you from liability for the unpaid balance. If you refinance or take on any additional debt on this property, you may lose this protection and have to pay any debt remaining even after foreclosure. You may want to consult a lawyer for more information.
☐ state law does not protect you from liability for the unpaid balance.

Refinance
Refinancing this loan will depend on your future financial situation, the property value, and market conditions. You may not be able to refinance this loan.

Tax Deductions
If you borrow more than this property is worth, the interest on the loan amount above this property's fair market value is not deductible from your federal income taxes. You should consult a tax advisor for more information.

Contact Information

	Lender	Mortgage Broker	Real Estate Broker (B)	Real Estate Broker (S)	Settlement Agent
Name	Ficus Bank		Omega Real Estate Broker Inc.	Alpha Real Estate Broker Co.	Epsilon Title Co.
Address	4321 Random Blvd. Somecity, ST 12340		789 Local Lane Sometown, ST 12345	987 Suburb Ct. Someplace, ST 12340	123 Commerce Pl. Somecity, ST 12344
NMLS ID					
ST License ID			Z765416	Z61456	Z61616
Contact	Joe Smith		Samuel Green	Joseph Cain	Sarah Arnold
Contact NMLS ID	12345				
Contact ST License ID			P16415	P51461	PT1234
Email	joesmith@ ficusbank.com		sam@omegare.biz	joe@alphare.biz	sarah@ epsilontitle.com
Phone	123-456-7890		123-555-1717	321-555-7171	987-555-4321

Confirm Receipt

By signing, you are only confirming that you have received this form. You do not have to accept this loan because you have signed or received this form.

_____   _____   _____   _____
Applicant Signature   Date   Co-Applicant Signature   Date

additional three business days must be added. For example, if the closing is set for Friday, October 25, the Closing Disclosure must be actually received by the borrower no later than Tuesday, October 22. However, if it is mailed, three business days must be added so that the Closing Disclosure needs to be mailed no later than Friday, October 18.[5]

Under certain conditions, a new Closing Disclosure needs to be sent, triggering a new three-day delivery schedule. Among the things that can trigger a new Closing Disclosure are (1) the annual percentage rate changes by more than one-eighth of a percent, (2) the loan product changes in a way that makes the disclosure inaccurate, or (3) a prepayment penalty is added. Obviously, the need for a new Closing Disclosure document will also cause the closing date to move to a later date.

It was generally the practice in residential real estate closings that the HUD-1 was prepared by the closing agent (frequently an employee of the title company). Because of the additional financial information required on the Closing Disclosure, the lender may very well now prepare this document. The long-term effects on closing procedures are not yet well known. One prominent real estate professional has opined that the new disclosure requirements may cause most residential closings to be done in an escrow, rather than in a formal, round table closing.

Closing Commercial Real Estate Transactions

The disclosure requirements for residential real estate closings do not apply to commercial transactions. Most commercial real estate transactions are conducted in a formal closing, with all of the interested parties or their representatives present. This allows for last-minute adjustments, as the decision makers are all in one place and can immediately resolve issues as they arise. Commercial real estate transactions do not typically have the emotional gravitas that surround residential closings. After all, most commercial real estate deals are a business decision and do not affect people's dwelling places.

---

5. Saturday counts as a "business day" for purposes of calculating delivery date.

Ethical Considerations in Real Estate Closings in Ohio

Ethical issues can arise for people who are involved in closing real estate transactions. It is impossible to exhaustively list all of the ethical concerns here, but discussing a few is in order.

Witnessing Documents

Some documents may require that they be witnessed or notarized. Witnessing is simply the act of observing that a person signed a document and that they were not under any disability—such as undue influence, intoxication, unsound mind, and so forth. A witness should actually observe the signature being written and the condition of the signer. A person should never sign as a witness to a signature that the witness did not actually see being written. All too often, people are asked to sign as a witness when the document has already been signed and the signatory is no longer present. Often the individual will agree to sign as a witness as an accommodation. This is unethical. The correct thing to do is to have the person return and sign again, perhaps above the older signature.

Notary publics serve an important function in real estate closings. For example, deeds must be notarized to effect transfer of the realty to the new owner. Notaries in Ohio receive a commission from the state after passing an exam. A notary has the authority to place an official seal on a document and certify to the identity of the person signing. If you are a notary, you either know the signatory personally or verify their identity with a picture ID. Other duties of a notary are to accept sworn statements. The notary should make sure that the person making the sworn statement affirmatively states that it is true and perform some outward sign to show their sincerity, such as raising their right hand. Notaries are sometimes asked to notarize a document that has already been signed and by someone that they do not know. This is unethical and can put the notary in jeopardy of losing their commission, and perhaps other damages.

Conflicts of Interest

If the person conducting a closing has an interest in the outcome, they should recuse themselves from the transaction. Even if everything is above board and fair, it can give the impression of impropriety to an outside ob-server. It is far better to let someone else handle this matter. Likewise, the same attorney should not represent both a lender and a borrower in the same trans-action. Both parties can waive this conflict of interest in writing, but the bet-ter thing to do is to simply not accept such an assignment.

Confidentiality

People involved in a real estate closing will necessarily have access to personal and confidential information about the buyers and sellers. A person's credit rating, bank account information, details about their loan and down pay-ment—all of this information is confidential and must be kept secret. Some-times a real estate professional may learn juicy details about a person that is tempting to send out on the grapevine. Do not be tempted to do so, except to those who have a need to know in connection with the real estate transaction.

Money

In a closing, it is common for the closing agent to receive and control large sums of money. The buyer's bank may send loan proceeds to be held until the closing; the buyer may provide a down payment; the seller may also need to bring money to the transaction. The closing agent must keep these funds in a separate account and cannot mix them with personal funds or office operat-ing money. It may seem easier to do otherwise, or even tempting to "borrow" money from the escrow to meet office expenses. Don't do it. Period.

Discussion Questions

1. Explain the difference between a formal closing and an escrow closing.
2. Explain the doctrine of relation back.
3. What are the purposes of a walk-through?
4. You are working in a county that uses a 360-day year to calculate prora-tions. The annual property tax for a property is $5,400. Seller has lived on the property for 45 days. How much should Buyer be credited to cover Seller's prorated taxes?
5. Compare when the HUD-1 form and the Closing Disclosure form must be delivered to a residential buyer. How do the new closing rules help a buyer in preparing for a closing?

Key Terms

Closing
Closing disclosure
Closing protection insurance
Doctrine of relation back
Dodd–Frank Act
Escrow agent
Escrow closing
Escrow instructions
Formal closing
Good faith estimate
HUD-1
Loan estimate
Prorations
RESPA
Round table closing
Settlement
Truth in lending
Underwater
Walk-through

Chapter 14

Real Estate and Probate

In Chapter 3 we learned that real property *always* has an owner, and that the owner can be determined with certainty. But if a property owner dies, who is the new owner? How is that new owner determined? How do we let the rest of the world know that the property has transferred? At first these questions may seem difficult, but as you will soon see, they have readily determinable answers. It is quite impossible to deal with Ohio real estate law without also considering the effect of **probate**[1] on ownership and transfer of realty.

Testate and Intestate Succession

You may be surprised to learn that *everyone* who lives in Ohio has an estate plan. If you have a **will**, a document that determines how you want your property to be distributed after you die, you certainly have an estate plan, at least of sorts. But if you do not have a will, the State of Ohio has a default estate plan that will kick in upon your death. A person who dies with a will is said to be **testate**, whereas a person who dies without a will is said to be **intestate**. If you die intestate, the laws of **intestate succession**, sometimes called the law of **descent and distribution**, will provide your estate plan.

Of course, one size does not fit all. Not every person will be happy with the estate plan that the State of Ohio provides through the laws of intestate succession. No problem—just write a will. As you no doubt know, a will specifies to whom you would like your property to be distributed upon your demise.

---

1. The word *probate* means "to prove"—consider the root word, *probe*. So, the literal purpose of probate is to prove the validity of a will. However, it is more commonly used to describe the process of dealing with an estate, paying its bills, and distributing the proceeds.

What Law Applies?

At first, determining what state's law applies seems like an easy question—and it is, but with a couple of interesting twists. First, for a will to be valid, it must comply with the laws of the state in which a person resided at the time the will was made—the **domicile** of the **testator**. A testator is a person who makes a will, and a domicile is that person's permanent residence. Everyone has a domicile, even people who live in an RV and travel from state to state. Surely they have a "home base"—where the RV is registered and the state that issued their driver's license. So, the domicile of the testator at the time a will is made determines which state's laws are used to determine if a will is valid, even if the testator has a different state of domicile when he or she dies.

Next, we need to look at particular items of property and determine if they are personalty or realty. The law of the state of domicile of a **decedent**[2] at the time of death will be used to administrate the decedent's personalty, while the law of the state in which *realty is located* will determine how the realty is distributed.

So, a person can be domiciled in State A when they make a will, own realty in State B, and move to State C, where they are domiciled upon death. State A's law will be used to determine the validity of the will, State B's laws will apply to the distribution of the realty in State B, and State C's laws will be used to determine how the decedent's personal property will be distributed. Thus, administration of an estate can involve laws from three states, or even more if realty is located in multiple states.

Requirements for a Valid Will in Ohio

A will is actually a pretty simple legal document, at least in comparison to, say, a contract to purchase commercial real property. A valid will in Ohio It can has only five basic requirements:

---

2. The legal name for a person who has died is *decedent*.

Requirement	Comments
Testator must be of sound mind	This means that, at the time that the will is made, the testator knows: 1. That they are making a will 2. What property they own, in general 3. Who is their immediate family—those persons who would inherit under intestate succession Sound mind is measured at the time that the will is made; a person who is otherwise not of sound mind could have a lucid moment and make a will at that time. A person who is under duress, undue influence, or otherwise acting under outside pressure does not have the requisite sound mind to make a will. The standard for sound mind to make a will is a fairly low hurdle.
Testator must be at least 18 years old	This means that a 17-year-old rock star that is worth millions of dollars cannot make a will. The laws of intestate succession will distribute that person's property.
The will must be in writing	The few exceptions to this rule are not relevant here, as real property cannot be distributed by an oral will. Written wills need not be on paper. Wills have been successfully probated that have been written in lipstick on a pillowcase, on the jailhouse wall, in the margin of a cookbook, and many other places.
The testator must sign the will *at the end*	A signature can be anything that the testator intends to be a signature; even an X will suffice. If the testator cannot physically sign the will, another person can sign on the testator's behalf, provided they do so in the testator's presence and at the testator's direction. The signature must be *after* the last provision in the will that disposes of property. A signature along the side margin of every page will not suffice to create a valid will in Ohio. It is common practice for witnesses to sign after the testator—this does not invalidate the will, so long as no additional gifts are made after the testator's signature.
Two witnesses must attest to the will	The witnesses serve two purposes: (1) they add to the seriousness of making a will so it is not done lightly, and (2) they can later testify as to the testator's sound mind. The witnesses attest that the testator signed the will and observe that the testator did so freely.

I think that a will could be spray painted on the side of a cow, so long as the person doing so is of sound mind, is over 18, signs at the end, and has two witnesses. This is an extreme example, of course, but it does illustrate the minimal requirements for a valid will in Ohio.

Changing a Will in Ohio

A testator can change his or her will at any time before death, and for any reason. The traditional way to change a will is by making a **codicil**, which is essentially an amendment to an already existing will. The codicil requires the same formalities as a will itself—sound mind, of age, writing, signed at the end, and witnesses. Thus, a complete will consisted of the original will, together with all of the codicils.

Using a codicil made sense at a time when wills were tediously typed out, but makes less sense these days with word processors and high-speed printers. It is usually easier to simply make a new will and revoke the previous one.

Ohio Law of Intestate Succession

As mentioned earlier, if a person domiciled in Ohio dies without a will, the Ohio law of intestate succession, sometimes called the law of descent and distribution, kicks in to determine to whom the decedent's property goes. Here are the basics of the Ohio law:

If the decedent is survived by	Property goes to
No spouse, but **lineal descendents**[3]	Lineal descendents, **per stirpes**[4]
Spouse and no children	Surviving spouse
Spouse and lineal descendents of the decedent and surviving spouse	Surviving spouse
Spouse and *one* lineal descendent of the decedent who is not the child of the surviving spouse	Surviving spouse gets $20,000 plus half of the balance Lineal descendent gets the rest

---

3. A lineal descendent is a child, grandchild, great-grandchild, etc. of the decedent.

4. *Per stirpes* means "by right of representation." Assume the descendent had three children, A, B, and C, and C predeceased the decedent, leaving two grandchildren of the decedent, D and E. The distribution will then be as follows: A gets one-third, B gets one-third, and D and E each get one-sixth (half of the one-third that C would have received).

Spouse and *more than one* lineal descendent of the decedent who *are not* the children of the surviving spouse	Surviving spouse gets $20,000 plus one-third of the balance Lineal descendents get the rest, per stirpes
Spouse and *more than one* lineal descendent of the decedent, at least one of whom *is* the child of the surviving spouse	Surviving spouse gets $60,000 Lineal descendents get the rest, per stirpes
No spouse, no lineal descendents	Parents of decedent
No spouse, no lineal descendents, no parents	Brothers and sisters of decedent
No spouse, no lineal descendents, no parents, no siblings	Grandparents of decedent
No spouse, no lineal descendents, no parents, no siblings, no grandparents	Next of kin[5]
No spouse, no lineal descendents, no parents no siblings, no grandparents, no next of kin	Step-children of the decedent
None of the above	Escheats to the State of Ohio

Of course, simply making a will can always change this scheme.

Intentionally Omitted Spouse

In Ohio, it is not really possible to exclude a surviving spouse from an estate. As you can see from the Ohio law of intestate succession, if a spouse survives the decedent, the spouse will receive a substantial portion of the estate. But you may wonder if you can effectively exclude a spouse by leaving them out of a will. The short answer is that you can leave a spouse out, but that person will have rights that make the intentional omission ineffective, for two reasons—the spouse's elective share and the family protection provisions of Ohio law.

A surviving spouse has a choice: he or she can take what was given under a will, or choose to take an elective share of the estate. The elective share is essentially the same as the intestate amount, but it cannot exceed half of the value of the estate if there is one lineal descendant of the decedent, or cannot exceed one-third of the value of the estate if there is more than one lineal de-

---

5. *Next of kin* means the people who are most closely related by blood. This is complex and beyond the scope of this text.

scendant of the decedent. So, even if a person hates his or her spouse and wants him or her to get nothing, the surviving spouse can choose to take an elective share, which can be substantial.

In addition, the surviving members of a decedent's family, including a spouse, can receive an allowance for support while the estate is being probated. This is intended to make sure that the family can afford to continue to meet the expenses of living in the meanwhile. The amount of the family support in Ohio is sizable, as the next chart shows.

#	Ohio Family Allowance
1	$40,000 cash
2	The surviving spouse may remain in the family home rent-free for one year.[6]
3	The surviving spouse may take up to two automobiles owned by the decedent, not to exceed a value of $40,000.[7]
4	One watercraft (boat)
5	One boat trailer (really!)
6	One outboard motor (really!)

These items are available to the surviving spouse and the family even before the estate probate process gets started. So, I suspect the lesson is that if a person domiciled in Ohio hates his or her spouse, they should be sure to terminate the marriage by annulment, dissolution, or divorce before dying, because the surviving spouse can receive a substantial part of the estate, even if the decedent had other intentions.

You may rightly ask what would happen if item 1 in the family allowance consumes all of the value of the estate. The answer is simple. The family allowance will be paid out of the estate and that ends the probate matter. When the assets of an estate are exhausted, no one further down the line gets anything.

---

6. This is true even if the home was the sole property of the decedent and given to someone else in the will. The person to whom the home was given will be the owner, but the surviving spouse may remain there for one year rent-free. Guess who gets to pay the real estate taxes: the owner, not the surviving spouse

7. The amount in item 1 is reduced by the fair market value of the lower-valued automobile taken.

Figure 14-1—Trust

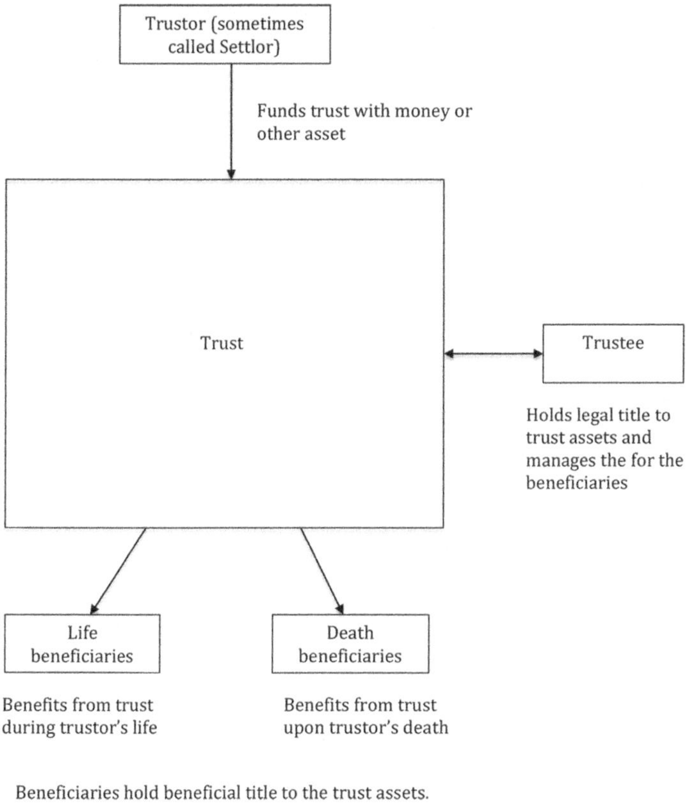

Trustor (sometimes called Settlor)

Funds trust with money or other asset

Trust

Trustee

Holds legal title to trust assets and manages the for the beneficiaries

Life beneficiaries

Benefits from trust during trustor's life

Death beneficiaries

Benefits from trust upon trustor's death

Beneficiaries hold beneficial title to the trust assets.

Trusts

A **trust** is simply an arrangement by which one person holds legal title to property for the benefit of someone else. A trust is not a legal entity but rather a concept, an arrangement, where title to property is logically split into two parts—legal title and beneficial title.

As you can see in Figure 14-1, several people can be involved in a trust. The **trustor** (sometimes called **settlor**) establishes the trust and places money or other assets, including real estate, in the trust. The **trustee** holds legal title to the trust assets and manages them, while the **beneficiaries** hold beneficial title to the trust assets but have no management rights to them.

Beneficiaries are split into two groups: **life beneficiaries** and **death beneficiaries**. The life beneficiaries receive the benefits of the trust assets during the life of the trustor, and the death beneficiaries receive the benefits of the trust upon the death of the trustor, and perhaps after that.

In Ohio, the same person can play multiple roles in a trust, with a couple of exceptions. First, the same person cannot be the sole trustee and the sole beneficiary of a trust. To do so would destroy the trust, because one person would hold all of the legal title and beneficial title to the trust assets. Next, the same person cannot be both the trustor and the death beneficiary. Since the death beneficiary benefits from the trust assets upon the death of the trustor, this person cannot also be the trustor for logical reasons that will yield to a little thought.

Why would someone want to set up a trust? There are several reasons. For example, suppose Jacob has a rather large estate, say $1 million, and wants the money to benefit his 19-year-old son's college education and provide a nest egg after that. If Jacob simply left the money to the son, it is quite likely that the son would foolishly spend the money and not have anything left to attend college. Jacob could leave the $1 million in trust by something as simple as the following language in his will:

> I hereby leave $1 million in trust to my brother Ebenezer for the benefit of my son Tim. Ebenezer shall use the trust assets to pay for Tim's college expenses, including tuition, room, board, books, and fees. The balance of the trust assets, if any, shall be paid to Tim on his 35th birthday.

It is that easy in its simplest form. Ebenezer has a **fiduciary duty** to Tim, one of the highest loyalty and trust. This trust will make sure that Tim's college expenses are paid and the balance of the trust paid to Tim when he reaches age 35, on the assumption that he will be more mature and prudent with money by then. In this example, Jacob is the trustor, Ebenezer is the trustee, and Tim is the death beneficiary. Because this trust was created in a will, there is no life beneficiary.

A person can also use a special kind of trust, commonly called a **living trust**, to simplify the probate process somewhat. In a living trust, the trustor is also the life beneficiary and, typically, the trustee as well. The following could create a living trust:

> I hereby declare that I have transferred all of my assets to myself, as trustee, who shall use the trust assets as the trustee deems appropriate for my benefit during my lifetime. Upon my death, the trust assets shall be paid as follows: <who gets what after death>.

The advantage of this arrangement is that, if done properly, it completely avoids the probate process, as everything that the person owns is held in trust and automatically passes to the death beneficiaries. Anything that automatically passes on death is not subject to probate.[8]

Probating an Estate in Ohio

When a person who is domiciled in Ohio dies, their estate becomes subject to the jurisdiction of the **probate court** in the county of domicile. All **probate assets** (assets that do not automatically pass upon death) become assets of the decedent's estate and are used to pay that person's remaining bills, final expenses, and finally distributed under the will if there is one, or by intestate succession if there is no will.

The probate court will appoint a **personal representative** to administer the estate and handle the assets. If the decedent died testate, the personal representative is known as an **executor**. If the decedent died intestate, the personal representative is known as an **administrator**.

From a real estate law perspective, any realty in another state will be passed according to the laws of that state. An additional probate matter will need to be opened in each state where the decedent owned realty. These additional matters are referred to as **ancillary administration**.

Transfers due to Death of Owner

The old adage "you can't take it with you" certainly applies to real property. When the owner of Ohio real property dies, ownership immediately and automatically passes to someone. You will recall from Chapter 1 that the owner of real property must always be knowable, stemming from the days of knight servitude and such. These days, we must know who is responsible for paying real estate taxes and assessments. That "person" may be an heir or the estate[9] itself.

---

8. The actual mechanics of a living trust would probably be much more complicated than the brief statement here, including arrangements for a successor trustee in the event of incompetence of the trustor, provisions for a guardian of the person of the trustor if he or she becomes incompetent, a list of powers of the trustee, details of how the trust assets would be distributed at death, and provisions for adding additional assets acquired by the trustor to the trust. I will leave the details of living trusts to an Estates and Probate course.

9. Unfortunately the term *estate* can have different meanings depending on context. As it is used here, it refers to all of the real and personal property owned by the decedent at the time of death and that is being administrated with the assistance of the probate court. Dis-

If the decedent died with a will that named someone to inherit the real property, and the property has not been sold to pay debts of the estate, that person will receive title to the property. If the decedent did not have a will, the Ohio law of intestate succession will determine who will receive the property. Of course, a person can always refuse to accept the property from the estate. In that case, the will or Ohio state law will determine who would receive the property instead.

If someone inherits real property from an estate, will they receive a deed? In Ohio, the answer is no. When the probate court approves the distribution of real property, it will issue a Certificate of Transfer, which serves to show title of the real property in the new owner (see Figure 14-2). The Certificate of Transfer is recorded at the county recorder's office, just like a deed. But unlike a deed, the Certificate of Transfer does not itself cause the transfer to happen—the approval by the probate court causes the transfer of ownership, and the Certificate of Transfer merely documents that fact.

This can be a bit confusing, because we become accustomed to thinking of a deed as the document that transfers ownership of real property. But, think of it this way—when the probate court approves the distribution of real property, ownership immediately transfers to the new owner. The court order transfers ownership. So, the Certificate of Transfer merely documents that fact and can be recorded to put the whole world on notice of the identity of the new owner. The "Authentication" section of the Certificate of Transfer form may confuse you. Perhaps this will help—the probate judge signs an original Certificate of Transfer, which is then kept on file by the probate court clerk. The probate court clerk will then prepare a copy of the Certificate of Transfer, and the "Authentication" section will be completed to indicate the authenticity of the copy. This authenticated copy is the one that will be recorded by the county recorder, as the probate court clerk keeps and files the original.[10]

Powers of Attorney

One type of document you may see from time to time in an Ohio real estate practice is a **power of attorney**. This document, which must be witnessed

---

tinguish that use with the term *estate* that refers to the various estates in land discussed in Chapter 3, such as life estate, estate by the entireties, and so forth.

10. It may seem that the Certificate of Transfer accomplishes the same thing as a deed, but this is not quite true. The act of signing, sealing, and delivering a deed is what transfers of real property to another person. In the case of transfers due to death, the probate court's court order transfers the property; the Certificate of Transfer is simply recorded in the recorder's office to put the world on notice as to who owns the property.

Figure 14-2—Certificate of Transfer

PROBATE COURT OF _____ COUNTY, OHIO
_____, JUDGE

ESTATE OF _____ ,DECEASED

CASE NO. _____

CERTIFICATE OF TRANSFER

NO. _____

[Check one of the following]

☐ Decedent died intestate.

☐ Decedent died testate.

Decedent died on _____ owning the real property described in this certificate. The persons to whom such real property passed by devise, descent or election are as follows:

Name	Residence Address	Transferee's share of decedent's interest

[Complete if applicable] The real property described in this certificate is subject to a charge of $_____ in favor of decedent's surviving spouse, _____ in respect of the unpaid balance of the specific monetary share which is part of the surviving spouse's total intestate share.

12.1 - CERTIFICATE OF TRANSFER

Amended: March 1, 2014

Discard all previous versions of this form

and notarized, gives a person, called an **attorney-in-fact**, the power to act on behalf of someone else. A power of attorney might be used, for example, if a married couple is selling real property and one of the spouses is out of town

Figure 14-2—Certificate of Transfer, *continued*

(Reverse of Form 12.1)

CASE NO._____

The legal description of decedent's interest in the real property subject to this certificate is: **[use extra sheets, if necessary]**.

Prior Instrument Reference:

Parcel No: _____

This instrument was prepared by _____

ISSUANCE

This Certificate of Transfer is issued this _____ day of _____, 20_____.

_____
Probate Judge

AUTHENTICATION

I certify that this document is a true copy of the original Certificate of Transfer No. _____ issued on _____ and kept by me as custodian of the official records of this Court.

_____   _____
Date   Probate Judge

                                    By _____
                                         Deputy Clerk

                                                        [Print Form]

12.1 - CERTIFICATE OF TRANSFER
PAGE 2

Amended: March 1, 2014
Discard all previous versions of this form

for an extended time. By providing the other spouse with a power of attorney, a real estate transaction can be completed with only one spouse present.

Powers of attorney are very specific in the powers and rights that are given to the attorney-in-fact and are strictly construed by the courts. For example, if a power of attorney gives the right to accept an offer, it does not also give the power to sign a deed. It is best to have an attorney-at-law draw up powers of attorney to make sure that the document will accomplish what is needed. A power of attorney can be revoked at any time by the person granting the power and will automatically become void if that person dies or becomes disabled to act on his or her own behalf. As a simple way to look at this—could the person granting the power exercise it if they were present in person? If not, the power of attorney will not be effective. Suppose the grantor of the power lapses into senile dementia and is unable to act on his or her own without the appointment of a guardian. In that case, the power of attorney would be ineffective, because the person could not act on his or her own.

A special form of power of attorney is called a **durable power**. This is exactly the same in all respects as a normal power of attorney, but will remain in effect after the incapacity of the person granting the power. This can be accomplished by including "the powers granted by this document shall not be affected by my disability." Of course, the person making the power of attorney has to have capacity at the time of making the durable power.

Summary

This has been a rather whirlwind tour of some of the concerns surrounding death of an owner of real property. Indeed, this entire book has been only a mere glimpse into the *Fundamentals of Ohio Real Estate Law*. I trust that you enjoyed the journey at least partly as much as I have enjoyed guiding you on it. I wish you every success in your expedition through Ohio real estate law.

Loveland, Ohio
2015

Discussion Questions

1. A resident of Ohio died owning real property in Kentucky and Tennessee.
    a. Where will the estate be administered?
    b. Which state's law applies to the distribution of the decedent's personal property?
    c. Which state's laws apply to the distribution of the decedent's real property?
2. Explain all of the elements for a valid will in Ohio.

3. Bob and Martha were married and had no children together. Bob was married before and has a son named Fred from a previous marriage. Bob died intestate in Ohio. His estate was worth $60,000. How much will Martha and Fred receive from Bob's estate? (Ignore any rules about support allowance.)

4. Explain the concept of a living trust. What advantage is there to having a living trust?

5. Explain why someone who inherits real property in a will does not receive a deed from the executor. What document is used instead of a deed in this circumstance?

6. Describe a situation in which a person would receive a fiduciary deed from an estate.

Key Terms

Administrator
Ancillary administration
Attorney-in-fact
Beneficiary
Certificate of Transfer
Codicil
Death beneficiary
Decedent
Descent and distribution
Domicile
Durable power
Executor
Fiduciary duty
Intestate
Intestate succession
Life beneficiary
Living trust
Per stirpes
Personal representative
Power of attorney
Probate
Probate asset
Settlor
Testate
Testator

Trust
Trustee
Trustor
Will

Part II

Real Estate Prelicensing Material

Ohio Real Estate Salesperson Prelicensing Notes

Part I of this book is a basic overview of Ohio real estate law and is intended to be used as an undergraduate text in a general introduction to Ohio-specific real estate concepts and laws. Part II contains three additional chapters that are required in a four-semester-credit Ohio Real Estate Law course for salesperson prelicensing. In addition, I have included links to additional material that may be helpful in a salesperson prelicensing course.

The Law & You — Ohio State Bar Association

https://www.ohiobar.org/General%20Resources/LawandYou/TLAY_Complete.pdf

This document covers the basics of the US legal system, with particular emphasis on Ohio-specific law and procedure, in a readable format. This material is typically taught in a separate Basic Legal Principles course but should be included in a prelicensing course.

Agency — Ohio Association of Realtors

http://ohiorealtors.org/legal/agency-law-resources/

I have found this material to be quite helpful in discussing the specifics of the agency relationships between consumers, salespersons, and brokers. In particular, I like to use copies of the Ohio Agency Disclosure Statement and the various iterations of the Consumer Guide to Agency Relationships in discussing the sometimes-confusing varieties of agency relationships that can be created in Ohio. By walking through the disclosure documents and describing the agency relationship that each establishes, the students not only gain a good understanding of the topic but they also get to use actual practice forms.

Residential Property Disclosure—Ohio Association of Realtors

http://ohiorealtors.org/consumers/required-disclosures/

Students generally enjoy walking through the required Ohio residential property disclosure form and describing various situations that would need to be disclosed.

Fair Housing

A table of the basic Fair Housing laws is included as Appendix H. I have found that students' understanding of this material increases when they carefully review this document and use hypothetical situations to identify which of the Fair Housing laws are involved. Chapter 16 contains a few hypothetical examples, and students seem to enjoy creating additional hypotheticals in class. My general admonition to students is to simply not violate any of the fair housing laws, but the licensing exam seems to focus on which of the laws are violated and how they are enforced in various situations.

Chapter 15

Real Estate Agency and Licensing

Agency

Here's something that you may find surprising—an Ohio real estate agent is usually not an "agent" in the legal sense. An **agent** is someone who is authorized to act on behalf of another person and has the power to bind that other person in a contract. That other person is known as a **principal**. Think of a purchasing agent at a company—that person can enter into contracts on behalf of the company, and the company will be the principal and be bound by the contracts. Note that for the principal to be bound by the acts of the agent, the principal must give the power to the agent; an agent cannot assume the power on his or her own.

Authority in agency relationships comes in several flavors—**actual authority**, **implied authority**, **apparent authority**, and **ratification**. The first two are pretty easy to understand. Actual authority is exactly what it says; the principal has actually given the agent the authority to act on the principal's behalf. A purchasing agent has been given actual authority by his or her employer to act on behalf of the company. Implied authority, on the other hand, is incidental to the agent's other duties. For example, suppose you are the manager of a store and have been given actual authority to hire and fire employees, set prices for merchandise, and so forth. If the front window of the store was broken in a storm, you will probably have implied authority to have the window repaired, even if the owner of the store did not specifically authorize you to do so.

Apparent authority exists when the principal does something that makes a third party reasonably believe that an agency relationship is in place when it is not. For example, suppose a candidate for a sales job, who has not yet been hired, is taken on a customer call so that the hiring manager can see him or her in action. If the candidate is allowed to make a sales presentation and sign an order while the hiring manager is watching, the contract for the sale will be valid, even though the candidate was not actually an employee and did not have actual authority. The fact that the customer was led to believe that the candidate was acting on behalf of the company, and the hiring manager did nothing to clarify the relationship, means that the customer could reasonably believe that an agency relationship was in place.

Agency by ratification occurs when a person who is not an agent acts without authority of any kind and manages to enter into a contract with a third party ostensibly on behalf of a principal. The contract will be binding on the purported agent, but not the principal, unless the principal decides to accept the contract, thereby ratifying it. Suppose Ron, a real go-getter, convinces someone to purchase an industrial product at a particular price from Acme Products, and even enters into a contract with him or her, when Ron has no business relationship at all with Acme. Ron might then go to Acme and say, "I have a buyer lined up for you to purchase the industrial product. If you are willing to pay me a commission, I'll make sure the deal goes through." Of course Acme has no obligation to accept the proposed transaction, but if Acme does accept it, Ron would be an agent by ratification. Essentially, Acme would authorize the transaction and accept its benefits.

You will notice that in all of these cases, the principal must have acted—granted actual authority, allowed implied authority, created the impression in a third party of an existing agency relationship for apparent authority, or accepted the benefits of a deal where no agency existed, thereby ratifying the authority.

The table below contains summaries of the various forms of authority as they relate to real estate agents.

Authority	Example
Actual Authority	"Sell my house."
Implied Authority	List the house on MLS, put sign in yard, install lockbox, and so forth.
Apparent Authority, Ratification	Probably not a consideration for real estate agents.

Agency relationships are pretty common—suppose you told me that you were going to the local fast-food restaurant for lunch and asked if I wanted anything. If I were to give you a $10 bill and tell you simply, "Bring back something for me," you would be my agent and I would be the principal. You would have the power to spend my money on "something" (probably food for my lunch). What's more, I would be bound by the choice you made for me. I gave you the authority to act on my behalf and spend my money.

Even though real estate agents are not normally true agents, in some instances a real estate agent may indeed be an agent in the legal sense. If I am selling my house, I want my real estate agent to go out and find potential buyers; I do not want them to accept offers on my behalf. Yet, if they are authorized to accept contracts on behalf of a property owner, a true agency relationship may be in place. However, in the interest of simplicity, in this book, I will use the term *real estate agent* in the looser sense that it is commonly understood—a salesperson of real property.

So if real estate agents are not true agents in the legal sense of the word, what are they? Essentially, they are subagents of the brokerage. A real estate agent, who obtains a listing of a property, is acting on behalf of the broker for whom they work, and the listing is actually that of the broker and not the agent. In fact, as you will see in the next chapter, any For Sale sign must display the brokerage name as prominently as that of the agent.

In Ohio it is illegal for real estate agents to represent a client directly; they must always work through their broker. What's more, they must operate using the business model that their particular broker has chosen to use. As we will see in the next section, brokers can use several business models in Ohio, each with different relationships between the broker and the client. Each brokerage will select one of the permitted business models and will engage with buyers and sellers only in accordance with their particular business models.

Real Estate Brokerage Business Models

Traditionally, a real estate broker (and the real estate agents working under that broker) actually represented only sellers. Buyers didn't always realize that the real estate agent they were using to help them with a property purchase transaction was actually looking out for the seller's best interests. Fortunately, the law has changed in Ohio, and brokerages can now represent buyers as well as sellers. This creates the potential for some conflicts of interest—can the same person represent the best interests of both the buyer and the seller in the same transaction? When it comes to real estate brokerages, the answer is yes. You may find this unusual, because even the basic issue as to the purchase price of the property would seem to be at odds, as the seller wants the highest price possible and the buyer wants the lowest. Some of the brokerage business models do have protections in place to help mitigate this problem. For what it's worth, an attorney would not be allowed to represent both sides of a legal matter, so these relationships are rather unique in the world of real estate brokerages.

In Ohio, the relationships between the brokerage and sellers and buyers must be disclosed, using standardized forms prepared by the Ohio Division of Real Estate. I have included the template supplied by the Ohio Division of Real Estate for each of the permitted business models. These templates are intended to be completed by putting the brokerage name in the places indicated. A real estate agent working with a particular brokerage will have a supply of the Consumer Guide to Agency Relationships disclosure form that is appropriate for that brokerage's business model, but not the others.

As you look at these disclosure documents, you will notice that they are very much the same in that they describe the various business models that brokerages can take, but the section labeled "Working with (Brokerage)" is specific to the business model of a particular brokerage. I suggest that you take time to read each of the disclosure forms carefully, paying careful attention to how the different business models are described.

Exclusive Seller's Agent

As the name suggests, a real estate brokerage that has chosen this business model represents only sellers. This was the traditional business model for real estate brokerages. The disclosure form in Figure 15-1 needs to be supplied to the seller before the brokerage markets or shows the property.

The section "Working with (Brokerage)" describes how this business model works, which is perhaps the simplest model to understand. A brokerage that exclusively represents sellers can still work with buyers as customers and provide nonconfidential information to the buyer. The buyer is expected to look out for their own best interests. The flow of confidential information will be from the seller through the real estate agent to the broker, but not down to the buyer. Furthermore, anything the buyer tells the real estate agent can be told to the seller, so the buyer should not reveal anything confidential to the real estate agent in this business model. As an example, the buyer should not tell the real estate agent the highest amount they are willing to pay for the property, as that information will be passed on to the seller. Figure 15-2 shows how information flows in this model. You will notice that confidential information does not flow to the buyer, and there is no such thing as confidential information from the buyer.

Figure 15-1—Exclusive Seller

Exclusive Seller

CONSUMER GUIDE TO AGENCY RELATIONSHIPS

Brokerage Name

We are pleased you have selected (brokerage) to help you with your real estate needs. Whether you are selling, buying or leasing real estate, (brokerage) can provide you with expertise and assistance. Because this may be the largest financial transaction you will enter into, it is important to understand the role of the agents and brokers with whom you are working. Below is some information that explains the various services agents can offer and their options for working with you.

For more information on agency law in Ohio you can also contact the Ohio Division of Real Estate & Professional Licensing at (614) 466-4100, or on their website www.com.state.oh.us.

Representing Sellers
Most sellers of real estate choose to list their home for sale with a real estate brokerage. When they do so, they sign a listing agreement that authorizes the brokerage and the listing agent to represent their interests. As the seller's agent, the brokerage and listing agent must: follow the seller's lawful instructions, be loyal to the seller, promote the seller's best interests, disclose material facts to the seller, maintain confidential information, act with reasonable skill and care and, account for any money they handle in the transaction. In rare circumstances, a listing broker may offer "subagency" to other brokerages which would also represent the seller's interests and owe the seller these same duties.

Representing Buyers
When purchasing real estate, buyers usually choose to work with a real estate agent as well. Often the buyers want to be represented in the transaction. This is referred to as buyer's agency. A brokerage and agent that agree to represent a buyer's interest in a transaction must: follow the buyer's lawful instructions, be loyal to the buyer, promote the buyer's best interests, disclose material facts to the buyer, maintain confidential information and, account for any money they handle in the transaction.

Dual Agency
Occasionally the same agent and brokerage who represents the seller also represents the buyer. This is referred to as dual agency. When a brokerage and its agents become "dual agents," they must maintain a neutral position between the buyer and the seller. They may not advocate the position of one client over the best interests of the other client, or disclose any personal or confidential information to the other party without written consent.

Representing Both the Buyer & Seller
On occasion, the buyer and seller will each be represented by two different agents from the same brokerage. In this case the agents may each represent the best interest of their respective clients. Or, depending on company policy, the agents may both act as dual agents and remain neutral in the transaction. When either of the above occurs, the brokerage will be considered a dual agent. As a dual agent the brokerage and its managers will maintain a neutral position and cannot advocate for the position of one client over another. The brokerage will also protect the confidential information of both parties.

Working With (brokerage)
(brokerage) only represents sellers. It does not represent buyers of real estate. Therefore, (brokerage) will never act as a dual agent representing both parties in a transaction. Instead it will only act as the seller's agent in the sale of real estate. Even though (brokerage) only lists properties for sellers, it can still work with buyers as customers. (brokerage) can provide such buyers with non-confidential information and write offers at the buyer's direction, but will not act as the agent of these buyers. Instead such buyers will represent their own best interests. It is also important for buyers to

Figure 15-1—Exclusive Seller, *continued*

understand that because the listing agent has a duty of full disclosure to the seller, buyers should not share any information with the listing agent that they would not want the seller to know.

Working With Other Brokerages

When (brokerage) lists property for sale it also cooperates with, and offers compensation to, other brokerages that represent buyers. (brokerage) does reserve the right, in some instances, to vary the compensation it offers to other brokerages. As a seller, you should understand that just because (brokerage) shares a fee with a brokerage representing the buyer, it does not mean that you will be represented by that buyer's brokerage. Instead that company will be looking out for the buyer and (brokerage) will be representing your interests.

Fair Housing Statement

It is illegal, pursuant to the Ohio Fair Housing Law, division (H) of Section 4112.02 of the Revised Code and the Federal Fair Housing Law, 42 U.S.C.A. 3601, as amended, to refuse to sell, transfer, assign, rent, lease, sublease or finance housing accommodations, refuse to negotiate for the sale or rental of housing accommodations, or otherwise deny or make unavailable housing accommodations because of race, color, religion, sex, familial status as defined in Section 4112.01 of the Revised Code, ancestry, military status as defined in that section, disability as defined in that section, or national origin or to so discriminate in advertising the sale or rental of housing, in the financing of housing, or in the provision of real estate brokerage services. It is also illegal, for profit, to induce or attempt to induce a person to sell or rent a dwelling by representations regarding the entry into the neighborhood of a person or persons belonging to one of the protected classes.

We hope you find this information to be helpful to you as you begin your real estate transaction. When you are ready to enter into a transaction, you will be given an Agency Disclosure Statement that specifically identifies the role of the agents and brokerages. Please ask questions if there is anything you do not understand.

Because it is important that you have this information, Ohio law requires that we ask you to sign below, acknowledging receipt of this Consumer Guide. Doing so will not obligate you to work with our company if you do not choose to do so.

_____   _____
Name   (Please Print)   Name   (Please Print)

_____   _____
Signature   Date   Signature   Date

Figure 15-2 — Exclusive Seller Information Flow

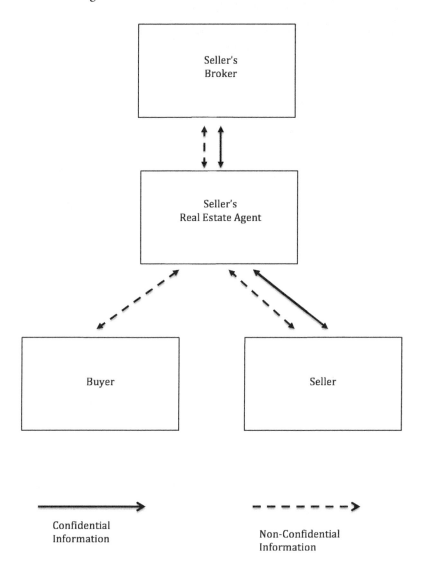

Exclusive Buyer's Agent

Once again, the name of this business model is pretty self-explanatory. A brokerage that has chosen this model will represent only buyers and not sellers. The disclosure form in Figure 15-3 needs to be supplied to the buyer at the **first substantive contact.**[1]

Here also, the section "Working with (Brokerage)" lays out the particulars of this business model. Note that the brokerage will attempt to negotiate for a seller-paid fee. Ordinarily, sellers of real estate pay a commission to their agent. It is common practice for that commission to be split between the seller's agent and the buyer's agent. Even if the seller pays all or part of the buyer-agent's fees, the agent represents only the buyer.

Here, the flow of confidential information is between the buyer, the agent, and the broker. No confidential information will pass to the seller. Figure 15-4 shows how confidential and nonconfidential information flows in this business model. Note that the seller should not provide any confidential information to the buyer's agent, as anything the seller says can be communicated to the buyer. This is true even though it is not expressly stated in Figure 15-3.

Dual Agency

In a dual agency situation, the same brokerage represents both the buyer and seller in a transaction. A real estate agent and that agent's broker must maintain a neutral position in a dual agency. The agent cannot advocate for either side and cannot disclose any confidential information to either side. In a dual agency, the broker and all agents working in the brokerage represent both the buyer and the seller. So, even if one agent of the brokerage is working for a buyer and another agent in the brokerage is working for the seller, both agents are considered to be dual agents, representing both the buyer and the seller. Figure 15-5 is the disclosure form used by brokerages that use this business model.

In a dual agency, who is looking out for the best interest of the buyer? Who is looking out for the best interest of the seller? In short, both the buyer and seller are responsible for protecting themselves, and the agents and brokerage are operating in a neutral position, not doing anything that would place one

---

1. "First substantive contact" means (1) the buyer is prequalified for financing, (2) the real estate agent receives specific information from the buyer, (3) the property is shown to the buyer (except in an open house), (4) the agent discusses an offer with the buyer, or (5) the agent submits an offer to purchase realty to a seller.

Figure 15-3—Exclusive Buyer

Exclusive Buyer

CONSUMER GUIDE TO AGENCY RELATIONSHIPS

Brokerage Name

We are pleased you have selected (brokerage) to help you with your real estate needs. Whether you are buying or leasing real estate, (brokerage) can provide you with expertise and assistance. Because this may be the largest financial transaction you will enter into, it is important to understand the role of the agents and brokers with whom you are working. Below is some information that explains the various services agents can offer and their options for working with you.

For more information on agency law in Ohio you can also contact the Ohio Division of Real Estate & Professional Licensing at (614) 466-4100, or on their website www.com.state.oh.us.

Representing Sellers
Most sellers of real estate choose to list their home for sale with a real estate brokerage. When they do so, they sign a listing agreement that authorizes the brokerage and the listing agent to represent their interests. As the seller's agent, the brokerage and listing agent must: follow the seller's lawful instructions, be loyal to the seller, promote the seller's best interests, disclose material facts to the seller, maintain confidential information, act with reasonable skill and care and, account for any money they handle in the transaction. In rare circumstances a listing broker may offer "subagency" to other brokerages which would also represent the seller's interests and owe the seller these same duties.

Representing Buyers
When purchasing real estate, buyers usually choose to work with a real estate agent as well. Often the buyers want to be represented in the transaction. This is referred to as buyer's agency. A brokerage and agent that agree to represent a buyer's interest in a transaction must: follow the buyer's lawful instructions, be loyal to the buyer, promote the buyer's best interests, disclose material facts to the buyer, maintain confidential information and, account for any money they handle in the transaction.

Dual Agency
Occasionally the same agent and brokerage who represents the seller also represents the buyer. This is referred to as dual agency. When a brokerage and its agents become "dual agents," they must maintain a neutral position between the buyer and the seller. They may not advocate the position of one client over the best interests of the other client, or disclose any personal or confidential information to the other party without written consent.

Representing Both the Buyer & Seller
On occasion, the buyer and seller will each be represented by two different agents from the same brokerage. In this case the agents may each represent the best interest of their respective clients. Or, depending on company policy, the agents may both act as dual agents and remain neutral in the transaction. When either of the above occurs, the brokerage will be considered a dual agent. As a dual agent the brokerage and its managers will maintain a neutral position and cannot advocate for the position of one client over another. The brokerage will also protect the confidential information of both parties.

Working With (brokerage)
(brokerage) only represents buyers. It does not represent sellers or list property for sale. Therefore, (brokerage) will never act as a dual agent representing both parties in a transaction. Instead it will only act as the buyer's agent in the purchase of real estate.

When acting as a buyer's agent, (brokerage) will seek its compensation from the listing broker. If the property is not listed with any broker, or the listing broker does not offer compensation, we will attempt to negotiate for a seller-paid fee. However, even if the listing broker or seller pays us, (brokerage) still represents only the buyer. If (brokerage) is not

Figure 15-3—Exclusive Buyer, *continued*

compensated by the listing broker or the seller, its compensation will be paid by the buyer, pursuant to a written agreement with the buyer.

Fair Housing Statement
It is illegal, pursuant to the Ohio Fair Housing Law, division (H) of Section 4112.02 of the Revised Code and the Federal Fair Housing Law, 42 U.S.C.A. 3601, as amended, to refuse to sell, transfer, assign, rent, lease, sublease or finance housing accommodations, refuse to negotiate for the sale or rental of housing accommodations, or otherwise deny or make unavailable housing accommodations because of race, color, religion, sex, familial status as defined in Section 4112.01 of the Revised Code, ancestry, military status as defined in that section, disability as defined in that section, or national origin or to so discriminate in advertising the sale or rental of housing, in the financing of housing, or in the provision of real estate brokerage services. It is also illegal, for profit, to induce or attempt to induce a person to sell or rent a dwelling by representations regarding the entry into the neighborhood of a person or persons belonging to one of the protected classes.

We hope you find this information to be helpful to you as you begin your real estate transaction. When you are ready to enter into a transaction, you will be given an Agency Disclosure Statement that specifically identifies the role of the agents and brokerages. Please ask questions if there is anything you do not understand.

Because it is important that you have this information, Ohio law requires that we ask you to sign below, acknowledging receipt of this Consumer Guide. Your signature will not obligate you to work with our company if you do not choose to do so.

Name   (Please Print)   Name   (Please Print)

Signature   Date   Signature   Date

EQUAL HOUSING
OPPORTUNITY

Figure 15-4—Exclusive Buyer Information Flow

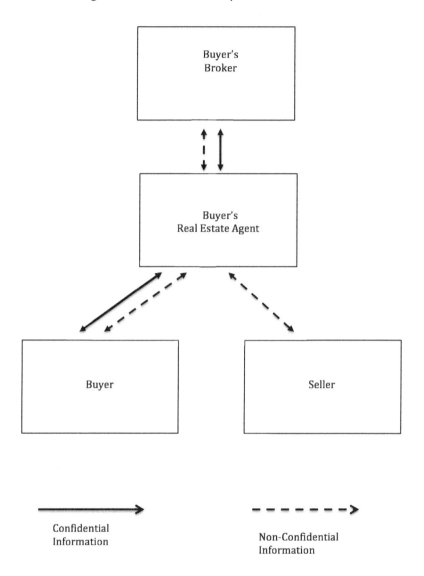

Figure 15-5—Dual Agency

Dual Agency

CONSUMER GUIDE TO AGENCY RELATIONSHIPS

Brokerage Name

We are pleased you have selected (brokerage) to help you with your real estate needs. Whether you are selling, buying or leasing real estate, (brokerage) can provide you with expertise and assistance. Because this may be the largest financial transaction you will enter into, it is important to understand the role of the agents and brokers with whom you are working. Below is some information that explains the various services agents can offer and their options for working with you.

For more information on agency law in Ohio you can also contact the Ohio Division of Real Estate & Professional Licensing at (614) 466-4100, or on their website www.com.state.oh.us.

Representing Sellers
Most sellers of real estate choose to list their home for sale with a real estate brokerage. When they do so, they sign a listing agreement that authorizes the brokerage and the listing agent to represent their interests. As the seller's agent, the brokerage and listing agent must: follow the seller's lawful instructions, be loyal to the seller, promote the seller's best interests, disclose material facts to the seller, maintain confidential information, act with reasonable skill and care and, account for any money they handle in the transaction. In rare circumstances, a listing broker may also offer "subagency" to other brokerages which would also represent the seller's interests and owe the seller these same duties.

Representing Buyers
When purchasing real estate, buyers usually choose to work with a real estate agent as well. Often the buyers want to be represented in the transaction. This is referred to as buyer's agency. A brokerage and agent that agree to represent a buyer's interest in a transaction must: follow the buyer's lawful instructions, be loyal to the buyer, promote the buyer's best interests, disclose material facts to the buyer, maintain confidential information and account for any money they handle in the transaction.

Dual Agency
Occasionally the same agent and brokerage who represents the seller also represents the buyer. This is referred to as dual agency. When a brokerage and its agent become "dual agents," they must maintain a neutral position between the buyer and the seller. They may not advocate the position of one client over the best interests of the other client, or disclose any personal or confidential information to the other party without written consent.

Representing Both the Buyer & Seller
On occasion, the buyer and seller will each be represented by two different agents from the same brokerage. In this case the agents may each represent the best interest of their respective clients. Or, depending on company policy, the agents may both act as dual agents and remain neutral in the transaction. When either of the above occurs, the brokerage will be considered a dual agent. As a dual agent the brokerage and its managers will maintain a neutral position and cannot advocate for the position of one client over another. The brokerage will also protect the confidential information of both parties.

Working With (brokerage)
(brokerage) does represent both buyers and sellers. When (brokerage) lists property for sale all agents in the brokerage represent the seller. Likewise when a buyer is represented by a (brokerage) agent, all of the agents represent that buyer. Therefore, when a buyer represented by a (brokerage) agent wishes to purchase property listed by our company, the agent(s) involved act as dual agents. This is true whether one agent is representing both parties or two separate agents are involved.

In the event that both the buyer and seller are represented by (brokerage) agents these agents and (brokerage) will act as dual agents but only if both parties agree. As dual agents they will treat both parties honestly, prepare and present offers at the direction of the parties, and help the parties fulfill the terms of any contract. They will not, however, disclose any

Figure 15-5—Dual Agency, *continued*

confidential information that will place one party at an advantage over the other or advocate or negotiate to the detriment of either party.

If dual agency occurs you will be asked to consent to it in writing. If you do not agree to your agent acting as a dual agent, you can seek representation from another brokerage.

As a buyer, you may also choose to represent yourself on properties (brokerage) has listed. In that instance (brokerage) will represent the seller and you would represent your own best interests. Because the listing agent has a duty of full disclosure to the seller you should not share any information with the listing agent that you would not want the seller to know.

Working With Other Brokerages

(brokerage) does offer representation to both buyers and sellers. When (brokerage) lists property for sale it also cooperates with, and offers compensation to, other brokerages that represent buyers. (brokerage) does reserve the right, in some instances, to vary the compensation it offers to other brokerages. As a seller, you should understand that just because (brokerage) shares a fee with a brokerage representing the buyer, it does not mean that you will be represented by that buyer's brokerage. Instead that company will be looking out for the buyer and (brokerage) will be representing your interests. When acting as a buyer's agent, (brokerage) also accepts compensation offered by the listing broker. If the property is not listed with any broker, or the listing broker does not offer compensation, we will attempt to negotiate for a seller-paid fee.

Fair Housing Statement

It is illegal, pursuant to the Ohio Fair Housing Law, division (H) of Section 4112.02 of the Revised Code and the Federal Fair Housing Law, 42 U.S.C.A. 3601, as amended, to refuse to sell, transfer, assign, rent, lease, sublease or finance housing accommodations, refuse to negotiate for the sale or rental of housing accommodations, or otherwise deny or make unavailable housing accommodations because of race, color, religion, sex, familial status as defined in Section 4112.01 of the Revised Code, ancestry, military status as defined in that section, disability as defined in that section, or national origin or to so discriminate in advertising the sale or rental of housing, in the financing of housing, or in the provision of real estate brokerage services. It is also illegal, for profit, to induce or attempt to induce a person to sell or rent a dwelling by representations regarding the entry into the neighborhood of a person or persons belonging to one of the protected classes.

We hope you find this information to be helpful to you as you begin your real estate transaction. When you are ready to enter into a transaction, you will be given an Agency Disclosure Statement that specifically identifies the role of the agents and brokerages. Please ask questions if there is anything you do not understand.

Because it is important that you have this information, Ohio law requires that we ask you to sign below, acknowledging receipt of this Consumer Guide. Doing so will not obligate you to work with our company if you do not choose to do so.

Name	(Please Print)	Name	(Please Print)

Signature	Date	Signature	Date

EQUAL HOUSING
OPPORTUNITY

party at an advantage over the other. For a dual agency situation to occur, both the buyer and seller will need to agree to the arrangement in writing. Perhaps this alone might alert the parties that they are on their own. While the brokerage and agents will follow the lawful and ethical instructions of the parties, preparing and presenting offers and helping to fulfill the terms of a contract, the buyer and seller are essentially on their own. But the agents cannot comment on the advisability of accepting any particular contract or commenting on the terms proposed by the other side in a contract.

If this seems odd to you, you are not alone. Just considering the purchase price of a piece of realty—the buyer wants the lowest price possible and the seller wants the highest. These are at cross-purposes. So, you may ask, why would a brokerage agree to do business with this model? The short, and somewhat cynical, answer is that the brokerage would be able to receive both the seller's commission and the buyer's commission.

The information flow in a dual agency model is shown in Figure 15-6, which presumes two different agents from the same brokerage to show how confidential and nonconfidential information is shared within the brokerage. Note that confidential information is shared among all of the agents, but that it does not flow out to the buyer and seller. In a dual agency relationship, all agents of the brokerage are deemed to know all of the confidential information from both sides but cannot share any of it with the buyer or seller. If only one agent was representing both buyer and seller, the information flow would be the same—confidential information flows up from the parties through the agent to the broker, but not back down to the parties. Figure 15-7 shows the information flow in a dual agency model with only one agent.

Split Agency but No Dual Agency

Split agency but no dual agency allows two real estate agents in the same brokerage to represent the buyer and seller in the transaction, which is similar to dual agency except that each agent looks out for the best interests of his or her own individual client. In a sense it is like working with real estate agents from two different brokerages in that an agent is advocating for each of the buyer and seller. But, the brokerage itself is considered to be acting as a dual agent. Figure 15-8 is the disclosure form used in this situation.

In this business model, the brokerage will not allow one real estate agent to represent both buyer and seller. Some real estate professionals consider this to be the best arrangement in that it allows the brokerage to potentially receive both the buyer-agent's commission and the seller-agent's commission,

Figure 15-6—Dual Agency Information Flow with Two Agents

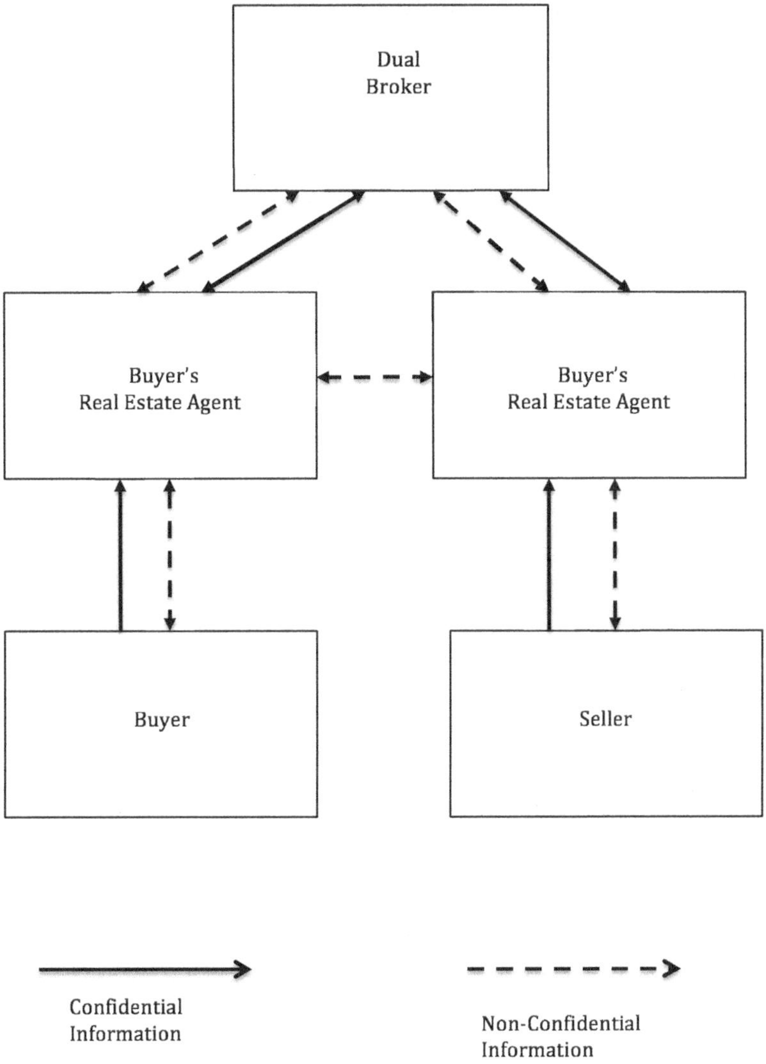

yet still have agents who are looking out for the best interest of their respective clients.

Figure 15-9 shows how information flow works in a split agency. Note that although confidential information flows up to the broker, it does not flow down to the other agents. For example, a buyer can share confidential infor-

Figure 15-7—Dual Agency Information Flow with One Agent

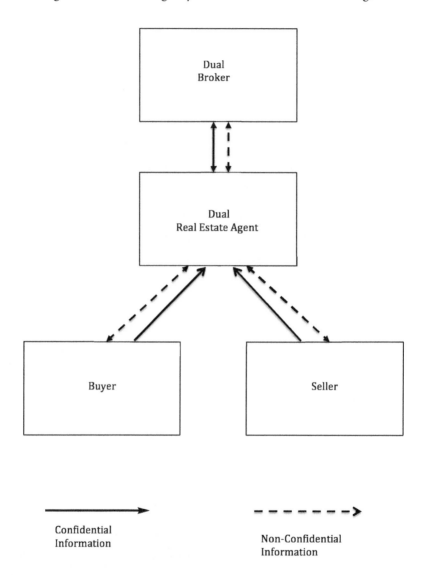

Figure 15-8—Split Agency but No Dual Agency

Split Agency No Dual

CONSUMER GUIDE TO AGENCY RELATIONSHIPS

Brokerage Name

We are pleased you have selected (brokerage) to help you with your real estate needs. Whether you are selling, buying or leasing real estate, (brokerage) can provide you with expertise and assistance. Because this may be the largest financial transaction you will enter into, it is important to understand the role of the agents and brokers with whom you are working. Below is some information that explains the various services agents can offer and their options for working with you.

For more information on agency law in Ohio you can also contact the Ohio Division of Real Estate & Professional Licensing at (614) 466-4100, or on their website www.com.state.oh.us.

Representing Sellers
Most sellers of real estate choose to list their home for sale with a real estate brokerage. When they do so, they sign a listing agreement that authorizes the brokerage and the listing agent to represent their interests. As the seller's agent, the brokerage and listing agent must: follow the seller's lawful instructions, be loyal to the seller, promote the seller's best interests, disclose material facts to the seller, maintain confidential information, act with reasonable skill and care and, account for any money they handle in the transaction. In rare circumstances, a listing broker may offer "subagency" to other brokerages which would also represent the seller's interests and owe the seller these same duties.

Representing Buyers
When purchasing real estate, buyers usually choose to work with a real estate agent as well. Often the buyers want to be represented in the transaction. This is referred to as buyer's agency. A brokerage and agent that agree to represent a buyer's interest in a transaction must: follow the buyer's lawful instructions, be loyal to the buyer, promote the buyer's best interests, disclose material facts to the buyer, maintain confidential information and, account for any money they handle in the transaction.

Dual Agency
Occasionally the same agent and brokerage who represents the seller also represents the buyer. This is referred to as dual agency. When a brokerage and its agents become "dual agents," they must maintain a neutral position between the buyer and the seller. They may not advocate the position of one client over the best interests of the other client, or disclose any personal or confidential information to the other party without written consent.

Representing Both the Buyer & Seller
On occasion, the buyer and seller will each be represented by two different agents from the same brokerage. In this case the agents may each represent the best interest of their respective clients. Or, depending on company policy, the agents may both act as dual agents and remain neutral in the transaction. When either of the above occurs, the brokerage will be considered a dual agent. As a dual agent the brokerage and its managers will maintain a neutral position and cannot advocate for the position of one client over another. The brokerage will also protect the confidential information of both parties.

Working With (brokerage)
(Brokerage) does offer representation to both buyers and sellers. Therefore, the potential exists for one agent to represent a buyer who wishes to purchase property listed with another agent in our company. If this occurs each agent will represent their own client, but (brokerage) and its managers will act as a dual agent. This means the brokerage and its managers will maintain a neutral position and not take any actions that will favor one side over the other. However, (brokerage) will still supervise both agents to assure that their clients are being fully represented.

While it is the policy of (brokerage) to allow a buyer and seller in the same transaction to be represented by two agents in our brokerage, it does not permit one agent to represent both parties. Therefore, a listing agent working directly with a

Figure 15-8—Split Agency but No Dual Agency, *continued*

buyer will represent only the seller's interests. In this situation the agent will still be able to provide the buyer with non-confidential information, prepare and present offers at their direction and assist the buyer in the financing and closing process. However, the buyer will be a customer, representing their own interests. Because the listing agent has a duty of full disclosure to the seller, a buyer in this situation should not share any information with the listing agent that they would not want the seller to know. If a buyer wishes to be represented, another agent in (brokerage) can be appointed to act as their agent or they can seek representation from another brokerage.

Working With Other Brokerages
(brokerage) does offer representation to both buyers and sellers. When (brokerage) lists property for sale it also cooperates with, and offers compensation to, other brokerages that represent buyers. (brokerage) does reserve the right, in some instances, to vary the compensation it offers to other brokerages. As a seller, you should understand that just because (brokerage) shares a fee with a brokerage representing the buyer, it does not mean that you will be represented by that buyer's brokerage. Instead that company will be looking out for the buyer and (brokerage) will be representing your interests.

When acting as a buyer's agent, (brokerage) also accepts compensation offered by the listing broker. If the property is not listed with any broker, or the listing broker does not offer compensation, we will attempt to negotiate for a seller-paid fee.

Fair Housing Statement
It is illegal, pursuant to the Ohio Fair Housing Law, division (H) of Section 4112.02 of the Revised Code and the Federal Fair Housing Law, 42 U.S.C.A. 3601, as amended, to refuse to sell, transfer, assign, rent, lease, sublease or finance housing accommodations, refuse to negotiate for the sale or rental of housing accommodations, or otherwise deny or make unavailable housing accommodations because of race, color, religion, sex, familial status as defined in Section 4112.01 of the Revised Code, ancestry, military status as defined in that section, disability as defined in that section, or national origin or to so discriminate in advertising the sale or rental of housing, in the financing of housing, or in the provision of real estate brokerage services. It is also illegal, for profit, to induce or attempt to induce a person to sell or rent a dwelling by representations regarding the entry into the neighborhood of a person or persons belonging to one of the protected classes.

We hope you find this information to be helpful to you as you begin your real estate transaction. When you are ready to enter into a transaction, you will be given an Agency Disclosure Statement that specifically identifies the role of the agents and brokerages. Please ask questions if there is anything you do not understand.

Because it is important that you have this information, Ohio law requires that we ask you to sign below, acknowledging receipt of this Consumer Guide. Doing so will not obligate you to work with our company if you do not choose to do so.

_____
Name   (Please Print)

_____
Name   (Please Print)

_____
Signature   Date

_____
Signature   Date

EQUAL HOUSING
OPPORTUNITY

Figure 15-9—Split Agency Information Flow

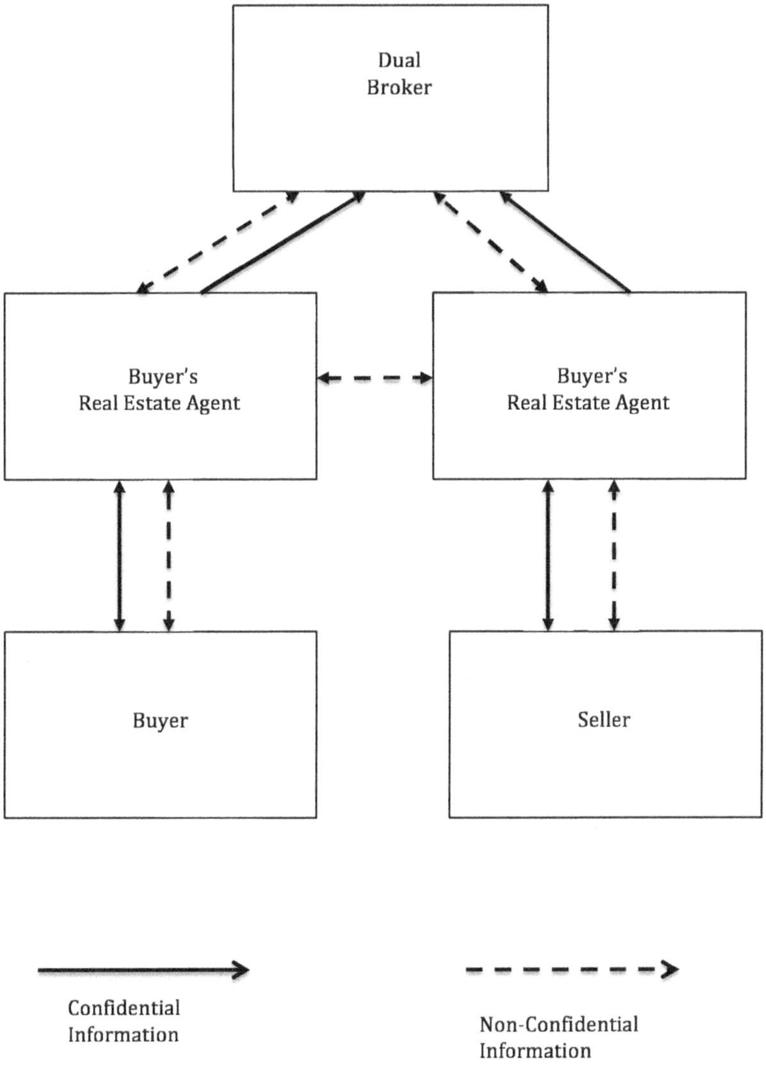

Confidential
Information

Non-Confidential
Information

Figure 15-10—Split Agency

Split Agency

CONSUMER GUIDE TO AGENCY RELATIONSHIPS

Brokerage Name

We are pleased you have selected (brokerage) to help you with your real estate needs. Whether you are selling, buying or leasing real estate, (brokerage) can provide you with expertise and assistance. Because this may be the largest financial transaction you will enter into, it is important to understand the role of the agents and brokers with whom you are working. Below is some information that explains the various services agents can offer and their options for working with you.

For more information on agency law in Ohio you can also contact the Ohio Division of Real Estate & Professional Licensing at (614) 466-4100, or on their website www.com.state.oh.us.

Representing Sellers
Most sellers of real estate choose to list their home for sale with a real estate brokerage. When they do so, they sign a listing agreement that authorizes the brokerage and the listing agent to represent their interests. As the seller's agent, the brokerage and listing agent must: follow the seller's lawful instructions, be loyal to the seller, promote the seller's best interests, disclose material facts to the seller, maintain confidential information, act with reasonable skill and care and, account for any money they handle in the transaction. In rare circumstances, a listing broker may offer "subagency" to other brokerages which would also represent the seller's interests and owe the seller these same duties.

Representing Buyers
When purchasing real estate, buyers usually choose to work with a real estate agent as well. Often the buyers want to be represented in the transaction. This is referred to as buyer's agency. A brokerage and agent that agree to represent a buyer's interest in a transaction must: follow the buyer's lawful instructions, be loyal to the buyer, promote the buyer's best interests, disclose material facts to the buyer, maintain confidential information and account for any money they handle in the transaction.

Dual Agency
Occasionally the same agent and brokerage who represents the seller also represents the buyer. This is referred to as dual agency. When a brokerage and its agents become "dual agents," they must maintain a neutral position in the transaction. They may not advocate the position of one client over the best interests of the other client, or disclose any confidential information to the other party without written consent.

Representing Both the Buyer & Seller
On occasion, the buyer and seller will each be represented by two different agents from the same brokerage. In this case the agents may each represent the best interest of their respective clients. Or, depending on company policy, the agents may both act as dual agents and remain neutral in the transaction. When either of the above occurs, the brokerage will be considered a dual agent. As a dual agent the brokerage and its managers will maintain a neutral position and cannot advocate for the position of one client over another. The brokerage will also protect the confidential information of both parties.

Working With (brokerage)
(brokerage) does offer representation to both buyers and sellers. Therefore the potential exists for one agent to represent a buyer who wishes to purchase property listed with another agent in our company. If this occurs each agent will represent their own client, but (brokerage) and its managers will act as a dual agent.

This means the brokerage and its managers will maintain a neutral position and not take any actions that will favor one side over the other. (brokerage) will still supervise both agents to assure that their respective clients are being fully represented and will protect the parties' confidential information.

In the event that both the buyer and seller are represented by the same agent, that agent and (brokerage) will act as dual agents but only if both parties agree. As dual agents they will treat both parties honestly, prepare and present offers at the direction of the parties, and help the parties fulfill the terms of any contract. They will not, however, disclose any

Figure 15-10 — Split Agency, *continued*

confidential information that would place one party at an advantage over the other or advocate or negotiate to the detriment of either party.

If dual agency occurs you will be asked to consent to it in writing. If you do not agree to your agent acting as a dual agent, you can ask that another agent in our company be assigned to represent you or you can seek representation from another brokerage.

As a buyer, you may also choose to represent yourself on properties (brokerage) has listed. In that instance (brokerage) will represent the seller and you would represent your own best interests. Because the listing agent has a duty of full disclosure to the seller you should not share any information with the listing agent that you would not want the seller to know.

Working With Other Brokerages

When (brokerage) lists property for sale it also cooperates with, and offers compensation to, other brokerages that represent buyers. (Brokerage) does reserve the right, in some instances, to vary the compensation it offers to other brokerages. As a seller, you should understand that just because (brokerage) shares a fee with a brokerage representing the buyer, it does not mean that you will be represented by that brokerage. Instead that company will be looking out for the buyer and (brokerage) will be representing your interests. When acting as a buyer's agent, (brokerage) also accepts compensation offered by the listing broker. If the property is not listed with any broker, or the listing broker does not offer compensation, we will attempt to negotiate for a seller-paid fee.

Fair Housing Statement

It is illegal, pursuant to the Ohio Fair Housing Law, division (H) of Section 4112.02 of the Revised Code and the Federal Fair Housing Law, 42 U.S.C.A. 3601, as amended, to refuse to sell, transfer, assign, rent, lease, sublease or finance housing accommodations, refuse to negotiate for the sale or rental of housing accommodations, or otherwise deny or make unavailable housing accommodations because of race, color, religion, sex, familial status as defined in Section 4112.01 of the Revised Code, ancestry, military status as defined in that section, disability as defined in that section, or national origin or to so discriminate in advertising the sale or rental of housing, in the financing of housing, or in the provision of real estate brokerage services. It is also illegal, for profit, to induce or attempt to induce a person to sell or rent a dwelling by representations regarding the entry into the neighborhood of a person or persons belonging to one of the protected classes.

We hope you find this information to be helpful to you as you begin your real estate transaction. When you are ready to enter into a transaction, you will be given an Agency Disclosure Statement that specifically identifies the role of the agents and brokerages. Please ask questions if there is anything you do not understand.

Because it is important that you have this information, Ohio law requires that we ask you to sign below, acknowledging receipt of this Consumer Guide. Your signature will not obligate you to work with our company if you do not choose to do so.

_____   _____
Name   (Please Print)   Name   (Please Print)

_____   _____
Signature   Date   Signature   Date

EQUAL HOUSING
OPPORTUNITY

mation with the buyer's agent, which will be shared with the broker, but the broker will not share that information with the seller's agent.

Split Agency

The split agency business model name can be confusing. Perhaps it would be better named "split agency with dual agency." This business model is a hybrid of the previous business model when two agents are from the same brokerage, with one agent acting on behalf of the buyer and another agent acting on behalf of the seller. What's more, this business model allows one real estate agent to represent both buyer and seller. In this case, the agent and the entire brokerage becomes a dual agent. As a dual agent, this person may not advocate for either side, may not disclose any confidential information, and must maintain a neutral position, all as discussed in the Dual Agency section above.

The information flow in a split agency business model is also a hybrid. If two agents are involved, the information flow is the same as in Figure 15-9, but if only one agent represents both buyer and seller, the information flow is the same as in Figure 15-7. You may be thinking that the split agency business model works well when two agents are involved, but if one agent is representing both the buyer and the seller, the disadvantages of a dual agency arrangement kicks in. And you would be right.

What Is the Best Agency Choice?

I believe that it is not in the best interest of either a buyer or a seller to agree to a dual agency relationship, because each of them would be essentially looking out for themselves, and the dual agent would at best be accommodating the transaction. In Ohio, an attorney who attempted to represent both sides of a transaction would be subject to discipline including disbarment. An exclusive agency arrangement or a split agency arrangement would seem to make the most sense, because someone would be looking out for their individual best interests. After all, if an attorney cannot represent both sides, it would seem prudent not to have a real estate agent doing so.

Regardless of the type of agency relationship in a particular transaction, both the buyer and seller in a residential real estate sale must receive an Agency Disclosure Statement that sets out who is representing whom in the deal. The form required in Ohio is shown in Figure 15-11. You will notice that this form has three different sections. Only one of these sections will be filled out, corresponding to the specifics of the transaction. Section I is used with two agents from two different brokerages, Section II is used with two agents from the

Figure 15-11—Agency Disclosure Statement

 AGENCY DISCLOSURE STATEMENT

EQUAL HOUSING OPPORTUNITY

The real estate agent who is providing you with this form is required to do so by Ohio law. You will not be bound to pay the agent or the agent's brokerage by merely signing this form. Instead, the purpose of this form is to confirm that you have been advised of the role of the agent(s) in the transaction proposed below. (For purposes of this form, the term "seller" includes a landlord and the term "buyer" includes a tenant.)

Property Address: _____

Buyer(s): _____

Seller(s): _____

I. TRANSACTION INVOLVING TWO AGENTS IN TWO DIFFERENT BROKERAGES

The buyer will be represented by _____, and _____.
                                   AGENT(S)   *BROKERAGE*

The seller will be represented by _____, and _____.
                                   AGENT(S)   *BROKERAGE*

II. TRANSACTION INVOLVING TWO AGENTS IN THE SAME BROKERAGE

If two agents in the real estate brokerage _____
represent both the buyer and the seller, check the following relationship that will apply:

☐ Agent(s)_____ work(s) for the buyer and
    Agent(s)_____ work(s) for the seller. Unless personally
    involved in the transaction, the broker and managers will be "dual agents", which is further explained on the back of this form.
    As dual agents they will maintain a neutral position in the transaction and they will protect all parties' confidential information.

☐ Every agent in the brokerage represents every "client" of the brokerage. Therefore, agents _____
    and _____ will be working for both the buyer and seller as "dual agents". Dual agency is explained
    on the back of this form. As dual agents they will maintain a neutral position in the transaction and they will protect all parties'
    confidential information. Unless indicated below, neither the agent(s) nor the brokerage acting as a dual agent in this transaction
    has a personal, family or business relationship with either the buyer or seller. *If such a relationship does exist, explain:*
    _____

III. TRANSACTION INVOLVING ONLY ONE REAL ESTATE AGENT

Agent(s) _____ and real estate brokerage _____ will

☐ be "dual agents" representing both parties in this transaction in a neutral capacity. Dual agency is further explained on the back of
    this form. As dual agents they will maintain a neutral position in the transaction and they will protect all parties' confidential
    information. Unless indicated below, neither the agent(s) nor the brokerage acting as a dual agent in this transaction has a
    personal, family or business relationship with either the buyer or seller. *If such a relationship does exist, explain:* _____
    _____

☐ represent only the (*check one*) ☐ **seller** or ☐ **buyer** in this transaction as a client. The other party is not represented and agrees to
    represent his/her own best interest. Any information provided the agent may be disclosed to the agent's client.

CONSENT

I (we) consent to the above relationships as we enter into this real estate transaction. If there is a dual agency in this transaction, I (we) acknowledge reading the information regarding dual agency explained on the back of this form.

_____   _____   _____   _____
BUYER/TENANT   *DATE*   *SELLER/LANDLORD*   *DATE*

_____   _____   _____   _____
BUYER/TENANT   *DATE*   *SELLER/LANDLORD*   *DATE*

Page 1 of 2   Effective 01/01/05

Figure 15-11—Agency Disclosure Statement, *continued*

DUAL AGENCY

Ohio law permits a real estate agent and brokerage to represent both the seller and buyer in a real estate transaction as long as this is disclosed to both parties and they both agree. This is known as dual agency. As a dual agent, a real estate agent and brokerage represent two clients whose interests are, or at times could be, different or adverse. For this reason, the dual agent(s) may not be able to advocate on behalf of the client to the same extent the agent may have if the agent represented only one client.

As a dual agent, the agent(s) and brokerage shall:
- Treat both clients honestly;
- Disclose latent (not readily observable) material defects to the purchaser, if known by the agent(s) or brokerage;
- Provide information regarding lenders, inspectors and other professionals, if requested;
- Provide market information available from a property listing service or public records, if requested;
- Prepare and present all offers and counteroffers at the direction of the parties;
- Assist both parties in completing the steps necessary to fulfill the terms of any contract, if requested.

As a dual agent, the agent(s) and brokerage shall not:
- Disclose information that is confidential, or that would have an adverse effect on one party's position in the transaction, unless such disclosure is authorized by the client or required by law;
- Advocate or negotiate on behalf of either the buyer or seller;
- Suggest or recommend specific terms, including price, or disclose the terms or price a buyer is willing to offer or that a seller is willing to accept;
- Engage in conduct that is contrary to the instructions of either party and may not act in a biased manner on behalf of one party.

Compensation: Unless agreed otherwise, the brokerage will be compensated per the agency agreement.

Management Level Licensees: Generally the broker and managers in a brokerage also represent the interests of any buyer or seller represented by an agent affiliated with that brokerage. Therefore, if both buyer and seller are represented by agents in the same brokerage, the broker and manager are dual agents. There are two exceptions to this. The first is where the broker or manager is personally representing one of the parties. The second is where the broker or manager is selling or buying his own real estate. These exceptions only apply if there is another broker or manager to supervise the other agent involved in the transaction.

Responsibilities of the Parties: The duties of the agent and brokerage in a real estate transaction do not relieve the buyer and seller from the responsibility to protect their own interests. The buyer and seller are advised to carefully read all agreements to assure that they adequately express their understanding of the transaction. The agent and brokerage are qualified to advise on real estate matters. IF LEGAL OR TAX ADVICE IS DESIRED, YOU SHOULD CONSULT THE APPROPRIATE PROFESSIONAL.

Consent: By signing on the reverse side, you acknowledge that you have read and understand this form and are giving your voluntary, informed consent to the agency relationship disclosed. If you do not agree to the agent(s) and/or brokerage acting as a dual agent, you are not required to consent to this agreement and you may either request a separate agent in the brokerage to be appointed to represent your interests or you may terminate your agency relationship and obtain representation from another brokerage.

Any questions regarding the role or responsibilities of the brokerage or its agents should be directed to an attorney or to:
Ohio Department of Commerce
Division of Real Estate & Professional Licensing
77 S. High Street, 20th Floor
Columbus, OH 43215-6133
(614) 466-4100

EQUAL HOUSING OPPORTUNITY

same brokerage, and Section III is used when only one real estate agent is involved. Section I is pretty self-explanatory. In Section II, the first box is checked in a split agency relationship, and the second box is checked in a dual agency situation. The first box in Section III is checked when only one agent is acting as a dual agent, and the second box is checked when only one agent is representing either the buyer or seller.

When this form is completed, only Section I, Section II, or Section III should be completed, and the other two sections need to be crossed out or left blank. Furthermore, only one of the two boxes in either Section II or Section III should be checked and the corresponding information completed. I suggest that if an error is made in filling out this form, you tear it up and prepare another copy from scratch.

Unlike the various Consumer Guides to Agency Relationships that are specific to the particular business model that a brokerage is using, the Agency Disclosure Statement is specific to a particular transaction. If the transaction doesn't close and the buyer elects to purchase a different house, a new form should be completed to reflect that transaction.

Becoming a Real Estate Agent in Ohio

As is spelled out in more detail in Chapter 17, a person who wants to become a real estate agent in Ohio must meet several qualifications, as summarized below:

1. Be at least 18 years old.
2. Have a broker sponsor their application.
3. Not have a record of criminal conviction, but it is possible to convince the superintendent of the Division of Real Estate that the individual has been rehabilitated.
4. Not have a record of violation of real estate licensing laws, but again it may be possible to convince the superintendent of the Division of Real Estate of rehabilitation.
5. Not have a court judgment of violation of Fair Housing laws. But it may be possible to wait two years and convince the superintendent of the Division of Real Estate that they have regained their good reputation and sign an affidavit that they will not violate Fair Housing laws in the future.

6. Successfully complete four college-level classes—Ohio Real Estate Law, Principles and Practices of Ohio Real Estate, Real Estate Finance, and Real Estate Appraisal—within 12 months of licensure.
7. Pass the salesperson's exam with a score of at least 75 percent
8. Complete a 10-hour consumer issues course after passing the license exam.

Becoming a Real Estate Broker in Ohio

To become an Ohio real estate broker, a person must first be a real estate agent and meet the following additional qualifications:

1. Work for a broker for at least two out of the preceding five years as a full-time agent, working at least 30 hours per week.
2. Complete at least 20 real estate transactions as a real estate agent, or demonstrate equivalent experience.
3. Successfully complete 40 hours of classroom instruction on Ohio Real Estate Law, Civil Rights Law, Case Law on Housing Discrimination, and Desegregation.
4. Successfully complete 20 hours of classroom instruction on Real Estate Appraisal.
5. Successfully complete 20 hours of classroom instruction on Real Estate Finance.
6. Successfully complete college-level instruction in Financial Management, Human Resource Management, Applied Business Economics, and Business Law.
7. Pass the broker's examination with a score of at least 75 percent.
8. Complete a 10-hour real estate brokerage course after passing the license exam.

Ethical Duties of Real Estate Agents and Brokers in Ohio

Real estate agents have fiduciary duties to their principals, as summarized in the following chart, which can be remembered by the mnemonic OLD CAR.

Duty	Meaning
Obedience	The agent must obey the lawful and ethical instructions of the principal.
Loyalty	The agent must keep the best interests of the principal ahead of anyone else, including the agent.
Disclosure	The agent must disclose material facts to the principal.[2]
Confidentiality	The agent must not disclose confidential information learned in the agency relationship about the principal to anyone. This duty essentially lasts forever.
Accountability	The agent must account for the whereabouts of all documents and money relating to the transaction.
Reasonable Care	The agent must use the level of care with respect to the principal that is normally expected of licensed real estate professionals.

Fraud and Misrepresentation

In Ohio, the concept of *caveat emptor* (let the buyer beware) is still in effect. A buyer is expected to inspect real estate carefully before purchasing it. If there is a **patent defect** (one that would be discovered in a reasonable inspection) the buyer is expected to find it. Even if the buyer doesn't see the patent defect or doesn't recognize it as a problem, the buyer is held to have notice of the defect and to have accepted the property with the defect. For example, if a buyer looks at a house he is considering purchasing and it has two feet of water in the basement, that would be a patent defect, and if the buyer buys the house anyway, they accept that defect. Likewise with other obvious problems, like seriously bulging walls, large foundation cracks, major holes in the roof, and so forth.

Not all defects are obvious and therefore patent defects. Many defects are not apparent or not visible in a reasonable inspection. Such defects are called **latent defects**. Both the buyer's agent and the seller's agent have a duty to tell the buyer about latent defects of which they are aware. You will remember from Chapter 6 that fraud is lying (or failing to disclose something you have a duty to disclose), intending that someone will rely on it; they do rely and are harmed. A real estate agent who fails to notify a buyer of a known latent defect is at risk of a claim for fraud.

Misrepresentation, sometimes called **deceit,** is basically the first two elements of fraud—lying (or failing to disclose), intending that someone rely on

---

2. In this context, a "material fact" is one that a reasonable person would want to know in making a decision to buy or sell.

it. A bit less heinous than fraud, misrepresentation can give rise to a lawsuit against the real estate agent. The prudent real estate agent will scrupulously disclose known defects to avoid a claim of fraud or misrepresentation.

Sellers of residential property of up to four dwelling units are required to prepare a Residential Property Disclosure form, which needs to be made available to every prospective buyer before entering into a purchase contract. If the buyer receives the disclosure form after entering into a purchase contract, the buyer may cancel the contract by sending the seller a signed and dated letter before the closing, so long as it is within 30 days of acceptance of the purchase contract and no later than 3 days after receiving the disclosure form. Thus the importance of preparing and timely delivering this form cannot be overstated. The required form is shown in Figure 15-12.

A real estate agent needs to understand that the disclosures are those of the seller, and the agent should provide only minimal assistance in helping a seller prepare the form. Otherwise, the disclosures could be seen as having been made by the real estate agent and not the seller. This could result in potential liability for the real estate agent. In particular, the agent should not advise the seller on how to word any particular disclosure. As to whether something should be disclosed, a good rule of thumb is, "When in doubt, disclose." It is better to disclose minor problems, because what may seem minor to a seller may be seen as a major problem to a buyer.

The form provides for such things as the water supply, the sewer system, wood-destroying insects, mechanical systems, hazardous materials, drainage, flood plains, underground storage tanks, wells, zoning, homeowners' associations, and boundary line disputes. The answers provided by a seller on this form can be the basis for making the real estate agents and potential buyers aware of latent defects in the property. Most of the answers on the form are to the actual knowledge of the seller, and many of the answers are limited to occurrences within the past five years. Even though the form is quite detailed, at the end of the form is a space for "other known material defects," which is defined as "any non-observable physical condition existing on the property that could be dangerous to anyone occupying the property or any non-observable physical condition that could inhibit a person's use of the property."

I cannot overemphasize the importance of this form as a safety net for real estate agents. Since the disclosures are made by the seller, ideally without assistance from the seller's agent, they are statements made by the seller and not either the buyer's or seller's agent. If a buyer later determines that one or more of the disclosures was incorrect or incomplete, the buyer may have a claim against the seller, and the agents should be without blame. On the other hand,

Figure 15-12—Residential Property Disclosure

STATE OF OHIO

<u>2013</u>

DEPARTMENT OF COMMERCE

RESIDENTIAL PROPERTY DISCLOSURE FORM

Purpose of Disclosure Form: This is a statement of certain conditions and information concerning the property actually known by the owner. An owner may or may not have lived at the property and unless the potential purchaser is informed in writing, the owner has no more information about the property than could be obtained by a careful inspection of the property by a potential purchaser. Unless the potential purchaser is otherwise informed, the owner has not conducted any inspection of generally inaccessible areas of the property. This form is required by Ohio Revised Code Section 5302.30.

THIS FORM IS NOT A WARRANTY OF ANY KIND BY THE OWNER OR BY ANY AGENT OR SUBAGENT REPRESENTING THE OWNER.   THIS FORM IS NOT A SUBSTITUTE FOR ANY INSPECTIONS.   **POTENTIAL PURCHASERS ARE ENCOURAGED TO OBTAIN THEIR OWN PROFESSIONAL INSPECTION(S).**

Owner's Statement: The statements contained in this form are made by the owner and are not the statements of the owner's agent or subagent. The statements contained in this form are provided by the owner only to potential purchasers in a transfer made by the owner. The statements are not for purchasers in any subsequent transfers. The information contained in this disclosure form does not limit the obligation of the owner to disclose an item of information that is required by any other statute or law to be disclosed in the transfer of residential real estate.

OWNER INSTRUCTIONS

Instructions to Owner: (1) Answer ALL questions. (2) Report known conditions affecting the property. (3) Attach additional pages with your signature if additional space is needed. (4) Complete this form yourself. (5) If some items do not apply to your property, write NA (not applicable). If the item to be disclosed is not within your actual knowledge, indicate Unknown.

Owner's Initials _____ Date _____   Purchaser's Initials _____ Date _____
Owner's Initials _____ Date _____   Purchaser's Initials _____ Date _____

(Page 1 of 5)

Figure 15-12—Residential Property Disclosure, *continued*

**STATE OF OHIO DEPARTMENT
OF COMMERCE**

RESIDENTIAL PROPERTY DISCLOSURE FORM

Pursuant to section 5302.30 of the Revised Code and rule 1301:5-6-10 of the Administrative Code.

TO BE COMPLETED BY OWNER (*Please Print*)
Property Address:

Owners Name(s):

Date: _____, 20_____

Owner ☐ is ☐ is not occupying the property. If owner is occupying the property, since what date: _____

If owner is not occupying the property, since what date: _____

THE FOLLOWING STATEMENTS OF THE OWNER ARE BASED ON OWNER'S ACTUAL KNOWLEDGE

A) WATER SUPPLY: The source of water supply to the property is (check appropriate boxes):

☐ Public Water Service   ☐ Holding Tank   ☐ Unknown

☐ Private Water Service   ☐ Cistern   ☐ Other _____

☐ Private Well   ☐ Spring   _____

☐ Shared Well   ☐ Pond   _____

Do you know of any current leaks, backups or other material problems with the water supply system or quality of the water? ☐ Yes
☐ No If "Yes", please describe and indicate any repairs completed (but not longer than the past 5 years): _____

Is the quantity of water sufficient for your household use? (NOTE: water usage will vary from household to household) ☐ Yes ☐ No

B) SEWER SYSTEM: The nature of the sanitary sewer system servicing the property is (check appropriate boxes):

☐ Public Sewer   ☐ Private Sewer   ☐ Septic Tank

☐ Leach Field   ☐ Aeration Tank   ☐ Filtration Bed

☐ Unknown   ☐ Other _____

If not a public or private sewer, date of last inspection: _____ Inspected By: _____

Do you know of **any previous or current** leaks, backups or other material problems with the sewer system servicing the property?
Yes ☐ No ☐ If "Yes", please describe and indicate any repairs completed (but not longer than the past 5 years): _____

**Information on the operation and maintenance of the type of sewage system serving the property is available from the
department of health or the board of health of the health district in which the property is located.**

C) ROOF: Do you know of **any previous or current** leaks or other material problems with the roof or rain gutters? ☐ Yes ☐ No
If "Yes", please describe and indicate any repairs completed (but not longer than the past 5 years): _____

D) WATER INTRUSION: Do you know of **any previous or current** water leakage, water accumulation, excess moisture or other
defects to the property, including but not limited to any area below grade, basement or crawl space? ☐ Yes ☐ No
If "Yes", please describe and indicate any repairs completed: _____

Owner's Initials _____ Date _____   Purchaser's Initials _____ Date _____
Owner's Initials _____ Date _____   Purchaser's Initials _____ Date _____

(Page 2 of 5)

Figure 15-12—Residential Property Disclosure, *continued*

Property Address_____

Do you know of any water or moisture related damage to floors, walls or ceilings as a result of flooding; moisture seepage; moisture condensation; ice damming; sewer overflow/backup; or leaking pipes, plumbing fixtures, or appliances? ☐Yes ☐No
If "Yes", please describe and indicate any repairs completed: _____

Have you ever had the property inspected for mold by a qualified inspector?   ☐Yes ☐No
If "Yes", please describe and indicate whether you have an inspection report and any remediation undertaken: _____

Purchaser is advised that every home contains mold. Some people are more sensitive to mold than others. If concerned about this issue, purchaser is encouraged to have a mold inspection done by a qualified inspector.

E) STRUCTURAL COMPONENTS (FOUNDATION, BASEMENT/CRAWL SPACE, FLOORS, INTERIOR AND EXTERIOR WALLS): Do you know of **any previous or current** movement, shifting, deterioration, material cracks/settling (other than visible minor cracks or blemishes) or other material problems with the foundation, basement/crawl space, floors, or interior/exterior walls?
☐ Yes ☐ No   If "Yes", please describe and indicate any repairs, alterations or modifications to control the cause or effect of any problem identified (but not longer than the past 5 years):_____

Do you know of **any previous or current** fire or smoke damage to the property? ☐Yes ☐No
If "Yes", please describe and indicate any repairs completed: _____

F) WOOD DESTROYING INSECTS/TERMITES: Do you know of **any previous/current** presence of any wood destroying insects/termites in or on the property or any existing damage to the property caused by wood destroying insects/termites? ☐Yes ☐No
If "Yes", please describe and indicate any inspection or treatment (but not longer than the past 5 years):_____

G) MECHANICAL SYSTEMS: Do you know of **any previous or current** problems or defects with the following existing mechanical systems? If your property does not have the mechanical system, mark N/A (Not Applicable).

	YES	NO	N/A		YES	NO	N/A
1) Electrical	☐	☐	☐	8) Water softener	☐	☐	☐
2) Plumbing (pipes)	☐	☐	☐	a. Is water softener leased?	☐	☐	☐
3) Central heating	☐	☐	☐	9) Security System	☐	☐	☐
4) Central Air conditioning	☐	☐	☐	a. Is security system leased?	☐	☐	☐
5) Sump pump	☐	☐	☐	10) Central vacuum	☐	☐	☐
6) Fireplace/chimney	☐	☐	☐	11) Built in appliances	☐	☐	☐
7) Lawn sprinkler	☐	☐	☐	12) Other mechanical systems	☐	☐	☐

If the answer to any of the above questions is "Yes", please describe and indicate any repairs to the mechanical system (but not longer than the past 5 years): _____

H) PRESENCE OF HAZARDOUS MATERIALS: Do you know of the **previous or current** presence of any of the below identified hazardous materials on the property?

	Yes	No	Unknown
1) Lead-Based Paint	☐	☐	☐
2) Asbestos	☐	☐	☐
3) Urea-Formaldehyde Foam Insulation	☐	☐	☐
4) Radon Gas	☐	☐	☐
a. If "Yes", indicate level of gas if known _____			
5) Other toxic or hazardous substances	☐	☐	☐

If the answer to any of the above questions is "Yes", please describe and indicate any repairs, remediation or mitigation to the property: _____

Owner's Initials _____ Date _____   Purchaser's Initials _____ Date _____
Owner's Initials _____ Date _____   Purchaser's Initials _____ Date _____

(Page 3 of 5)

Figure 15-12—Residential Property Disclosure, *continued*

Property Address_____

I) UNDERGROUND STORAGE TANKS/WELLS: Do you know of any underground storage tanks (existing or removed), oil or natural gas wells (plugged or unplugged), or abandoned water wells on the property? ☐Yes ☐ No
If "Yes", please describe: _____

Do you know of any oil, gas, or other mineral right leases on the property? ☐Yes ☐ No

Purchaser should exercise whatever due diligence purchaser deems necessary with respect to oil, gas, and other mineral rights. Information may be obtained from records contained within the recorder's office in the county where the property is located.

J) FLOOD PLAIN/LAKE ERIE COASTAL EROSION AREA: Yes   No   Unknown
Is the property located in a designated flood plain?
Is the property or any portion of the property included in a Lake Erie Coastal Erosion Area?   ☐   ☐   ☐

K) DRAINAGE/EROSION: Do you know of **any previous or current** flooding, drainage, settling or grading or erosion problems affecting the property? ☐Yes ☐No
If "Yes", please describe and indicate any repairs, modifications or alterations to the property or other attempts to control any problems (but not longer than the past 5 years):_____

L) ZONING/CODE VIOLATIONS/ASSESSMENTS/HOMEOWNERS' ASSOCIATION: Do you know of any violations of building or housing codes, zoning ordinances affecting the property or any nonconforming uses of the property? ☐Yes ☐No
If "Yes", please describe: _____

Is the structure on the property designated by any governmental authority as a historic building or as being located in an historic district? (NOTE: such designation may limit changes or improvements that may be made to the property). ☐Yes ☐ No
If "Yes", please describe: _____

Do you know of **any recent or proposed** assessments, fees or abatements, which could affect the property? ☐Yes ☐ No
If "Yes", please describe: _____

List any assessments paid in full (date/amount)_____
List any current assessments: _____ monthly fee _____ Length of payment (years _____ months _____)

Do you know of any recent or proposed rules or regulations of, or the payment of any fees or charges associated with this property, including but not limited to a Community Association, SID, CID, LID, etc.   ☐Yes ☐ No
If "Yes", please describe (amount)_____

M) BOUNDARY LINES/ENCROACHMENTS/SHARED DRIVEWAY/PARTY WALLS: Do you know of any of the
following conditions affecting the property?   Yes   No   Yes   No

1) Boundary Agreement   ☐ ☐   4) Shared Driveway   ☐ ☐
2) Boundary Dispute   5) Party Walls
3) Recent Boundary Change   6) Encroachments From or on Adjacent Property
If the answer to any of the above questions is "Yes", please describe: _____

N) OTHER KNOWN MATERIAL DEFECTS: The following are other known material defects in or on the property:
_____

For purposes of this section, material defects would include any non-observable physical condition existing on the property that could be dangerous to anyone occupying the property or any non-observable physical condition that could inhibit a person's use of the property.

Owner's Initials _____ Date_____   Purchaser's Initials _____ Date _____
Owner's Initials _____ Date_____   Purchaser's Initials _____ Date _____

(Page 4 of 5)

Figure 15-12—Residential Property Disclosure, *continued*

Property Address_____

CERTIFICATION OF OWNER

Owner certifies that the statements contained in this form are made in good faith and based on his/her actual knowledge as of the date signed by the Owner. Owner is advised that the information contained in this disclosure form does not limit the obligation of the owner to disclose an item of information that is required by any other statute or law or that may exist to preclude fraud, either by misrepresentation, concealment or nondisclosure in a transaction involving the transfer of residential real estate.

OWNER: _____   DATE: _____

OWNER: _____   DATE: _____

RECEIPT AND ACKNOWLEDGEMENT OF POTENTIAL PURCHASERS

Potential purchasers are advised that the owner has no obligation to update this form but may do so according to Revised Code Section 5302.30(G). Pursuant to Ohio Revised Code Section 5302.30(K), if this form is not provided to you prior to the time you enter into a purchase contract for the property, you may rescind the purchase contract by delivering a signed and dated document of rescission to Owner or Owner's agent, provided the document of rescission is delivered <u>prior</u> to all three of the following dates: 1) the date of closing; 2) 30 days after the Owner accepted your offer; and 3) within 3 business days following your receipt or your agent's receipt of this form or an amendment of this form.

Owner makes no representations with respect to any offsite conditions. Purchaser should exercise whatever due diligence purchaser deems necessary with respect to offsite issues that may affect purchaser's decision to purchase the property.

Purchaser should exercise whatever due diligence purchaser deems necessary with respect to Ohio's Sex Offender Registration and Notification Law (commonly referred to as "Megan's Law"). This law requires the local Sheriff to provide written notice to neighbors if a sex offender resides or intends to reside in the area. The notice provided by the Sheriff is a public record and is open to inspection under Ohio's Public Records Law. If concerned about this issue, purchaser assumes responsibility to obtain information from the Sheriff's office regarding the notices they have provided pursuant to Megan's Law.

Purchaser should exercise whatever due diligence purchaser deems necessary with respect to abandoned underground mines. If concerned about this issue, purchaser assumes responsibility to obtain information from the Ohio Department of Natural Resources.   The Department maintains an online map of known abandoned underground mines on their website at www.dnr.state.oh.us.

I/WE ACKNOWLEDGE RECEIPT OF A COPY OF THIS DISCLOSURE FORM AND UNDERSTAND THAT THE STATEMENTS ARE MADE BASED ON THE OWNERS ACTUAL KNOWLEDGE AS OF THE DATE SIGNED BY THE OWNER.

My/Our Signature below does not constitute approval of any disclosed condition as represented herein by the owner.

PURCHASER: _____   DATE: _____

PURCHASER: _____   DATE: _____

(Page 5 of 5)

if the agents provide material assistance in preparing the form, then the disclosures could be seen as having been made by the agents, potentially giving rise to liability for the agents.

I suggest that you take time to look at the disclosure form in some detail to become familiar with the things that are found there. You will see that some of the knowledge requirements are limited to the past five years, for example, repairs to mechanical systems, while other sections are not time limited, for example, presence of hazardous materials.

Ohio Real Estate Administrative Agencies

Ohio has two administrative agencies that regulate real estate brokers and agents. These are the **Ohio Real Estate Commission** and the **Ohio Division of Real Estate**. Both of these agencies are part of the Ohio Department of Commerce. We will examine each of these agencies in the following sections.

Ohio Real Estate Commission

This agency is the decision- and rule-making body that deals with real estate brokers and agents. It consists of five members appointed by the governor. Four members are licensed real estate brokers and the fifth member is a nonlicensed member of the public. The Real Estate Commission sets standards for licensing and continuing education, as well as dealing with suspension and revocation of licenses. It may be helpful to think of the Real Estate Commission as a parallel to the legislative and judicial branches of government.

Ohio Division of Real Estate

The Division of Real Estate is governed by the superintendent, who is appointed by the director of commerce from among three names submitted by the Ohio Real Estate Commission. The Division of Real Estate is the enforcement arm of the commission. It deals with administration of license laws, investigation of complaints against brokers and agents, maintaining an investigation and audit bureau, and carrying out orders of the commission. Think of the Division of Real Estate as a parallel to the executive branch of government.

License Revocation, Suspension, and On Deposit

When the Division of Real Estate investigates complaints against brokers and agents, it can refer the case to the Real Estate Commission to determine if discipline is warranted. Among other things, the commission may decide to revoke or suspend licenses. A **license revocation** is the permanent termination of a license. Grounds for license revocation are set out in Ohio Revise Code Section 4735.18, which is discussed in Chapter 16. A person whose license has been revoked may apply to the commission for a new license, but that new license may be denied.

A **license suspension** is a temporary interruption of a licensee's right to practice, for a set period of time, after which the license is reactivated. The licensee may have to pay a fine or take some other action, such as completing continuing education, before the suspension is lifted. The commission has broad discretion to suspend licenses. A license may be suspended for any of the following reasons, among others:

1. Not paying disciplinary fines or citations
2. Not completing postlicensure education
3. Not completing required continuing education
4. Not timely renewing a license

In addition to license revocation and suspension, the commission can impose other discipline such as citations (fines), additional education, and a public reprimand. A prudent real estate agent will be diligently aware of the statutory duties outlined in Chapter 16 and not engage in any activity that would put his or her license at risk.

License On Deposit or Inactive

A real estate broker who wishes to stop acting as a broker and wants to become a real estate agent under another broker can place his or her broker **license on deposit** with the Division of Real Estate and reactivate the real estate agent license. The broker's license can remain on deposit indefinitely, but the licensee must meet continuing education requirements and renew the license when it becomes due.

Likewise, a broker or real estate agent can place their license on deposit during active military service. The license will remain inactive until after the licensee is honorably discharged from active military duty and the license next comes up for renewal.

Any real estate agent who no longer wants to practice or whose broker no longer wants to sponsor the agent can return his or her license to the Division of Real Estate and go **inactive**. The license can remain inactive indefinitely, but the licensee must meet continuing education requirements and renew the license when it becomes due.

Ancillary Trustee

If a brokerage no longer has at least one licensed broker, due to the death of a broker or loss of license, the superintendent of the Division of Real Estate can appoint an **ancillary trustee** to manage the business of the brokerage. The ancillary trustee can work only to complete existing transactions and obligations of the brokerage and cannot enter into new agreements or transactions. In essence, the ancillary trustee's duty is limited to managing the orderly winding up and termination of the brokerage's business.

Discussion Questions

1. Explain the difference between actual authority, implied authority, apparent authority, and ratification.

2. Explain the difference between the dual agency and split agency business models.

3. Explain the ethical duties of an Ohio real estate agent.

4. Explain the differences between the Ohio Real Estate Commission and the Ohio Division of Real Estate.

5. Explain the difference between license revocation, suspension, on deposit, and inactive.

Key Terms

Actual authority
Agent
Ancillary trustee
Apparent authority
Deceit

Dual agency
Exclusive buyer's agent
Exclusive seller's agent
First substantive contact
Fraud
Implied authority
Inactive license
Latent defect
License on deposit
License revocation
License suspension
Misrepresentation
Ohio Division of Real Estate
Ohio Real Estate Commission
Patent defect
Principal
Ratification
Split agency
Split agency but no dual agency

Chapter 16

Fair Housing

Surely real estate agents want to treat everyone equally. After all, we all want to be treated fairly ourselves. Unfortunately, many traps are hidden from unwary real estate agents, who can find themselves embroiled in lengthy litigation, sometimes with the federal government on the other side. This can place their real estate license in jeopardy and give rise to monetary damages that can easily exceed their personal assets. This topic is one that the Ohio Real Estate Commission and the Ohio Division of Real Estate take very seriously, requiring continuing education on fair housing laws and providing for discipline for violating the laws.

It is especially important for a real estate agent to not allow client prejudices to put the agent in jeopardy. Sometimes, a client may give their real estate agent instructions that run counter to fair housing laws, such as telling the agent that they will not sell their house to a person of a particular ethnicity. If the agent follows the client's direction and does not show the property to people of that ethnic persuasion, the agent will have violated fair housing laws. When this activity results in litigation, the agent and the agent's brokerage will clearly be in the crosshairs, as plaintiffs see the agents and brokerages as having deeper pockets than the client who gave the instructions.

The Ohio real estate agent license examination has historically had a heavy focus on fair housing issues, so a prudent person preparing for the exam will study this material carefully. Questions on the exam sometimes lay out a set of facts and ask which fair housing laws are violated. A cautious person practicing real estate law will simply treat everyone equally and fairly, thus not ever violating any particular law. But, this material is ripe for the examiners to prepare questions that deal with the fine-line distinctions between the various fair housing laws.

Appendix H contains a chart that shows the various fair housing laws, together with their exemptions. You may want to carefully review this chart before sitting for the real estate license exam to help solidify the differences between the laws and their exemptions.

Constitutional Background

At the end of the Civil War, three amendments to the US Constitution were adopted. The Thirteenth Amendment abolished slavery; the Fourteenth Amendment guaranteed due process, equal protection of the laws, and protected privileges and immunities of citizenship; and the Fifteenth Amendment guaranteed the right to vote irrespective of race.

At first glance, it would seem that these amendments created a level playing field in all areas of life. But, there are a couple of problems. First, the amendments protected citizens against actions undertaken by a state and not by an individual. So, a person could refuse to sell their house to a person of a particular ethnicity, and even create deed restrictions that prevented future owners of the property from doing so. This was not a constitutional violation, because it was the act of an individual and not the state.

Second, several states (primarily in the South) enacted **Jim Crow laws**, which perpetuated racial segregation and other unfair treatments, mostly against African Americans. Segregated facilities, while claiming to be "separate but equal," were often inferior or underfunded. While the constitutional amendments provided certain guarantees, they were, for almost all purposes, a set of empty promises.

As US citizens, we enjoy certain **fundamental rights**, such as the right of free speech, the right to travel, the right to peaceably assemble, the right to practice religion, and several others. But surprisingly, we do not have a fundamental right to housing. If we did, our country would not have a homeless population, as everyone would be assured a place to live. Rather, we have equal opportunity to seek housing, with no guarantee that the search will be successful.

Civil Rights Act of 1866

Congress recognized some of these problems and enacted the Civil Rights Act of 1866 (1866 Act), passing it over the veto of President Andrew Johnson. This act was intended to give all citizens the same rights to make and enforce contracts, sue and be sued, and give evidence in court. The relevant part of the 1866 Act relating to real estate (Section 1982) reads, "All citizens of the United States shall have the same right in every State and Territory as is enjoyed by White citizens thereof to inherit, lease, sell, hold, and convey real ... property." Even though this chapter of the book is focused on residential housing, the 1866 Act covers *all* real property, including residential, commercial, and unimproved land.

In 1968, the US Supreme Court held that the 1866 Act applies to discrimination by individuals and not just state actors. So, an individual's refusal to sell his house to an African American because of that person's race would be a violation of Section 1982 of the 1866 Act.

Because the act specifically mentions "White citizens," it was originally understood to apply only to racial discrimination, in particular African Americans, as opposed to Caucasians. In 1987, the US Supreme Court held that the 1866 Act also applies to **ancestry**. Thus, it protects Italian Americans, Irish Americans, and other Caucasian groups.

If someone claims discrimination in violation of the 1866 Act, they must sue in federal district court; this act cannot be enforced in state court. But Ohio law does enter into the picture. No particular federal statute of limitations exists for claims under the 1866 Act, but the analogous state law is relied upon. Thus, in Ohio, a claim must be made in federal court within one year of the alleged discrimination, because the Ohio Civil Rights Act has a one-year statute of limitations.

Civil Rights Act of 1968

The next fair housing statute we will examine is known by two names—the Civil Rights Act of 1968, and the Federal Fair Housing Act. We are especially concerned about Title VIII of the Civil Rights Act of 1968, because it covers discrimination in real estate transactions. You may see this particular act called any of the preceding names, but for simplicity I will refer to it as Title VIII in this text.

The primary thing to remember about Title VIII is that it expanded on the protection against discrimination in housing provided by the 1866 Act because it covers discrimination based on race, color,[1] gender, national origin, disability,[2] marital status, and familial status.[3]

---

1. "Color" is indeed distinct from "race." For example, light-skinned African Americans have been known to discriminate against dark-skinned African Americans. This is a discrimination based color and not race.

2. "Disability" means a substantial limitation in one or more major life functions due to a physical or mental impairment. This is a broad category of impairments that includes such things as hearing, vision, or mobility impairment, terminal illness, and so forth.

3. "Familial status" means families that include children under 18 who live with a parent or guardian, or pregnant women. However, provisions allow senior housing to exclude families with children under 18 and pregnant women. Thus, a retirement community that is intended for people ages 62 years or older can exclude families with children under age 18 and pregnant women without violating Title VIII. However, the community still must not

Title VIII covers both residential property and unimproved land to be developed into residential property. This is different from the 1866 Act, which covers *all* real estate, including commercial property.

Title VIII requires all brokerages to display a fair housing poster in the public part of their offices. Figure 16-1 is the fair housing poster made available by the Ohio Division of Real Estate. In addition, all real estate advertisements are required to include the Equal Housing Opportunity logo, which is found at the top of Figure 16-1.

Title VIII includes a long list of acts that constitute illegal discrimination if they are based on race, color, gender, national origin, disability, marital status, and familial status:

1. Refusing to rent or sell residential property after receiving a bona fide offer.
2. Refusing to negotiate with a person for the sale or rental of residential property.
3. Advertising for the sale or rental of residential property in a way that indicates a preference based on one of the protected classes.
4. Stating that residential property is not available for sale or rental when it actually is available.
5. Discrimination on the terms or conditions of sale or rental.
6. Denying access to a multiple listing service.
7. Inducing or attempting to induce someone to sell or rent residential property because of someone of a protected class moving into the neighborhood.[4]
8. Refusing to make a loan to purchase, repair, improve, or maintain residential property.[5]
9. Coercing, intimidating, threatening, or interfering with anyone who seeks protestation against discrimination under Title VIII.
10. Taking any action that would make residential property unavailable or denying it to any person (a catchall category).

A person claiming discrimination under Title VIII can bring suit in either federal or state court, or can seek administrative remedies from either the Federal Department of Housing and Urban Development (HUD) or the Ohio Civil Rights Commission. If the administrative remedy approach is taken, the claim must brought within one year of the alleged violation of Title VIII. A lawsuit in state or federal court must be brought within two years of the alleged violation of Title VIII. Unlike some other areas of the law that require a

---

discriminate on the basis of race, color, gender, national origin, disability, or marital status.
  4. This is considered *blockbusting*, which is discussed later in this chapter.
  5. This is considered *redlining*, which is discussed later in this chapter.

Figure 16-1—Fair Housing Poster

EQUAL HOUSING
OPPORTUNITY

It Is Illegal To Discriminate Against Any Person Because of Race, Color, Religion, Sex, Familial Status, National Origin, Military Status, Disability or Ancestry

- In the sale or rental of housing or residential lots
- In advertising the sale or rental of housing
- In the financing of housing
- In the provision of real estate brokerage services

Blockbusting is also illegal.

The Broker and Sales Associates are licensed by the Ohio Department of Commerce, Division of Real Estate & Professional Licensing. The division may be contacted for inquiries and complaints and for information on the Real Estate Recovery Fund (Section 4735.12 of the Revised Code) as a source of satisfaction for unsatisfied civil judgments against a licensee.

Ohio Department of Commerce Division of Real Estate & Professional Licensing

77 S. High Street, 20th Floor
Columbus, OH 43215-6133
(614) 466-4100

www.com.ohio.gov/real

PROVIDED BY THE OHIO REAL ESTATE COMMISSION

Effective 3/25/2008

person to exhaust administrative remedies before suing in court, a claim can be made under Title VIII directly in federal or state court.

Exemptions

Some exemptions from the strict rules in Title VIII are intended to recognize that some circumstances do not justify stringently applying Title VIII. These are summarized below:

1. A sale or rental of a single-family residential property by the owner, provided that (a) the person owns three or fewer residential properties, and (b) the transaction does not use a broker or real estate agent. If the owner is not the most recent occupant, this exemption can be used only once every 24 months.
2. Residential property owned by a religious organization can discriminate in favor of members of that religion. For example, a church rectory can be limited to members of the clergy of that faith.
3. Private clubs with lodging not open to the public and not operated for a profit can discriminate in favor of members of that club. For example, a Masonic retirement home can be limited to masons.
4. Rental of a room or unit in residential property where the owner also lives, provided that (a) there are no more than four units, and (b) the transaction does not use a broker or real estate agent.[6]

Ohio Fair Housing — Ohio Civil Rights Act

Federal law, including constitutional law, sets out minimum protections — states can always enact legislation that provides additional protections, so long as they do not interfere with other federal laws. Ohio has enacted its own fair housing statutes, found in Chapter 4112 of the Ohio Revised Code, sometimes called the Ohio Civil Rights Act.

Ohio fair housing laws generally reflect the same restrictions as Title VIII, in that housing discrimination based on race, color, religion, gender, national

---

6. This is known as the "Mrs. Murphy exemption" — Senator Aiken of Vermont coined the term when he suggested that Congress "integrate the Waldorf and other large hotels, but permit the 'Mrs. Murphys,' who run small rooming houses all over the country, to rent their rooms to those they choose." Robert Loevy, *To End All Segregation: The Politics of the Passage of the Civil Rights Act of 1964*, 51 (1990).

origin, marital status, familial status, ancestry, and disability are prohibited. The enumerated acts that are prohibited under Title VIII also violate Ohio fair housing, which covers residential property and unimproved land.

A claim that someone has violated the Ohio Civil Rights Act can be brought with the Ohio Civil Rights Commission or in court, either federal or the Ohio Court of Common Pleas. There is no need to exhaust administrative remedy with the Ohio Civil Rights Commission before filing a lawsuit. The statute of limitations under the Ohio Civil Rights Act is one year, which is where the one-year statute of limitations for the Federal Civil Rights arises.

Exemptions

The Ohio Civil Rights Act recognizes only two exemptions—religions and private clubs. This means that the single-family sales by owner and Mrs. Murphy exemptions do not exist under Ohio fair housing.

License Exam Tip

I think it is time to take a quick break and look at some of the ways that fair housing laws are tested on the Ohio real estate agent license exam. As mentioned earlier, a prudent real estate agent simply will not discriminate against any of the protected classes, but the exam looks at a deeper understanding of how the laws interact. The examples below may help you to see how this is tested.

1. Suppose an owner of a store front refused to rent it to someone because that person is Methodist. What fair housing laws are violated? Let's look at each one in turn. The Civil Rights Act of 1866 is not violated, because it does not cover religion as a protected class. Neither Title VIII nor Ohio fair housing are violated, because these laws deal only with residential or unimproved land. So, while this is a bad practice and may result in a discrimination claim, it does not violate fair housing laws.
2. What if an apartment manager refused to rent a unit to a woman because she is pregnant—what fair housing laws are violated? The Civil Rights of 1866 is not violated, because it does not include familial status as a protected class. But, this example would violate Title VIII and Ohio fair housing, because both of them do include familial status, including pregnant women.
3. Imagine that a woman owns a boarding house with four units and lives in one of the units. She feels uncomfortable living in the same place as men

and refuses to rent rooms to males—what fair housing statutes are being violated? Again, the Civil Rights Act of 1866 does not include gender as a protected class, so it is not being violated, and Title VIII contains the Mrs. Murphy exemption, so it is not being violated. However, the Ohio Civil Rights Act is being violated because it includes gender as a protected class and does not include the Mrs. Murphy exemption.

4. Finally, suppose an owner of a house who is currently living there tells his real estate agent that he will not sell the house to an Italian American. What fair housing laws would be violated if the real estate agents refuses to show the house to anyone who has an Italian-sounding last name? The Civil Rights Act of 1866 would be violated because it has been interpreted by the US Supreme Court to include ancestry, which would include Caucasian Italian Americans. Title VIII would be violated because it covers national origin and the sale-by-owner exemption would not apply, since a real estate agent is involved. The Ohio Civil Rights Act would also be violated, because it includes national origin as a protected class. What's more, the real estate agent (and by extension, his or her broker) would probably be held more culpable than the homeowner because they are expected to know the fair housing laws. The real estate agent should simply not honor this illegal request from the homeowner and not disclose any information to the seller about the ancestry of a potential buyer.

Disparate Treatment and Disparate Impact

Housing discrimination comes in two basic flavors—**disparate treatment** and **disparate impact**. Disparate treatment discrimination is perhaps the easiest to understand. It is simply overtly treating someone differently because of membership in a particular protected class. For example, refusing to rent an apartment unit to someone *because* that person is of a particular race is disparate treatment.

On the other hand, disparate impact discrimination occurs when a decision seems to be neutral on its face but has the effect of discriminating against a protect class. For instance, suppose an apartment owner has a policy of renting units only to people with blue eyes. On its face, this seems acceptable, because eye color is not a protected class. But, it will have the *effect* of unpermitted discrimination because people of certain races, national origins, and ancestry will not have blue eyes. Such discrimination will violate fair housing laws because it has a disparate impact on protected classes. It is important to look beyond the actual basis for the discrimination to see what consequences may arise as a result.

Remember, however, that discrimination in and of itself is not wrongful. When I decide to sell my house to one person, I have discriminated against all of the other potential buyers. What's important is *why* I chose one purchaser over another. If I decide not to sell my home to someone because he or she owns three dogs, I have discriminated against dog owners, but that is not a protected class and thus permissible. And you can always discriminate on the basis of green—the color of money.

Remedies

Both compensatory and punitive damages are available for fair housing violations. As we discussed in Chapter 6, compensatory damages are designed to make the plaintiff whole and put them in the position they would have been in but for the violation. Surely the dollar amount of an underlying transaction will enter into a calculation of damages, but other considerations can increase the amount of compensatory damages recovered. Additional damages are often awarded for such things as being humiliated by the violation and the resulting loss of self-esteem, and such damages can easily exceed the monetary value of the underlying transaction itself.

Punitive damages, which are intended to punish wrongdoers, are also available to a person who was wronged by a fair housing violation. Since these damages are designed to punish, punitive damages are frequently calculated based on the financial wherewithal of real estate agents and brokers who willingly violate fair housing laws. If the real estate agent violated fair housing but the agent's broker did not authorize the violation, the broker may be on the hook for compensatory damages not for punitive damages.

Sometimes, a real estate agent and broker may claim damages in an amount equal to their lost commissions if their client was thwarted by someone else's fair housing violation. Occasionally, a victim of a fair housing violation will seek injunctive relief in the form of a restraining order preventing the sale or lease of the residential unit until the victim has the opportunity to make an offer.

Advertising

Advertising can cause a fair housing violation. Even though Title VIII and the Ohio Fair Housing Act contain some exemptions, the exemptions do not apply to advertising. For example, someone relying on the Mrs. Murphy exemption could not advertise that units are not available to people of a certain race.

Also, statements that seem innocuous on their face can give rise to claim of a fair housing violation. For example, an apartment that advertises that the complex does not include a play area may be factual but can be interpreted to mean that families with children are not welcome. Likewise, an advertisement that mentions that a house is near churches or synagogues could be understood to mean that people of only certain religions would be accepted. A cautious real estate agent will read advertisements carefully to make sure that statements of fact could not be construed to mean a fair housing violation.

Restrictive Deed Covenants

In Chapter 5, we discussed deed restrictions and covenants for such things as allowable fences, sheds, and similar things. Some deed restrictions and covenants would violate fair housing by, say, prohibiting the sale of a house to someone of a particular race. Until a 1948 US Supreme Court case, these deed restrictions were considered enforceable.[7] Since that time, however, any deed restriction or covenant that would violate fair housing is unenforceable and of no effect. A careful real estate agent will advise his or her client not to rely on such a restriction.

Steering, Blockbusting, and Redlining

Steering, blockbusting, and redlining are prohibited by both Title VIII and the Ohio Civil Rights Act. Unlike most of the other fair housing violations we have discussed, which are often perpetuated by owners, these three prohibitions are directed at real estate professionals. We will look at each of these in this section.

Steering

If a real estate agent shows properties only in particular areas because the agent believes that the potential buyer would want to live or not live in a particular area because of the demographics of persons in the protected classes living there, the agent is engaging in steering. For example, a real estate agent who shows a client houses in only an area where people of the same ethnicity

---

7. *Shelley v. Kramer*, 334 U.S. 1 (1948).

live is steering. Likewise, an agent who avoids showing houses in an area with residents of a different ethnicity from their client is steering. Steering can be based only on the protected classes—for example, showing a Jewish couple homes only near a synagogue is steering.

Now, this does not prohibit clients from indicating where they would like to live. If the Jewish couple tells the agent that they want to live near a synagogue, the agent can ask if they have a particular synagogue in mind and show properties that meet that criteria. If a client indicates, for example, that they want to live in an Italian neighborhood, a wise real estate agent will state that they do not know what an Italian neighborhood is and ask the client if they have a particular area in mind. The client can steer the agent, but not the other way around.

Blockbusting

Blockbusting occurs when real estate professionals use concerns about the changing demographics of a neighborhood to obtain listings. For example, an unscrupulous agent could go door-to-door and say, "Are you aware that the house at the end of the block was just sold to an undesirable person? You might want to sell your home right now, before property values go down any further and crime increases." This can induce panic selling and a self-fulfilling prophecy—with many homes being placed on the market in a short time, prices will surely fall. Some instances of blockbusting are more subtle than the direct approach in the example. An unscrupulous real estate agent might call residents in the area pretending to be a wrong number, looking for the "new Puerto Rican family." Some agents have gone so far as to purchase property in the neighborhood themselves and selling it to a minority buyer to create the situation.

Redlining

Redlining is discrimination in lending, where a lender refuses to make real estate loans in a particular area because of the ethnic composition of the area and the perceived declining property value and ability of owners to make payments. The term *redlining* comes from lenders who would use a red pencil to outline an area on a map in which they will not make loans. As additional lenders refuse to make loans in these areas, the values do indeed go down, as financing becomes unavailable to potential purchasers.

Redlining can occur also when insurance companies refuse to write homeowners' insurance policies in a particular area. The lack of available insurance has the effect of making loans unobtainable, because lenders require that real estate on which they lend money be insured.

This is not to say that lenders are prohibited from denying loans in areas with declining real estate values. But the decision not to make a loan must be based on genuine economic conditions and not the ethnic character of the neighborhood.

Testing

Testing refers to the use of individuals who, without any genuine intent to rent or purchase a dwelling, pose as prospective buyers or renters. This information may indicate whether a real estate agent is violating fair housing laws. Testing can be done by a variety of organizations, including the Civil Rights Division of the US Department of Justice.

Typically, a couple of a minority ethnicity will state that they are moving into the area and are seeking housing. The couple will claim to have been prequalified for a purchase of a certain amount and will describe the kind of residence they are looking for. They will make notes on the properties shown and how they were treated by the agent. Later, another couple of the majority ethnicity will make a similar claim, frequently stating a lower prequalification, and compare the properties they were shown and treatment by the real estate agent.

Since testers are not bona fide purchasers or renters, a violation of fair housing discovered using testing will not subject the real estate agent to discipline from the Ohio Real Estate Commission, but the agent may still be liable for monetary damages. According to the US Department of Justice, it has recovered more than $12.9 million, including more than $2.3 million in civil penalties and more than $10.5 million in other damages from its testing program.[8]

Standing to Sue

Standing to sue refers to the right of a plaintiff to bring a lawsuit. To have standing to sue, the plaintiff must have some real interest in the outcome of the case. At first glance, it would seem that only a person who has been denied residential housing as a result of a fair housing violation would have standing to sue for such violation. Perhaps surprisingly, a neighbor of a property that was not sold due to a fair housing violation has standing to sue because the

---

8. https://www.justice.gov/crt/fair-housing-testing-program-1

neighbor has been deprived of the opportunity to live in a diverse area. Fair housing has a very broad reach, indeed.

Discussion Questions

1. Discuss the differences between the Civil Rights Act of 1866, Title VIII, and the Ohio Civil Rights Act relating to fair housing.

2. Describe the exemptions from fair housing found in Title VIII and the Ohio Civil Rights Act.

3. Explain the difference between disparate treatment and disparate impact.

4. Explain steering, blockbusting, and redlining.

5. Give an example of how testing can result in a claim for violating fair housing laws.

6. Explain why a fair housing violation found by testing does not result in discipline by the Ohio Real Estate Commission.

Key Terms

Ancestry
Blockbusting
Disparate impact
Disparate treatment
Fundamental rights
Jim Crow laws
Redlining
Standing to sue
Steering

Chapter 17

Ohio Real Estate Agent and Broker Laws

Real estate agents are subject to a large body of statutory law. These laws are designed to protect the public, not the agent. The Ohio Division of Real Estate requires students preparing to sit for the license exam to be familiar with real estate consumer protection laws. Chapter 4735 of the Ohio Revised Code deals with these issues. This chapter of the book summarizes key laws found in Chapter 4735 of the Ohio Revised Code, including a cross-reference to the actual code sections. You are expected to have a general understanding of these statutes, but you are not expected to memorize the section numbers. They are provided here for your convenience in reading the actual statutes, which can be found online at http://codes.ohio.gov/orc/4735.

Definitions (Section 4735.01)

A **real estate broker** is someone who is engaged in the business of selling, exchanging, purchasing, and renting real estate. It includes someone who negotiates the sale, exchange, and purchase of real estate, lists property for sale, and deals with options to purchase real estate. Also included are people who operate, manage, or rent buildings to the public. A real estate broker is someone who advertises or holds him- or herself out as engaging in the above-mentioned business activities and who procures prospects or negotiates transactions for the sale, exchange, purchase, or rental of real estate. Real estate is broadly defined to be all interests of land in Ohio, excluding cemetery interment rights (grave sites).

A **real estate salesperson** is any person associated with a licensed real estate broker who engage in acts or transactions set out by the definition of a real estate broker, for compensation or otherwise. Real estate salespeople must work under the supervision of a broker and cannot practice on their own. A *real estate salesperson* is the term used in the statutes to mean what is commonly known as a real estate agent. For consistency with the statutes, I will use the term *salesperson* in this chapter instead of *real estate agent*.

Foreign real estate means any real estate not located in Ohio. **Foreign real estate dealer** and **foreign real estate salesperson** have the same meaning as an Ohio real estate broker and real estate salesperson, respectively, but who deal with property located outside Ohio.

Limited real estate salesperson is a person who deals only with cemetery interment rights.[1]

Everyone who engages in the business of a real estate broker or real estate salesperson in Ohio must be licensed, with the following exceptions:

1. A person selling their own property (For Sale by Owner—FSBO, pronounced "fizz-bow"). This can be an individual, a corporation, a partnership, or an association.
2. A court-appointed guardian, executor, administrator, bankruptcy trustee, or other person who has the authority to act on behalf of someone who cannot act for themselves in selling property owned by that person.
3. A public official performing that person's official duties, such as a sheriff selling property in foreclosure.
4. An attorney-at-law acting on behalf of a client, but this does not include the general power to act as a broker or salesperson.
5. A broker of the sale of business assets, but not including real estate interests.

Nonresident Commercial Brokers and Salespersons (Section 4735.022)

An out-of-state licensed broker dealing with commercial property may perform acts that would otherwise require an Ohio license if they do all of the following:

1. Work in cooperation with an Ohio real estate broker who holds a valid, active license.
2. Enter into a written agreement with the Ohio broker that includes the terms of cooperation, compensation, and a statement that the out-of-state commercial broker and its agents will agree to adhere to the laws of Ohio.

---

1. Ohio Rev. Code § 4767.031.

3. Furnish the Ohio broker with a copy of the out-of-state commercial broker's current certificate of good standing from the jurisdiction where the out-of-state commercial broker maintains an active real estate license.
4. File an irrevocable written consent with the Ohio broker that legal actions arising out of the conduct of the out-of-state commercial broker or its agents may be sued in Ohio.
5. Include the name of the Ohio broker on all advertising.
6. Deposit all escrow funds, security deposits, and other money received in trust or special accounts maintained by the Ohio broker.
7. Deposits all documentation required by this section, as well as records and documents related to the transaction with the Ohio broker.

The Ohio broker must maintain the records and documents related to the transactions for at least three years.

Complaint Procedure (Section 4735.051)

Anyone can file a complaint against a licensee with the Ohio Division of Real Estate, who investigates the complaint. If the investigation reveals reasonable evidence of a violation, the case is sent to the Ohio Real Estate Commission for a hearing. The commission hears testimony, considers written documentation, and decides what to do. This may result in the complaint being dismissed or the licensee being publicly reprimanded, being required to complete additional continuing education, having a civil penalty imposed, or having their license suspended or revoked.

Reciprocity (Section 4735.07)

The Ohio Real Estate Commission can enter into reciprocity agreements to waive the examination requirements for people licensed as brokers or salespersons from other states that have similar license requirements and whose states grant reciprocity with Ohio.

Real Estate Recovery Fund (Section 4735.12)

The real estate recovery fund is used to protect consumers who are harmed by a real estate licensee who violates the license laws and causes financial harm.

The fund is financed by a payment of $5 to $10 from each license renewal or transfer fee, up to a maximum of $2 million.

To claim a payment from the fund, there must be an unsatisfied judgment against a broker or salesperson for a violation of real estate licensing laws. The judgment must be final and nonappealable, the claimant must show that the licensee has not paid all or part of the judgment, and the claim must be made within one year of the date of the final judgment.

Up to $40,000 can be paid to a claimant from the fund, multiplied by the number of licensees involved. A licensee who has a payment made from the fund on his or her behalf shall have his or her license suspended until the fund is repaid. Bankruptcy of the licensee does not discharge this obligation.

License Usage (Section 4735.13)

Every broker in Ohio must have a physical place of business and display the broker's license in a public area—a broker cannot operate with a virtual office. The broker must notify the Ohio Division of Real Estate if his or her place of business changes. Each salesperson's license must be held and maintained by the sponsoring broker. A new salesperson's license is sent to the sponsoring broker and not the salesperson directly. If the salesperson is terminated by the broker, that person's license must be returned to the Ohio Division of Real Estate, who will then send it to the salesperson's new broker. The broker must return the license to the Ohio Division of Real Estate within three days of a salesperson's written request.

License Continuation (Section 4735.14)

A salesperson can engage in the practice of real estate so long as a broker continues to hold his or her license, and provided it is not suspended or revoked. Broker and salesperson licenses must be renewed every three years on the person's birthday. Renewal forms are mailed directly to the brokers and salespeople, who are responsible for renewing their own licenses.

Any broker, brokerage, or salesperson that fails to renew on or before the filing deadline will be automatically suspended by the Division of Real Estate. A suspended license may be reactivated within 12 months of the date of suspension by paying a renewal fee plus a penalty fee of 50 percent of the renewal fee. Failure to reactivate the license shall result in automatic revocation of the license.

Each licensee must notify the Ohio Division of Real Estate of their residence address and update that information if they move. Failure to do so may cause the renewal notice to not be delivered and does not excuse late or nonrenewal of licenses.

Continuing Education (Section 4735.141)

Both brokers and salespersons must complete 30 classroom hours of continuing education every three years. Of these 30 hours, three hours must be completed in each of the following areas: core laws, civil rights, and ethics. It is perhaps easiest to remember these requirements by the rule of 3s—every three years, 30 hours, three hours in each of the three special areas. The continuing education must be completed in an institution approved by the Ohio Real Estate Commission.

If the continuing education requirements are not fulfilled, the person's license is automatically suspended. If a broker's license is suspended for failure to complete continuing education requirements, all salespeople who are associated with that broker are also suspended, and the broker must notify the affected salespeople within three days.

For active licensees who are over 70 years old, the continuing education requirements are a bit more lax. These people need to take only the three special area courses—three hours in each of the following: core laws, civil rights, and ethics.

Business Advertising (Section 4735.16)

Each brokerage must have a sign plainly stating that it is a real estate brokerage. If the brokerage has multiple branch offices, each office must have such a sign. Any advertisement to buy, sell, or lease real estate by a broker or salesperson must include both the licensee's name and that of the brokerage. The name of the brokerage must be displayed as prominently as the name of the licensee. If a licensee is representing a seller, advertisements must not indicate that the property is "for sale by owner." A real estate broker or salesperson obtaining the signature of a party to a listing or other agreement involved in a real estate transaction shall furnish a copy of agreement to the party immediately after obtaining the party's signature.

Violation of the advertising rules in this section may result in a citation (fine) of between $200 per violation and $2,500 per violation imposed against the licensee, and other disciplinary action. Three violations in any consecutive 12 months will automatically result in disciplinary proceedings.

Every broker's office shall prominently display in the same area as it displays licenses a statement that it is illegal to discriminate against any person because of race, color, religion, sex, familial status, national origin, military status, disability, or ancestry in the sale or rental of housing or residential lots, in advertising the sale or rental of housing, in the financing of housing, or in the provision of real estate brokerage services and that blockbusting also is illegal. The statement shall bear the US Department of Housing and Urban Development Equal Housing Opportunity logo,[2] shall contain the information that the broker and the broker's salespersons are licensed by the Division of Real Estate and that the division can assist with any consumer complaints or inquiries, and shall provide the division's address and telephone number.

Licensed Nonresidents (Section 4735.17)

Licenses may be issued to nonresidents of Ohio, subject to the following requirements:

1. The licensee, if a broker, shall maintain an active place of business in this state. A post office box is not an active place of business for purposes of this section.
2. Every nonresident applicant shall file an irrevocable consent that he or she can be sued in Ohio.
3. A duplicate copy of any process or pleading served on the superintendent shall be immediately forwarded by certified mail to the main office of the licensee against which that process or pleading is directed.

Discipline (Section 4735.18)

As stated above, the Division of Real Estate must investigate every complaint against a licensee, and the Ohio Real Estate Commission must hold a hearing if there is reasonable evidence of a violation. The division can also initiate an investigation on its own. A licensee can have his or her license suspended or revoked If the licensee is found guilty of any of the following:

---

2. The Equal Housing Opportunity logo appears at the bottom of the business model disclosures found in Chapter 15.

1. Knowingly making any misrepresentation.
2. Making any false promises with intent to influence, persuade, or induce.
3. A continued course of misrepresentation or making false promises through agents, salespersons, advertising, or otherwise.
4. Acting for more than one party in a transaction except as permitted in a dual agency situation.
5. Failure within a reasonable time to account for or to remit any money in the licensee's possession that belongs to others.
6. Dishonest or illegal dealing, gross negligence, incompetency, or misconduct.
7. Violating the Fair Housing laws (discussed in Chapter 16), provided that the violation arose out of a situation wherein parties were engaged in bona fide efforts to purchase, sell, or lease real estate.
8. For any second violation of the Fair Housing laws, the commission shall suspend for a minimum of two months or revoke the license of the broker or salesperson. For any subsequent offense, the commission shall revoke the license of the broker or salesperson.
9. Obtaining a license for themselves or helping another to obtain a license by fraud, misrepresentation, or deceit.
10. Willfully disregarding or violating any provision of this Chapter 4735 of the Ohio Revised Code.
11. Demanding a commission to which the licensee is not entitled.
12. Paying commissions or fees to, or dividing commissions or fees with, anyone not licensed as a real estate broker or salesperson or who is not operating as a permitted out-of-state commercial real estate broker or salesperson.
13. Falsely representing membership in any real estate professional association of which the licensee is not a member; for example, using the term REALTOR® when the licensee is not a member of the National Association of Realtors®.
14. Accepting, giving, or charging any undisclosed commission, rebate, or profit.
15. Offering anything of value other than the consideration recited in the sales contract as an inducement to a person to enter into a contract for the purchase or sale of real estate.
16. Acting as an undisclosed principal in any transaction.
17. Guaranteeing future profits that may result from the resale of real property.
18. Advertising or placing a sign on any property offering it for sale or for rent without the consent of the owner or the owner's authorized agent.
19. Inducing anyone to breach an existing contract in order to enter into a different contract.

20. Negotiating directly a seller, purchaser, lessor, or tenant, knowing that that person is represented by another broker.
21. Offering real property for sale or for lease without the knowledge and consent of the owner or the owner's authorized agent, or on any terms other than those authorized.
22. Engaging in deceptive advertising in any form at all.
23. Knowingly falsifying any statement of account or invoice.
24. Threatening unjustified legal proceedings against competitors.
25. Failing to keep complete and accurate records of all transactions for a period of three years from the date of the transaction,
26. Failing to furnish all parties involved in a real estate transaction with true copies of all listings and other agreements at the time they are signed.
27. Failing to maintain an Ohio non-interest-bearing trust bank account that is separate from the brokerage account to deposit money held in a fiduciary capacity such as escrow funds, earnest money, and the like. This account shall be separate and distinct from any other account maintained by the broker.
28. If the broker is engaged in the management of real property on behalf of owners, failing to maintain an Ohio trust bank account, to be used exclusively for the deposit and maintenance of all rents, security deposits, escrow funds, and other moneys received by the broker in a fiduciary capacity in the course of managing real property. This account shall be separate and distinct from any other account maintained by the broker. This account may earn interest, which shall be paid to the property owners on a pro rata basis.
29. Failing to put definite expiration dates in all written listing agreements.
30. Having an unsatisfied final judgment or lien in any court of record against the licensee arising out of the licensee's conduct as a licensed broker or salesperson.
31. Failing to account for funds held by the licensee on behalf of a party to a transaction when demanded to do so by a party.
32. Failing to pay a real estate salesperson the salesperson's earned commission within a reasonable time after receiving it.
33. Engaging in the unauthorized practice of law.
34. Having been adjudicated incompetent.
35. Allowing an unlicensed person to act as an agent.
36. Knowingly inserting or participating in inserting any materially inaccurate term in a document.
37. Failing to inform his or her client of an offer or counteroffer or failing to present an offer or counteroffer in a timely manner, unless otherwise in-

structed by the client, provided the instruction is not in conflict with law, such as Fair Housing laws.

Right to Sue (Section 4735.21)

No one other than a real estate broker or foreign real estate dealer can sue to collect a real estate commission, including a person who was licensed at the time but whose license has now expired.

No salesperson or foreign real estate salesperson shall handle any money, except in the name of and with the consent of the licensed real estate broker or licensed foreign real estate dealer under whom the salesperson is licensed at the time. A salesperson or foreign real estate salesperson cannot sue buyers and sellers and can only sue a real estate broker or foreign real estate dealer under whom the salesperson is licensed as a salesperson at the time the cause of action arose.

A salesperson cannot not sell, assign, or otherwise transfer his or her interest in a commission to an unlicensed person. If a salesperson does so anyway, the broker shall not pay the unlicensed person. The unlicensed person or entity cannot sue the broker for not paying him or her.

Earnest Money (Section 4735.24)

When earnest money connected to a real estate purchase agreement is deposited in a broker's trust account, the broker shall maintain that money in the account is in accordance with the terms of the purchase agreement until one of the following occurs:

1. The transaction closes and the broker disburses the earnest money to the closing or escrow agent or otherwise disburses the money under the terms of the purchase agreement.
2. Both parties provide the broker with written instructions that specify how the broker is to disburse the earnest money and the broker acts under to those instructions.
3. The broker receives a copy of a final court order that specifies to whom the earnest money is to be awarded and the broker acts pursuant to the court order.
4. The earnest money becomes "unclaimed funds" as defined in the Ohio Revised Code, and the broker has reported the unclaimed funds to the Ohio Director of Commerce and has remitted all of the earnest money to the director.

A purchase agreement may provide that in the event of a dispute regarding the disbursement of the earnest money, the broker will return the money to the purchaser without notice to the parties unless the broker has received one of the following within two years of receiving the earnest money:

1. Written instructions signed by both parties specifying how the money is to be disbursed.
2. Written notice that a court action to resolve the dispute has been filed.

Foreign Real Estate (Section 4735.25)

Foreign real estate can be sold only by foreign real estate dealers and foreign real estate salespersons, except that an Ohio owner can sell his or her foreign real estate in a single FSBO transaction.

Duties Following Closing of Transaction (Section 4735.74)

Unless otherwise agreed in writing, a licensee owes no further duty to a client after performance of all duties or after any contract has terminated or expired, except for both of the following:

1. Providing the client with an accounting of all moneys and property relating to the transaction.
2. Keeping confidential all information received during the course of the transaction unless:
   a. The client permits disclosure.
   b. Disclosure is required by law or by court order.
   c. The information becomes public from a source other than the licensee.
   d. The information is necessary to prevent a crime the client intends to commit.
   e. Disclosure is necessary to defend the brokerage or its licensees against an accusation of wrongful conduct or to establish or defend a claim that a commission is owed on a transaction.
   f. Disclosure is regarding sales information requested by a registered or licensed real estate appraiser assistant for the purposes of performing an appraisal.

Discussion Questions

1. Provide examples of people who do not need a real estate license to sell realty.

2. Explain how the real estate recovery fund is used and how it is repaid.

3. Explain the continuing education requirements for Ohio brokers and salespersons.

4. Explain what a broker or salesperson must do to buy or sell realty for his or her own account.

5. Explain how a salesperson and brokerage name must appear in advertising.

Key Terms

Foreign real estate
Foreign real estate dealer
Foreign real estate salesperson
FSBO
Limited real estate salesperson
Real estate broker
Real estate salesperson

Appendix A

Sample Lease

THIS LEASE AGREEMENT (this "Agreement") made and entered into _____ 20___, by and between Linda Landlord ("Landlord") and Terry Tenant ("Tenant").

WHEREAS, Landlord is the fee owner of certain real property being, lying and situated in Hamilton County, Ohio, such real property having a street address of 234 Zebra Drive, Cincinnati, Ohio 45241 ("Premises").

WHEREAS, Landlord desires to lease the Premises to Tenant upon the terms and conditions as contained herein; and

WHEREAS, Tenant desires to lease the Premises from Landlord on the terms and conditions as contained herein;

NOW, THEREFORE, for and in consideration of the covenants and obligations contained herein and other good and valuable consideration, the receipt and sufficiency of which is hereby acknowledged, the parties hereto hereby agree as follows:

1. **TERM.** Landlord leases to Tenant and Tenant leases from Landlord the above-described Premises together with any and all appurtenances thereto, for a term of _____ years, such term beginning on _____ 20__, and ending at 11:59 PM _____ 20__.

2. **RENT.** The total rent for the term hereof is the sum of $_____ payable on the first day of each month of the term. All such payments shall be made to Landlord at Landlord's address as set forth at the end of this Agreement on or before the due date and without demand.

3. **DAMAGE DEPOSIT.** Upon the due execution of this Agreement, Tenant shall deposit with Landlord the sum of $_____, as security for any damage caused to the Premises during the term hereof ("Deposit"). The De-

posit shall be returned to Tenant, less any set off for damages to the Premises upon the termination of this Agreement. Landlord shall pay Tenant interest on Deposit at the rate of 5% per annum, paid on the annual anniversary of this Agreement.

4. **USE OF PREMISES.** The Premises shall be used and occupied by Tenant and Tenant's immediate family exclusively, as a private single family dwelling, and no part of the Premises shall be used at any time during the term of this Agreement by Tenant for the purpose of carrying on any business, profession, or trade of any kind, or for any purpose other than as a private single family dwelling. Tenant shall not allow any other person, other than Tenant's immediate family or transient relatives and friends who are guests of Tenant, to use or occupy the Premises without first obtaining Landlord's written consent to such use. Tenant shall comply with any and all laws, ordinances, rules and orders of any and all governmental or quasi-governmental authorities affecting the cleanliness, use, occupancy and preservation of the Premises.

5. **CONDITION OF PREMISES.** Tenant stipulates, represents and warrants that Tenant has examined the Premises, and that they are at the time of this Lease in good order, repair, and in a safe, clean and tenantable condition.

6. **ASSIGNMENT AND SUB-LETTING.** Tenant shall not assign this Agreement, or sublet or grant any license to use the Premises or any part thereof without the prior written consent of Landlord. Any consent by Landlord to one such assignment, subletting or license shall not be deemed to be consent to any subsequent assignment, subletting or license. An assignment, subletting or license without the prior written consent of Landlord or an assignment or subletting by operation of law shall be absolutely null and void and shall, at Landlord's option, terminate this Agreement.

7. **ALTERATIONS AND IMPROVEMENTS.** Tenant shall make no alterations to the buildings or improvements on the Premises or construct any building or make any other improvements on the Premises without the prior written consent of Landlord. Any and all alterations, changes, or improvements built, constructed or placed on the Premises by Tenant shall, unless otherwise provided by written agreement between Landlord and Tenant, be and become the property of Landlord and remain on the Premises at the expiration or earlier termination of this Agreement.

8. **NON-DELIVERY OF POSSESSION.** In the event Landlord cannot deliver possession of the Premises to Tenant upon the commencement of the Lease term, through no fault of Landlord or its agents, then Landlord or

its agents shall have no liability, but the rental herein provided shall abate until possession is given. Landlord or its agents shall have 30 days in which to give possession, and if possession is tendered within such time, Tenant agrees to accept the demised Premises and pay the rental herein provided from that date. In the event possession cannot be delivered within such time, through no fault of Landlord or its agents, then this Agreement and all rights hereunder shall terminate.

9. **HAZARDOUS MATERIALS.** Tenant shall not keep on the Premises any item of a dangerous, flammable or explosive character that might unreasonably increase the danger of fire or explosion on the Premises or that might be considered hazardous or extra hazardous by any responsible insurance company.

10. **UTILITIES.** Tenant shall be responsible for arranging for and paying for all utility services required on the Premises, including, but not limited to, water, gas, electric, and trash removal.

11. **MAINTENANCE AND REPAIR; RULES.** Landlord shall, at its sole expense, keep and maintain the Premises in a good and habitable condition. Tenant shall, at its sole expense, keep and maintain the Premises and appurtenances in good and sanitary condition and repair during the term of this Agreement and any renewal thereof. Without limiting the generality of the foregoing, Tenant shall:

(a) Keep all windows, glass, window coverings, doors, locks and hardware in good, clean order and repair;

(b) Not obstruct or cover the windows or doors;

(c) Not leave windows or doors in an open position during any inclement weather;

(d) Not hang any laundry, clothing, sheets, etc. from any window, rail, porch or balcony nor air or dry any of such things within any yard area or space;

(e) Not cause or permit any locks or hooks to be placed upon any door or window without the prior written consent of Landlord;

(f) Keep all heating and air conditioning filters clean and free from dirt;

(g) Keep all lavatories, sinks, toilets, and all other water and plumbing apparatus in good order and repair and shall use same only for the purposes for which they were constructed. Tenant shall not allow any sweepings, rubbish, sand, rags, ashes or other substances to be thrown or deposited in any plumbing apparatus. Any damage to any such apparatus and the cost of clearing stopped plumbing resulting from misuse shall be borne by Tenant;

(h) Regularly mow the lawn of the Premises and rake and dispose of leaves from the lawn of the Premises;

(i) Cause Tenant's family and guests at all times to maintain order in the Premises and at all places on the Premises, and shall not make or permit any loud or improper noises, or otherwise disturb the neighbors;

(j) Keep all radios, television sets, stereos, phonographs, etc., turned down to a level of sound that does not annoy or interfere with the neighbors;

(k) Deposit all trash, garbage, rubbish or refuse in proper containers, shall take such containers to the curb for pickup no earlier than the day before scheduled pick-up and shall not allow any trash, garbage, rubbish or refuse to be deposited or permitted to stand on the exterior of the Premises

12. **DAMAGE TO PREMISES.** In the event the Premises are destroyed or rendered wholly uninhabitable by fire, storm, earthquake, or other casualty not caused by the negligence of Tenant, this Agreement shall terminate from such time except for the purpose of enforcing rights that may have then accrued hereunder. The rental provided for herein shall then be accounted for by and between Landlord and Tenant up to the time of such injury or destruction of the Premises, Tenant paying rentals up to such date and Landlord refunding rentals collected beyond such date. Should a portion of the Premises thereby be rendered uninhabitable, the Landlord shall have the option of either repairing such injured or damaged portion or terminating this Lease. In the event that Landlord exercises its right to repair such uninhabitable portion, the rental shall abate in the proportion that the injured parts bears to the whole Premises, and such part so injured shall be restored by Landlord as speedily as practicable, after which the full rent shall recommence and the Agreement continue according to its terms.

13. **INSPECTION OF PREMISES.** Upon reasonable advance notice to Tenant, Landlord and Landlord's agents shall have the right at all reasonable times during the term of this Agreement and any renewal thereof to enter the Premises for the purpose of inspecting the Premises and for the purposes of making any repairs, additions or alterations as may be deemed appropriate by Landlord. Landlord and its agents shall further have the right to exhibit the Premises and to display the usual "for sale," "for rent," or "vacancy" signs on the Premises at any time within 45 days before the expi-

ration of this Lease. The right of entry shall likewise exist for the purpose of removing placards, signs, fixtures, alterations or additions that do not conform to this Agreement or to any restrictions, rules or regulations affecting the Premises.

14. **SUBORDINATION OF LEASE.** This Agreement and Tenant's interest hereunder are and shall be subordinate, junior and inferior to any and all mortgages, liens or encumbrances now or hereafter placed on the Premises by Landlord, all advances made under any such mortgages, liens or encumbrances (including, but not limited to, future advances), the interest payable on such mortgages, liens or encumbrances and any and all renewals, extensions or modifications of such mortgages, liens or encumbrances.

15. **TENANT'S HOLD OVER.** If Tenant remains in possession of the Premises with the consent of Landlord after the natural expiration of this Agreement, a new tenancy from month-to-month shall be created between Landlord and Tenant which shall be subject to all of the terms and conditions hereof except that rent shall then be due and owing at $_____per month and except that such tenancy shall be terminable upon 30 days written notice served by either party.

16. **SURRENDER OF PREMISES.** Upon the expiration of the term hereof, Tenant shall surrender the Premises in as good a state and condition as they were at the commencement of this Agreement, reasonable use and wear and tear thereof and damages by the elements excepted.

17. **ANIMALS.** Tenant shall be entitled to keep no more than a total of 2 pets of any kind, including domestic dogs, cats and birds on the Premises; however, at such time as Tenant shall actually keep any such animal on the Premises, Tenant shall pay to Landlord a pet fee of $_____, which shall be non-refundable.

18. **QUIET ENJOYMENT.** Tenant, upon payment of all of the sums referred to herein as being payable by Tenant and Tenant's performance of all Tenant's agreements contained herein and Tenant's observance of all rules and regulations, shall and may peacefully and quietly have, hold and enjoy said Premises for the term hereof.

19. **INDEMNIFICATION.** Landlord shall not be liable for any damage or injury of or to the Tenant, Tenant's family, guests, invitees, agents or employees or to any person entering the Premises or the building of which the Premises are a part or to goods or equipment, or in the structure or equipment of the structure of which the Premises are a part, and Tenant hereby agrees

to indemnify, defend and hold Landlord harmless from any and all claims or assertions of every kind and nature.

20. **DEFAULT**. If Tenant fails to comply with any of the material provisions of this Agreement, other than the covenant to pay rent, or of any present rules and regulations or any that may be hereafter prescribed by Landlord, or materially fails to comply with any duties imposed on Tenant by statute, within 7 days after delivery of written notice by Landlord specifying the non-compliance and indicating the intention of Landlord to terminate the Lease by reason thereof, Landlord may terminate this Agreement. If Tenant fails to pay rent when due and the default continues for 7 days thereafter, Landlord may, at Landlord's option, declare the entire balance of rent payable hereunder to be immediately due and payable and may exercise any and all rights and remedies available to Landlord at law or in equity or may immediately terminate this Agreement.

21. **LATE CHARGE**. In the event that any payment required to be paid by Tenant hereunder is not made within three 3 days of when due, Tenant shall pay to Landlord, in addition to such payment or other charges due hereunder, a late fee in the amount of $_____.

22. **ABANDONMENT**. If at any time during the term of this Agreement Tenant abandons the Premises or any part thereof, Landlord may, at Landlord's option, obtain possession of the Premises in the manner provided by law, and without becoming liable to Tenant for damages or for any payment of any kind whatever. Landlord may, at Landlord's discretion, as agent for Tenant, relet the Premises, or any part thereof, for the whole or any part thereof, for the whole or any part of the then unexpired term, and may receive and collect all rent payable by virtue of such reletting, and, at Landlord's option, hold Tenant liable for any difference between the rent that would have been payable under this Agreement during the balance of the unexpired term, if this Agreement had continued in force, and the net rent for such period realized by Landlord by means of such reletting. If Landlord's right of reentry is exercised following abandonment of the Premises by Tenant, then Landlord shall consider any personal property belonging to Tenant and left on the Premises to also have been abandoned, in which case Landlord may dispose of all such personal property in any manner Landlord shall deem proper and Landlord is hereby relieved of all liability for doing so.

23. **RIGHTS AND REMEDIES**. The rights and remedies under this lease are cumulative, and either party's using any one right or remedy shall not pre-

clude or waive that party's right to use any other. These rights and remedies are in addition to any other rights the parties may have by law, statute, ordinance, or otherwise.

24. **RECORDING OF AGREEMENT.** Tenant shall not record this Agreement on the Public Records of any public office. In the event that Tenant shall record this Agreement, this Agreement shall, at Landlord's option, terminate immediately and Landlord shall be entitled to all rights and remedies that it has at law or in equity.

25. **GOVERNING LAW.** This Agreement shall be governed, construed and interpreted by, through and under the Laws of the State of Ohio, excluding choice of law provisions.

26. **SEVERABILITY.** If any provision of this Agreement or the application thereof shall, for any reason and to any extent, be invalid or unenforceable, neither the remainder of this Agreement nor the application of the provision to other persons, entities or circumstances shall be affected thereby, but instead shall be enforced to the maximum extent permitted by law.

27. **BINDING EFFECT.** The covenants, obligations and conditions herein contained shall be binding on and inure to the benefit of the heirs, legal representatives, and assigns of the parties hereto.

28. **DESCRIPTIVE HEADINGS.** The descriptive headings used herein are for convenience of reference only and they are not intended to have any effect whatsoever in determining the rights or obligations of the Landlord or Tenant.

29. **CONSTRUCTION.** The pronouns used herein shall include, where appropriate, either gender or both, singular and plural.

30. **NON-WAIVER.** No indulgence, waiver, election or non-election by Landlord under this Agreement shall affect Tenant's duties and liabilities hereunder.

31. **MODIFICATION.** The parties hereby agree that this document contains the entire agreement between the parties and this Agreement shall not be modified, changed, altered or amended in any way except through a written amendment signed by all of the parties hereto.

32. **NOTICE.** Any notice required or permitted under this Lease or under state law shall be deemed sufficiently given or served if sent by United States certified mail, return receipt requested, addressed as follows:

If to Landlord to:
Linda Landlord

765 Tlokweng Road
Cincinnati, OH 45455

If to Tenant to:
Terry Tenant
234 Zebra Drive
Cincinnati, Ohio 45444

Landlord and Tenant shall each have the right from time to time to change the place notice is to be given under this paragraph by written notice thereof to the other party.

LANDLORD:

Sign: _____

Print: _____ Date: _____

TENANT:

Sign: _____

Print: _____ Date: _____

Appendix B

Contract to Purchase Real Estate

CONTRACT TO PURCHASE REAL ESTATE

This Contract to Purchase Real Estate is entered into as of this xxx day of xxx, 2016, by and between xxx, husband wife, (hereinafter referred to as "Seller") and xxx, husband and wife, (hereinafter referred to as "Buyer"), to purchase the real estate known and designated as xxx and known as Parcel No. xxx of the records of the Auditor of Hamilton County, Ohio (hereinafter referred to as "Premises"), under the following terms, provisions, covenants and conditions:

1. <u>Sale of Real Estate</u>. Seller agrees to sell and Buyer agrees to purchase the above described Premises, together with all improvements thereon and all appurtenant rights, and including all land, buildings, fixtures, heating, electrical and plumbing fixtures and facilities, window shades, blinds, awnings, curtain rods, screens, storm windows and storm doors, wall-to-wall carpeting, stair carpeting, built-in kitchen appliances, landscaping and shrubbery, kitchen refrigerator, and mudroom cabinets.

Seller certifies to Buyer that Seller owns all the above items included in the sale and that they will be free and clear of any debt, lien or encumbrance at closing.

EXCLUDED FROM SALE: xxx

2. <u>Purchase Price</u>. Buyer shall pay to Seller for the sale of the Premises the sum of xxx Dollars ($xxx), payable as follows:

A.   <u>Earnest Money</u>. The sum of $xxx shall be paid by Buyer to Seller at the time this Contract is executed. Said sum shall be paid to the account of xxx IOLTA account, and shall be held by xxx until its disposition or disbursement is directed by the mutual assent of the parties. Said sum shall apply to the purchase price and shall be nonrefundable unless there shall occur a breach of this

Contract to Purchase by Seller or unless a contingency of Buyer has become applicable. Buyer and Seller agree that said funds shall be deposited into a non-interest bearing checking account.

B.   Balance of Purchase Price. The balance of the purchase price shall be paid in cash, certified funds or title company check in full at the time of closing.

C.   Closing costs. Seller shall pay from the net proceeds at closing: (1) the deed preparation fee; (2) the Ohio conveyance fee; and, (3) the cost of a home warranty chosen and obtained by Buyer in an amount not to exceed $400.00. Buyer shall pay all other closing and lender costs, including the premium for an owner's policy of title insurance if selected by Buyer. Seller and Buyer both state and agree that no sales commission is owed to any broker or third party as a result of this Contract being executed by the parties or as a result of the closing of the Premises.

3. Contingencies:

A.   Financing Contingency. This contract is contingent upon Buyer obtaining financing of the purchase price and a mortgage loan covering the Premises in an amount not greater than 80% of the purchase price, for a term of not less than 30 years, and at a customary and market interest rate acceptable to Buyer. Buyer shall apply for and make a diligent effort to obtain said financing no later than 7 days from the date of this Contract. The commitment for said financing shall be obtained within thirty (30) days from the date of this Contract to Purchase Real Estate, unless the parties mutually agree to an extension of such time period.

A lender "pre-approval" letter issued by Buyer's intended lender shall be provided to Seller at the time this Contract is executed.

Unless Buyer notifies Seller otherwise in writing prior to the expiration of the said thirty (30) days, this contingency shall be deemed satisfied.

B.   Inspections: The Buyer has the option to have the Premises inspected, at Buyer's expense. Buyer shall have ten (10) days (Inspection Period) beginning the day following written Contract acceptance to conduct all inspections related to the Premises. Inspections regarding the physical material condition, insurability and cost of a casualty insurance policy, boundaries, and use of the Premises shall be the sole responsibility of the Buyer. Buyer is relying solely upon Buyer's examination of the Premises, the limited Seller's certification herein, and inspections herein requested by the Buyer or otherwise required, if any, for its physical condition and overall character. During the Inspection

Period, Buyer and Buyer's inspectors and contractors shall be permitted access to the Premises at reasonable times and upon reasonable notice. Buyer shall be responsible for any damage to the real estate caused by Buyer or Buyer's inspectors or contractors, which repairs shall be completed in a timely and workmanlike manner at Buyer's expense.

If Buyer is not satisfied with the condition of the Premises as revealed by the inspection(s) and desires corrections to material defect(s), Buyer shall provide written notification of any material defect(s) and the relevant portion(s) of the inspection report to Seller with a request for corrections desired within the Inspection Period. Buyer and Seller shall have five (5) days beginning the day following the date of delivery of the Post-Inspection Agreement or other written notice requesting corrections ("Settlement Period") to negotiate to reach a written agreement in settlement of the condition of the Premises. If written settlement of the condition of the Premises is not reached within the Settlement Period, Buyer shall have the option to withdraw the written request for corrections within the Settlement Period and accept the real estate as is. If written settlement is not reached, with signed copies of settlement agreement physically delivered to all parties, within the Settlement Period and Buyer has not withdrawn the request for corrections in writing, this Contract shall be terminated. Buyer shall have the right to terminate the contract during the Settlement Period.

If Buyer is satisfied with the results of the inspection(s), Buyer shall deliver written notification to Seller within the Inspection Period stating Buyer's satisfaction and waiver of the contingency. IF BUYER DOES NOT DELIVER WRITTEN NOTIFICATION AS IDENTIFIED ABOVE WITHIN THE INSPECTION PERIOD, THEN BUYER SHALL BE DEEMED TO BE SATISFIED WITH ALL INSPECTIONS AND THE CONTINGENCY SHALL BE CONSIDERED WAIVED. IF BUYER DOES NOT COMPLETE REAL ESTATE INSPECTION(S) DURING THE INSPECTION PERIOD, BUYER'S RIGHT TO INSPECT SHALL BE DEEMED WAIVED. IT IS NOT THE INTENT OF THIS PROVISION TO PERMIT THE BUYER TO TERMINATE THIS AGREEMENT FOR COSMETIC OR NON-MATERIAL DEFECTS OR CONDITIONS. BUYER AGREES THAT MINOR REPAIRS AND ROUTINE MAINTENANCE ITEMS ARE NOT TO BE CONSIDERED MATERIAL DEFECTS WITH REGARD TO THIS CONTINGENCY.

C.   Appraisal Contingency: Buyer's obligation to close this transaction is contingent upon Buyer obtaining, at Buyer's expense, an independent appraisal performed by an appraiser licensed in Ohio which results in the Real Estate appraising at an amount equal to or greater than the Purchase Price. In the event the Real Estate does not obtain an appraised value equal to or greater than the Purchase Price, Buyer shall have the right to terminate this Contract by delivering written notice to Seller on or before the expiration of (i) the time-frame set forth in Section 3 above for obtaining an appraisal in connection with a cash sale or (ii) the time-frame set forth in Section 3 above for obtaining a loan commitment (such applicable time period being referred to as the "Appraisal Contingency Period"). If Buyer does not deliver written notice to Seller that Buyer is terminating the Contract prior to the expiration of the Appraisal Contingency Period, then Buyer's right to terminate this Contract shall be deemed waived.

4. <u>Conveyance of Title</u>. Title to the above-described Premises shall be conveyed by general warranty deed on or before _____, 2014. Said title to be free, clear and unencumbered, free of building orders, subject to zoning regulations of record, and except easements and restrictions of record which do not adversely affect the use of the property.

5. <u>Possession</u>. Possession is to be given to Buyer on _____, 2016, unless Seller shall notify Buyer of an earlier date of possession.

6. <u>Prorations of Taxes and Assessments</u>: There shall be prorated between Seller and Buyer as of closing all real estate taxes and installments of assessments as shown on the latest available tax duplicate in the office of the county auditor.

7. <u>Representations and Warranties</u>. Buyer acknowledges that Seller is conveying the real estate, and included property, in an "AS IS" condition. Seller represents to Buyer that: (1) the Premises are not located in a historic district; (2) there are no home owner associations regarding the Premises; (3) the Premises are not currently designated to be located in a flood plain; and (4) there are no special assessments pending for certification other than assessments of record and appearing on the Auditor's tax duplicate, if any. Otherwise, Seller makes no representations or warranties to Buyer regarding the condition, character or intended use of the premises.

Buyer acknowledges receipt of a completed Ohio Real Property Disclosure form at least three (3) days prior to the execution of this Contract and finds no exceptions or objections. Seller makes no other representations or warranties of any other kind regarding the Premises, including but not limited to, matters relating to habitability, zoning, water and sewers, development of the land, construction of buildings, and the use or intended use of the Premises by Buyer. Further, any approvals, inspections, permits, licenses and/or certificates regarding the development, habitability, zoning, sewer, and/or use or intended use of the Premises shall be the sole responsibility of the Buyer.

8. <u>Time of the Essence</u>. Time is of the essence in all terms and conditions of this contract.

9. <u>Insurance</u>. All risk of loss or damage to the Premises after the date of closing shall be the sole responsibility of Buyer.

10. <u>Miscellaneous</u>. Seller agrees that at the time of transfer of title, the above-described real estate, and all items thereof, will be in the same condition as on the date of this contract, reasonable wear and tear excepted. This contract comprises the entire agreement between Seller and Buyer, and it is agreed that no other representations or agreement have been made or relied upon.

This contract constitutes a binding contract upon the parties, their heirs, personal representatives, executors, administrators and assigns.

This contract has been prepared by Seller's attorney, xxx. The Buyer should seek independent legal counsel and review if the Buyer has any questions or concerns regarding Buyer's rights and obligations hereunder.

_____

xxx—Seller

_____

xxx—Seller

_____

xxx—Buyer

_____

xxx—Buyer

Appendix C

Sketching Metes and Bounds Descriptions

A description of a tract of land always starts at a given point called the point of beginning (POB). The outline of the tract is then followed by using certain directions and measurements until you come back to the POB. It is important to remember that in using metes and bounds you must always start from the POB and follow the defined boundary lines until you come back to the POB.

Metes and Bounds Descriptions always have two parts—a direction and a distance, such as "North 30° East 200 feet." First, we should look at the direction part. "North 30° East" means that the direction of the boundary is 30° toward East from due North. (Directions are always East or West from either North or South.) See the figure below:

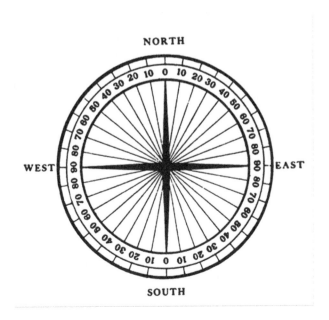

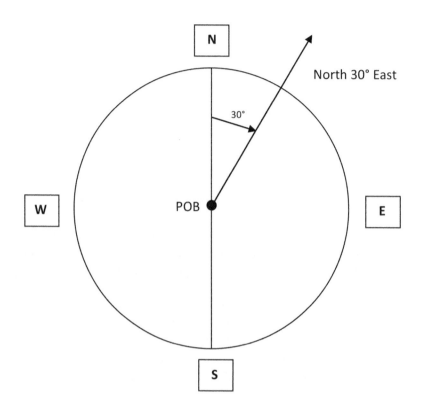

To plot North 30° East from the POB, make a dot on your paper to represent the POB. Then place the center dot of your protractor on the POB, with the protractor on the right (east) side, and the straight edge running vertically (north and south). Then, make a dot on your paper next to the 30° mark on your protractor.

Now, you need to draw the border from POB dot toward dot you just made at the 30° using your ruler. The length of this border is 200 feet (North 30° East 200 feet). Since you can't draw a 200 foot line, you will need to draw it to some scale. For our projects, you can use 1 inch to represent 100 feet. Thus, your 200 foot border will require a line 2 inches long. Draw a dot at the 2 inch mark to represent the corner of the tract. Finally, draw a straight line from the POB to the dot representing the corner. Be careful not to use the dot you placed that represented the direction.

Then, repeat the process by placing your protractor on the dot representing the end of the border, and sketch the next direction and length. Keep doing this until you return to the POB.

Remember to keep the straight edge of your protractor running north and south. Also, be sure to place your protractor on the left side for directions that include east. Measure angles from either North or South as the directions call for.

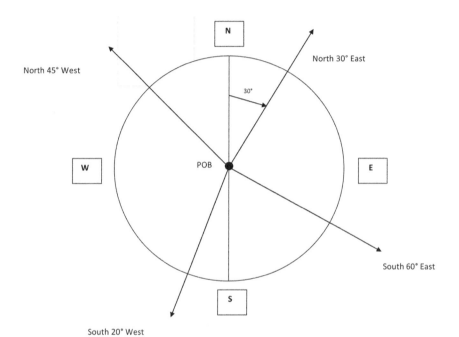

Appendix D

Sample Deed

QUIT CLAIM DEED

William H. Babson, an unmarried man, for valuable consideration paid, hereby quit claims to Donald Jones II (an unmarried man) and Angela Brown (an unmarried woman), for their joint lives, remainder to the survivor of them, whose tax mailing address is 1694 Montclair Avenue, Cincinnati, Ohio 45214, all of his right title and interest in the following described Real Property:

> Situated in the City of Cincinnati, Hamilton County, Ohio and being known and designated as Lot Number One Hundred Seventy Four (174) on the plat of lots made by Joseph A. James and recorded in the Records of Plats of Hamilton County, Ohio in Deed Book 151, Page 415. Said Lot No. 174 being twenty (20) feet in front on Montclair Street and extends back one hundred (100) feet in depth.
>
> Prior instrument reference: Official Records Book 4340 Page 593 of the Deed Records of Hamilton County, Ohio

IN WITNESS WHEREOF, William H. Babson sets his hand hereto this 6th Day of June, 2007.

_____
William H. Babson

STATE OF OHIO   )
) ss.
COUNTY OF HAMILTON   )

The foregoing instrument was personally acknowledged before me this 6th Day of June, 2007, by William H. Babson, who acknowledged the signing of the same to be his voluntary act and deed, for the uses and purposes therein mentioned.

IN TESTIMONY WHEREOF, I have hereunto subscribed my name and affixed my official seal.

_____

Notary Public

This instrument was prepared by:
Wm. Bruce Davis
Attorney-at-Law
2400 Clermont College Drive
Batavia, OH 45103
513-732-5305

Appendix E

Transfer Tax Exemptions

DTE Form 100 (EX)

Rev. 11/12
S.C. Date 12/12

STATEMENT OF REASON FOR EXEMPTION FROM REAL PROPERTY CONVEYANCE FEE

Revised Code Sec. 319.202 and 319.54 (G)(3)

SEE INSTRUCTIONS ON REVERSE SIDE

TYPE OR PRINT ALL INFORMATION WITH BLUE OR BLACK INK

FOR COUNTY AUDITOR'S USE ONLY   Date _____ Co. No. _____77_____ Number _____

Instr _____ Tax Dist. No. _____ Land _____ Bldg. _____ Tot. _____

D.T.E. CODE NO. _____ _____ Split/New Plat   #OF PARCELS _____

PARCEL AND ROUTING NOS.

FOLLOWING MUST BE COMPLETED BY GRANTEE OR HIS/HER REPRESENTATIVE

1. Grantor's Name _____ Phone Number _____

2. Grantee's Name _____ Phone Number _____

2a. Grantee's Address _____

3. Address of Property_____

4. Tax Billing Address _____

5. No conveyance fees shall be charged because the real property is transferred:

____ a. To or from the United States, this state, or any instrumentality, agency, or political subdivision of the United States or this State;

____ b. Solely in order to provide or release security for a debt or obligation;

____ c. To confirm or correct a deed previously executed and recorded;

____ d. To evidence a gift, in any form, between husband and wife, or parent and child or the spouse of either;

____ e. On sale for delinquent taxes or assessments;

____ f. Pursuant to court order, to the extent that such transfer is not the result of a sale effected or completed pursuant such order - Court Case Number _____

____ g. Pursuant to a reorganization of corporations or unincorporated associations or pursuant to the dissolution of a corporation to the extent that the corporation conveys the property to a stockholder as a distribution in kind of the corporation's assets in exchange for the stockholder's shares in the dissolved corporation;

____ h. By a subsidiary corporation to its parent corporation for no consideration, nominal consideration, or in sole consideration of the cancellation or surrender of the subsidiary's stock;

____ i. By lease, whether or not it extends to mineral or mineral rights, unless the lease is for a term of years renewable forever;

____ j. When the value of the real property or interest in real property conveyed does not exceed one hundred dollars;

____ k. Of an occupied residential property being transferred to the builder of a new residence when the former residence is traded as part of the consideration for the new residence;

____ l. To a grantee other than a dealer in real property, solely for the purpose of and as a step in, its prompt sale to others;

____ m. To or from a person when no money or other valuable and tangible consideration readily convertible into money is paid or to be paid for the real estate and the transaction is not a gift;

____ n. To an heir or devisee, between spouses or to a surviving spouse, from a person to himself and others, to a surviving tenant, or on the death of a registered owner;

____ o. To a trustee acting on behalf of minor children of the deceased;

____ p. Of an easement or right-of-way when the value of the interest conveyed does not exceed one thousand dollars;

____ q. Of property sold to a surviving spouse pursuant to section 2106.16 of the Revised Code;

____ r. To or from an organization exempt from federal income taxation under section 501(c)(3) of the Internal Revenue Code, provided such transfer is without consideration and is in furtherance of the charitable or public purpose of such organization;

____ s. Among the heirs at law or devisees, including a surviving spouse of a common decedent, when no consideration in money is paid or to be paid for the real property;

____ t. To a trustee of a trust, when the grantor of the trust has reserved an unlimited power to revoke the trust;

____ u. To the grantor of a trust by a trustee of the trust, when the transfer is made to the grantor pursuant to the exercise of the grantor's power to revoke the trust or to withdraw trust assets;

____ v. To the beneficiaries of a trust if the fee was paid on the transfer from the grantor of the trust to the trustee or pursuant to trust provisions that became irrevocable at the death of the grantor;

____ w. To a corporation for incorporation into a sports facility constructed pursuant to section 307.696 [307.69.6] of the Revised Code.

____ x. between persons pursuant to R.C. section 5302.18.

____ y. from a county land reutilization corporation organized under R.C. section 1724 third party.

6. Has the grantor indicated that this property is entitled to receive the senior citizen, disabled person, or surviving spouse homestead exemption for the preceding or current tax year? ☐Yes ☐No.   If yes, complete DTE Form 101.

7. Has the grantor indicated that this property is qualified for current agricultural use valuation for the preceding or current tax year? ☐Yes ☐No.   If yes, complete DTE Form 102.

8. Application for owner-occupancy (2.5% on qualified levies) reduction. (Notice: Failure to complete this application prohibits the owner from receiving this reduction until another proper and timely application is filed.) Will this property be grantee's principal residence by Jan. 1 of next year? ☐Yes ☐No   If yes, is the property a multi-unit dwelling?   ☐Yes ☐No

I declare under penalties of perjury that this statement has been examined by me and to the best of my knowledge and belief is a true, correct, and complete statement.

_____
SIGNATURE OF GRANTEE OR REPRESENTATIVE/DATE

INSTRUCTIONS TO GRANTEE OR REPRESENTATIVE FOR COMPLETING STATEMENT OF REASON FOR EXEMPTION FROM REAL PROPERTY CONVEYANCE FEE, DTE FORM (100)EX

COMPLETE LINES 1 THRU 8 ONLY

WARNING: ALL QUESTIONS MUST BE COMPLETED TO THE BEST OF YOUR KNOWLEDGE TO COMPLY WITH OHIO REVISED CODE SECTION 319.202. PERSONS WILLFULLY FAILING TO COMPLY OR FALSIFYING INFORMATION ARE GUILTY OF A MISDEMEANOR OF THE FIRST DEGREE (O.R.C. SECTION 319.99(B)).

LINE 1   List grantor's name as shown in the deed or other instrument conveying this real property.

LINE 2, 2a   List grantee's name as shown in the deed or other instrument conveying this real property and the grantee's mailing address.

LINE 3   List address of property conveyed by street number and street.

LINE 4   List complete name and address to which tax bills are to be sent. CAUTION: EACH PROPERTY OWNER IS RESPONSIBLE FOR PAYING THE PROPERTY TAXES ON TIME EVEN IF NO TAX BILL IS RECEIVED.

LINE 5   Check one of the exemptions (a) – (w), as appropriate. Keep in mind that a county auditor may inspect any and all documents in connection with the submission of a conveyance to determine whether the transfer is entitled to exemption. The auditor may exercise that discretionary power by requiring additional information in the form of affidavits, deeds, trust documents, purchase agreements, closing statements, court orders, resolutions from corporate boards of directors, articles of incorporation, Internal Revenue Service exemption certificates, or in any other form deemed necessary by the auditor that sufficiently substantiates the claim for exemption.

LINE 6   If the grantor has indicated that the property to be conveyed will receive the senior citizen, disabled person or surviving spouse homestead exemption for the proceeding or current tax year under O.R.C. section 323.152(A), grantor must complete DTE Form 101 or submit a statement which complies with the provisions of O.R.C. 319.202(A)(2), and the grantee must submit such form to the county auditor along with this statement.

LINE 7   If the grantor has indicated that the property to be conveyed was qualified for current agricultural use valuation for the preceding or current tax year under O.R.C. section 5713.30, the grantor must complete DTE Form 102 or a statement that complies with O.R.C. section 319.202(B)(2), and the grantee must submit such form to the county auditor alone with this statement.

LINE 8   Complete line 8 (Application For 2 ½% Reduction) only if the parcel is used for residential purposes. To receive the 2-½% homestead tax reduction for the next year, you must own and occupy your home as your principal place of residence (domicile) on January 1 of that year. A homeowner and spouse may receive this reduction on only one home in Ohio. Failure to complete this application prohibits the owner from receiving this reduction until another proper and timely application is filed.

Appendix F

Promissory Note

PROMISSORY NOTE

$120,000.00   March 5, 2016

1. BORROWER'S PROMISE TO PAY

In return for a loan that I have received, I promise to pay U.S. $ 120,000.00 (this amount is called "principal"), plus interest, to the order of the Lender. The Lender is **Laverne Lender**. I understand that the Lender may transfer this Note. The Lender or anyone who takes this Note by transfer and who is entitled to receive payments under this Note is called the "Note Holder".

2. INTEREST

Interest will be charged on unpaid principal until the full amount of principal has been paid. I will pay interest at a yearly rate of **4.25 %**.

The interest rate required by this Section 2 is the rate I will pay both before and after any default described in Section 6(B) of this Note.

3. PAYMENTS

(A) Time and Place of Payments
I will pay principal and interest by making payments every month.

I will make my monthly payments on the **1st** day of each month beginning on **April 1, 2016** I will make these payments every month until I have paid all of the principal and interest and any other charges described below that I may owe under this Note. My monthly payments will be applied to interest before principal. If, on **March 1 2046**, I still owe amounts under this Note, I will pay those amounts in full on that date, which is called the "maturity date".

I will make my monthly payments at **1123 Bank Street, Cashville, Ohio 45112** or at a different place if required by the Note Holder

(B) Amount of Monthly Payments

My initial monthly payment will be in the amount of U.S. $ **590.33** plus other monies payable monthly as described in the mortgage instrument.

4. BORROWER'S RIGHT TO PREPAY

I have the right to make payments of principal at any time before they are due. A payment of principal only is known as a "prepayment."

When I make a prepayment, I will tell the Note Holder in writing that I am doing so.

I may make a full prepayment or partial prepayments without paying any prepayment charge. The Note Holder will use all of my prepayments to reduce the amount of principal that I owe under this Note. If I make a partial prepayment, there will be no changes in the due date or in the amount of my monthly payment unless the Note Holder agrees in writing to those changes.

5. LOAN CHARGES

If a law, which applies to this loan and which sets maximum loan charges, is finally interpreted so that the interest or other loan charges collected or to be collected in connection with this loan exceed the permitted limits, then: (i) any such loan charge shall be reduced by the amount necessary to reduce the charge to the permitted limit; and (ii) any sums already collected from me/us which exceeded permitted limits will be refunded to me/us. The Note Holder may choose to make this refund by reducing the principal I owe under this Note or by making a direct payment to me/us. If a refund reduces principal, the reduction will be treated as a partial prepayment.

6. BORROWER'S FAILURE TO PAY AS REQUIRED

(A) Late Charge for Overdue Payments

If the Note Holder has not received the full amount of any monthly payment within **five (5)** calendar days after the date it is due, I will pay a late charge to the Note Holder. The amount of the charge will be **five percent**

(5%) of my overdue payment of principal and interest. I will pay this late charge promptly but only once on each late payment. This late charge is to compensate the Note Holder for their inconvenience and is not to be considered additional interest.

(B) Default

If I do not pay the full amount of each monthly payment within 25 days of the date it is due, I will be in default.

(C) Notice of Default

If I am in default, the Note Holder may, but is not required to, send me/us a written notice telling me/us that if I do not pay the overdue amount by a certain date, the Note Holder may require me/us to pay immediately the full amount of principal which has not been paid and all the interest that I owe on that amount.

(D) No Waiver by Note Holder

Even if, at a time when I am in default, the Note Holder does not require me/us to pay immediately in full as described above, the Note Holder will still have the right to do so if I am in default at a later time.

(E) Payment of Note Holder's Costs and Expenses

If the Note Holder has required me/us to pay immediately in full as described above, the Note Holder will have the right to be paid back by me/us for all of its costs and expenses in enforcing this Note to the extent not prohibited by applicable law. Those expenses include, for example, reasonable attorneys' fees.

7. GIVING OF NOTICES

Unless applicable law requires a different method, any notice that must be given to me/us under this Note will be given by delivering it or by mailing it by first class mail to me/us at the Property Address above or at a different address if I give the Note Holder a notice of my different address.

Any notice that must be given to the Note Holder under this Note will be given by mailing it by first class mail to the Note Holder at the address stated in Section 3(A) above or at a different address if I am given a notice of that different address.

8. OBLIGATIONS OF PERSONS UNDER THIS NOTE

If more than one person signs this Note, each person is fully and personally obligated to keep all of the promises made in this Note, including the promise to pay the full amount owed. Any person who is a guarantor, surety or endorser of this Note is also obligated to do these things. Any person who takes over these obligations, including the obligations of a guarantor, surety or endorser of this Note, is also obligated to keep all of the promises made in this Note. The Note Holder may enforce its rights under this Note against each person individually or against all of us together. This means that any one of us may be required to pay all of the amounts owed under this Note.

9. WAIVERS

I and any other persons who has obligations under this Note waive the rights of presentment and notice of dishonor. "Presentment" means the right to require the Note Holder to demand payment of amounts due. "Notice of dishonor" means the right to require the Note Holder to give notice to other persons that amounts due have not been paid.

10. SECURED NOTE

In addition to the protections given to the Note Holder under this Note, a Mortgage, (the "Instrument"), dated the same date as this Note, protects the Note Holder from possible losses which might result if I do not keep the promises which I make in this Note. That Instrument describes how and under what conditions I may be required to make immediate payment in full of all amounts I owe under this Note.

Some of those conditions are described as follows:

If all or any part of the Property or any interest in it is sold or transferred (or if a beneficial interest in Borrower is sold or transferred and Borrower is not a natural person) without Lender's prior written consent, Lender may, at its option, require immediate payment in full of all sums secured by this Instrument. However, this option shall not be exercised by Lender if exercise is prohibited by federal law as of the date of this Instrument.

If Lender exercises this option, Lender shall give Borrower notice of acceleration. The notice shall provide a period of not less than 30 days from the date the notice is delivered or mailed within which Borrower must pay all sums secured by this Instrument. If Borrower fails to pay these sums prior to the expiration of this period, Lender may invoke any remedies permitted by this Instrument without further notice or demand on Borrower.

Signed, sealed and delivered in the presence of:

Witness

_____

Wanda Witness

Borrower

_____

Betty Borrower

Appendix G

Mortgage

MORTGAGE

THIS MORTGAGE ("Instrument"), is made March 5, 2016 between the Mortgagor, **Betty Borrower**, ("Borrower"), and the Mortgagee, **Laverne Lender**, whose address is **1123 Bank Street, Cashville, Ohio 45112** ("Lender").

Whereas, Borrower is indebted to Lender in the principal sum of **one hundred twenty thousand dollars ($120,000.00)**, which indebtedness is evidenced by Borrower's note of even date herewith ("Note"), providing for monthly installments of principal and interest.

To secure to Lender (a) the repayment of the indebtedness evidenced by the Note, with interest thereon, and all renewals, extensions and modifications thereof; (b) the repayment of any future advances, with interest thereon, made by Lender to Borrower ("Future Advances"); (c) the payment of all other sums, with interest thereon, advanced in accordance herewith to protect the security of this Instrument; and (d) the performance of the covenants and agreements of Borrower herein contained, Borrower does hereby mortgage, grant, convey and assign to Lender the following described property located in **Grant County, Ohio:**

Lot 23 of Super Subdivision #3, Block B, as recorded in Plat Book D, Page 142 of the Plat Records of Grant County, Ohio.

Which has the address of **723 Circle Drive, Hillsdale, Ohio 45138**, ("Property Address").

TOGETHER with all buildings, improvements, hereditaments, appurtenances and tenements now or hereafter erected on the property, and all heretofore or hereafter vacated alleys and streets abutting the property, and all easements, rights, appurtenances, rents, royalties, mineral, oil and gas rights and profits ("Property").

Borrower covenants that Borrower is lawfully seized of the estate hereby conveyed and has the right to mortgage, grant, convey and assign the Property that the property is unencumbered and that Borrower will warrant and defend generally the title to the Property against all claims and demands, subject to any easements and restrictions listed in a schedule of exceptions to coverage in any title insurance policy insuring Lender's interest in the Property.

Borrower and Lender covenant and agree as follows:

1. PAYMENT OF PRINCIPAL AND INTEREST. Borrower shall promptly pay when due the principal of and interest on the indebtedness evidenced by the Note, any prepayment and late charges provided in the Note and all other sums secured by this Instrument. In the event the agreed payment is less than the interest due then the excess unpaid interest shall be added to the principal.

2. FUNDS FOR TAXES, INSURANCE AND OTHER CHARGES. Borrower shall pay to Lender on the day monthly installments of principal or interest are payable under the Note, until the Note is paid in full, a sum ("Funds") equal to one-twelfth of (a) the yearly water and sewer rates and taxes and assessments which may be levied on the Property, (b) the yearly ground rents, if any, (c) the yearly premium installments for fire and other hazard insurance, rent loss insurance and such other insurance covering the Property as Lender may require this Instrument, all as reasonably estimated initially and from time to time by Lender on the basis of assessments and bills and reasonable estimates thereof.

The Funds shall be held in an institution the deposits or accounts of which are insured or guaranteed by a Federal or state agency. Lender shall apply the Funds to pay said rates, rents, taxes, assessments, and insurance premiums so long as Borrower is not in breach of any covenant or agreement of Borrower in this Instrument. Lender shall not be required to pay Borrower any interest on the Funds. Lender shall give to Borrower, without charge, an annual accounting of the Funds in Lender's normal format showing credits and debits to the Funds and the purpose for which each debit to the Funds was made. The Funds are pledged as additional security for the sums secured by this Instrument. If at any time the amount of the Funds held by Lender shall be less than the amount deemed necessary by Lender to pay water and sewer rates, taxes, assessments and insurance premiums as they fall due, Borrower shall pay to Lender any amount necessary to make up the deficiency within 30 days after notice from Lender to Borrower requesting payment thereof.

Upon Borrower's breach of any covenant or agreement of Borrower in this Instrument, Lender may apply, in any amount and in any order as Lender shall determine in Lender's sole discretion, any Funds held by Lender at the time of application (i) to pay rates, taxes, assessments and insurance premiums which are now or will hereafter become due, or (ii) as a credit against sums secured by this Instrument.

Upon payment in full of all sums secured by this Instrument, Lender shall promptly refund to Borrower any Funds held by Lender.

3. APPLICATION OF PAYMENTS. Unless applicable law provides otherwise, all payments received by Lender from Borrower under the Note or this instrument shall be applied by Lender in the following order of priority: (i) amounts payable to Lender by Borrower; (ii) interest payable on the Note; (iii) principal of the Note; (iv) interest payable on advances; (v) principal of advances made; (vi) interest payable on any Future Advance, provided that if more than one Future Advance is outstanding, Lender may apply payments received among the amounts of interest payable on the Future Advances in such order as Lender, in Lender's sole discretion, may determine; (vii) principal of any Future Advance, provided that if more than one Future Advance is outstanding, Lender may apply payments received among the principal balances of the Future Advances in such order as Lender, in Lender's sole discretion, may determine; and (viii) any other sums secured by this Instrument in such order as Lender, at Lender's option, may determine.

4. CHARGES; LIENS. Borrower shall pay, when due, the claims of all persons supplying labor or materials to or in connection with the Property. Without Lender's prior written permission, Borrower shall not allow any lien inferior to this Instrument to be perfected against the Property.

5. HAZARD INSURANCE. Borrower shall keep the improvements now existing or hereafter erected on the Property insured by carriers at all times satisfactory to Lender against loss by fire, hazards included within the term

"extended coverage", rent loss and such other hazards, casualties, liabilities and contingencies as Lender shall require and in such amounts and for such periods as Lender shall require. All premiums on insurance policies shall be paid in the manner provided herein. All insurance policies and renewals thereof shall be in a form acceptable to Lender and shall include a standard mortgage clause in favor of and in form acceptable to Lender. Lender shall have the right to hold the policies, and Borrower shall promptly furnish to Lender all renewal notices and all receipts of paid premiums. At least thirty days prior to the expiration date of a policy, Borrower shall deliver to Lender a renewal policy in form satisfactory to Lender. In the event of loss, Borrower shall give immediate written notice to the insurance carrier and to Lender. Borrower hereby authorizes and empowers Lender as attorney-in-fact for Borrower to make proof of loss, to adjust and compromise any claim under insurance policies, to appear in and prosecute any action arising from such insurance policies, to collect and receive insurance proceeds, and to deduct therefrom Lender's expenses incurred in the collection of such proceeds; provided however, that nothing contained in this section shall require Lender to incur any expense or take any action hereunder. Borrower further authorizes Lender to apply the balance of such proceeds to the payment of the sums secured by this Instrument, whether or not then due, in the order of application set forth herein accounting to the mortgagor for any surplus. In the event the mortgagor does not renew the insurance policy then mortgagee may obtain loss payee insurance coverage only, which cost shall be payable by the mortgagor. Failure to reimburse the mortgagee for the cost of this policy within 30 calendar days after being mailed a bill for it shall constitute default under the mortgage.

If the insurance proceeds are applied to the payment of the sums secured by this Instrument, any such application of proceeds to principal shall not extend or postpone the due dates of the monthly installments or change the amounts of such installments. If the Property is sold or if Lender acquires title to the property, Lender shall have all of the right, title and interest of Borrower in and to such insurance policies and unearned premiums thereon and to the proceeds resulting from any damage to the Property prior to such sale and acquisition.

6. PRESERVATION AND MAINTENANCE OF PROPERTY Borrower (a) shall not commit waste or permit impairment or deterioration of the Property, (b) shall not abandon the Property, (c) shall restore or repair promptly and in a good and workmanlike manner all or any part of the Property to the equivalent of its original condition, or such other condition as Lender may approve

in writing, in the event of any damage, injury or loss thereto, whether or not insurance proceeds are available to cover in whole or in part the costs of such restoration or repair, (d) shall keep the Property, including improvements, fixtures, equipment, machinery and appliances thereon in good repair and shall replace fixtures, equipment, machinery and appliances on the Property when necessary to keep such items in good repair, (e) shall comply with all laws, ordinances, regulations and requirements of any governmental body applicable to the Property, and (f) shall give notice in writing to Lender of and, unless otherwise directed in writing by Lender, appear in and defend any action or proceeding purporting to affect the Property, the security of this Instrument or the rights or powers of Lender.

7. USE OF PROPERTY. Property may be used only for purposes permitted by law.

8. PROTECTION OF LENDER'S SECURITY. If Borrower fails to perform the covenants and agreements contained in this instrument, or if any action or proceeding is commenced which affects the Property or title thereto or the interest of Lender therein, including, but not limited to, eminent domain, insolvency, code enforcement, or arrangements or proceedings involving a bankrupt or decedent, then Lender at Lender's option may make such appearances, disburse such sums and take such action as Lender deems necessary, in its sole discretion to protect Lender's interest, including, but not limited to, (i) disbursement of attorney's fees, (ii) entry upon the Property to make repairs, (iii) procurement of satisfactory insurance as provided herein and may also (iv) declare all of the sums secured by this Instrument to be immediately due and payable without prior notice to Borrower, and Lender may invoke any remedies permitted by this Instrument.

Any amounts disbursed by Lender pursuant to this section, with interest thereon at the rate stated in the Note, shall become additional indebtedness of Borrower secured by this Instrument.

9. INSPECTION. Lender may make or cause to be made reasonable entries upon and inspections of the Property.

10. CONDEMNATION. Borrower shall promptly notify Lender of any action or proceeding relating to any condemnation or other taking, whether direct or indirect, of the Property, or part thereof, and Borrower shall appear in and

prosecute any such action or proceeding unless otherwise directed by Lender in writing. Borrower authorizes Lender, at Lender's option, as attorney-in-fact for Borrower, to commence, appear in and prosecute, in Lender's or Borrower's name, any action or proceeding relating to any condemnation or other taking of the Property, whether direct or indirect, and to settle or compromise any claim in connection with such condemnation or other taking. The proceeds of any award, payment or claim for damages, direct or consequential, in connection with any condemnation or other taking, whether direct or indirect, of the Property, or part thereof, or for conveyances in lieu of condemnation, are hereby assigned to and shall be paid to Lender.

Borrower authorizes Lender to apply such awards, payments, proceeds or damages, after the deduction of Lender's expenses incurred in the collection of such amounts, to payment of the sums secured by this Instrument, whether or not then due, in the order of application set forth herein, with the balance, if any, to Borrower. Unless Borrower and Lender otherwise agree in writing, any application of proceeds to principal shall not extend or postpone the due date of the monthly installments or change the amount of such installments. Borrower agrees to execute such further evidence of assignment of any awards, proceeds, damages or claims arising in connection with such condemnation or taking as lender may require.

11. BORROWER AND LIEN NOT RELEASED. From time to time, Lender may, at Lender's option, without giving notice to or obtaining the consent of Borrower, Borrower's successors or assigns or of any junior lienholder or guarantors, without liability on Lender's part and notwithstanding Borrower's breach of any covenant or agreement of Borrower in this Instrument, extend the time for payment of said indebtedness or any part thereof, reduce the payments thereon, release anyone liable on any of said indebtedness, accept a renewal note or notes therefor, modify the terms and time of payment of said indebtedness, release from the lien of this Instrument any part of the Property, take or release other or additional security, reconvey any part of the Property, consent to any map or plan of the Property, consent to the granting of any easement, join in any extension or subordination agreement, and agree in writing with Borrower to modify the rate of interest or period of amortization of the Note or change the amount of the monthly installments payable thereunder. Any actions taken by Lender pursuant to the terms of this section shall not affect the obligation of Borrower or Borrower's successors or assigns to pay the sums secured by this Instrument and to observe the covenants of Bor-

rower contained herein, shall not affect the guaranty of any person, corporation, partnership or other entity for payment of the indebtedness secured hereby, and shall not affect the lien or priority of lien hereof on the Property. Borrower shall pay Lender a reasonable service charge, together with such title insurance premiums and attorney's fees as may be incurred at Lender's option, for any such action if taken at Borrower's request.

12. FORBEARANCE BY LENDER NOT A WAIVER. Any forbearance by Lender in exercising any right or remedy hereunder, or otherwise afforded by applicable law, shall not be a waiver of or preclude the exercise of any right or remedy. The procurement of insurance or the payment of taxes or other liens or charges by Lender shall not be a waiver of Lender's right to accelerate the maturity of the indebtedness secured by this Instrument.

13. REMEDIES CUMULATIVE. Each remedy provided in this instrument is distinct and cumulative to all other rights or remedies under this Instrument, or afforded by law or equity and may be exercised concurrently, independently, or successively, in any order whatsoever.

14. ACCELERATION IN CASE OF BORROWER'S INSOLVENCY. If Borrower shall voluntarily file a petition under the Federal Bankruptcy Act, as such Act may from time to time be amended, or under any similar or successor Federal statue relating to bankruptcy, insolvency, arrangements or reorganizations, or under any state bankruptcy or insolvency act, or file an answer in an involuntary proceeding admitting insolvency or inability to pay debts, or if Borrower shall fail to obtain a vacation or stay of involuntary proceedings brought for the reorganization, dissolution or liquidation of Borrower, or if Borrower shall be adjudged a bankrupt, or if a trustee or receiver shall be appointed for Borrower or Borrower's property, or if the Property shall become subject to the jurisdiction of a Federal bankruptcy court or similar state court, or if Borrower shall make an assignment for the benefit of Borrower's creditors, or if there is an attachment, execution or other judicial seizure of any portion of Borrower's assets and such seizure is not discharged within ten days, then Lender may, at Lender's option, declare all of the sums secured by this Instrument to be immediately due and payable without prior notice to Borrower, and Lender may invoke any remedies permitted by this Instrument. Any attorney's fees and other expenses incurred by Lender in connection with Borrower's bankruptcy or any of the other aforesaid events shall be additional indebtedness of Borrower secured by this Instrument.

15. TRANSFERS OF THE PROPERTY OR BENEFICIAL INTERESTS IN BOR-ROWER; ASSUMPTION. On sale or transfer of (i) all or any part of the Property, or any interest therein, or (ii) beneficial interests in Borrower (if Borrower is not a natural person or persons but is a corporation, partnership, trust or other legal entity), Lender may, at Lender's option, declare all of the sums secured by this Instrument to be immediately due and payable, and Lender may invoke any remedies permitted by this Instrument.

16. NOTICE. Except for any notice required under applicable law to be given in another manner, (a) any notice to Borrower provided for in this Instrument or in the Note shall be given by mailing such notice by first class mail addressed to Borrower at Borrower's address stated below or at such other address as Borrower may designate by notice to Lender as provided herein, and (b) any notice to Lender shall be given by certified mail, return receipt requested, to Lender's address stated herein or to such other address as Lender may designate by notice to Borrower as provided herein. Any notice provided for in this Instrument or in the Note shall be deemed to have been given to Borrower or Lender when given in the manner designated herein.

17. SUCCESSORS AND ASSIGNS BOUND; JOINT AND SEVERAL LIA-BILITY; AGENTS; CAPTIONS. The covenants and agreements herein contained shall bind, and the rights hereunder shall inure to, the respective successors and assigns of Lender and Borrower, subject to the provisions hereof. All covenants and agreements of Borrower shall be joint and several. In exercising any rights here under or taking any actions provided for herein, Lender may act through its employees, agents or independent contractors as authorized by Lender. The captions and headings in this Instrument are for convenience only and are not to be used to interpret or define the provisions hereof.

18. GOVERNING LAW; SEVERABILITY. This Instrument shall be governed by the laws of the State of Ohio, without respect to choice of law provisions. In the event that any provision of this Instrument or the Note conflicts with applicable law, such conflict shall not affect other provisions of this Instrument or the Note which can be given effect without the conflicting provisions, and to this end the provisions of this Instrument and the Note are declared to be severable.

19. ACCELERATION; REMEDIES. Upon Borrower's breach of any covenant or agreement of Borrower in this instrument, including, but not limited to, the covenants to pay when due any sums secured by this Instrument, Lender at Lender's option may declare all of the sums secured by this Instrument to be immediately due and payable without further demand and may foreclose this Instrument by judicial proceeding and may invoke any other remedies permitted by applicable law or provided herein. Lender shall be entitled to collect all costs and expenses incurred in pursuing such remedies, including, but not limited to, attorney's fees, and costs of documentary evidence, abstracts and title reports.

20. RELEASE. Upon payment of all sums secured by this Instrument, Lender shall release this Instrument. Borrower shall pay Lender's reasonable costs incurred in releasing this Instrument.

21. ATTORNEY'S FEES. As used in this instrument and in the Note, "attorney's fees" shall include attorney's fees, if any, which may be awarded by an appellate court.

22. RIDERS TO THIS INSTRUMENT. If one or more riders are executed by borrower and recorded together with this Instrument, the covenants and agreements of each such rider shall be incorporated into and shall amend and supplement the covenants and agreements of this instrument as if riders were a part of this Instrument.

23. HAZARDOUS SUBSTANCES. Borrower shall not cause or permit the presence, use, disposal, storage or release of any Hazardous Substances on or in the Property. Borrower shall not do, or allow anyone else to do, anything affecting the Property that is in violation of any Environmental Law. The preceding two sentences shall not apply to the presence, use or storage on the Property of small quantity of Hazardous Substances that are generally recognized to be appropriate to normal residential uses and to maintenance of the Property.

Borrower shall immediately give Lender written notice of any investigation, claim, demand lawsuit or other action by any governmental or regulatory agency or private party involving the Property and any Hazardous Substance or Environmental Law of which Borrower has actual knowledge. If Borrower learns, or is notified by any governmental or regulatory authority, that any removal or other remediation of any Hazardous Substance affecting the Property is necessary, Borrower hall promptly take all necessary remedial actions in accordance with Environmental Law.

As used in this Instrument, "Hazardous Substances" are those substances defined as toxic or hazardous substances by Environmental Law and the following substances: gasoline, kerosene, other flammable or toxic petroleum products, toxic pesticides and herbicides, volatile solvents, materials containing asbestos or formaldehyde, and radioactive materials. As used in this Instrument "Environmental Law" means federal laws and laws of the jurisdiction where the property is located that relate to health, safety and environmental protection.

In Witness Whereof, Borrower has executed this Instrument or has caused the same to be executed by its representatives thereunto duly authorized.

Signed, sealed and delivered in the presence of:

Witness

_____

Wanda Witness

Borrower

_____

Betty Borrower

STATE OF OHIO   }
                       } ss:
COUNTY OF GRANT   }

I hereby certify that on this day, before me, an officer duly authorized in the state aforesaid and in the county aforesaid to take acknowledgements personally appeared **Betty Borrower** to me known to be the person described or who identified herself to be the persons described by means of an Ohio driver's license and who executed the foregoing instrument and acknowledged before me that she executed the same for the purpose expressed.

Witness my hand and official seal in the county and state aforesaid this _____day of _____ 20____

_____

Notary Public
My Commission Expires_____

(Seal)

Appendix H

Fair Housing Statutes

The only color you can discriminate on is green (money).

	Civil Rights Act of 1866 (§ 1982)	Federal Fair Housing Title VIII (Civil Rights Act of 1968)	Ohio Civil Rights Act
Prohibits Discrimination based on	Race, ancestry, color	Race, color, religion, gender, national origin, disability, marital status, familial status[1]	Race, color, religion, gender, national origin, marital status, familial status,[2] ancestry, disability
Applies to	Residential, commercial, and unimproved land	Residential and unimproved land to be used for residential construction	Residential and unimproved land
Enforced in	Federal courts only	Federal or state courts	Federal or state courts
Statute of Limitations	One year	One year to make administrative filing with HUD; two years to file in court	One year
Exemptions[3]	None	Single family residential sales by owner without broker,[4] religions,[5] private clubs,[6] owner occupied exemption[7]	Religions, private clubs

1. Families that include children under 18 or pregnant women (but exception for senior housing).

2. Families that include children under 18 or pregnant women (but exception for senior housing).

3. Exemptions do not apply to advertising, for example, Mrs. Murphy could not ad-

vertise that units were not available to people of a certain race.

4. Must own no more than three houses, if owner is not most recent occupant, this exemption can be used only once every 24 months.

5. Property owned by religions can limit occupancy to members of that religion.

6. Property owned by private clubs can give preference to members of that club, so long as lodging is not open to the general public.

7. Residence has four or fewer units and owner lives in one of the units, sometimes called the "Mrs. Murphy" exemption.

Glossary

Abandoned easement (Chapter 2)—One way to terminate an easement, in which the easement holder has discontinued use of the easement and intends to never use it again.

Acceleration clause (Chapter 12)—A clause in a promissory note that causes the entire balance of the loan to become due upon the event of a default.

Acceptance (Chapter 6)—An unconditional willingness to be bound by the other party's offer. It is one of the four elements required to form a contract. The terms of an acceptance must be exactly the same as the terms of the offer.

Accord and satisfaction (Chapter 6)—An agreement to substitute new performances for those originally contained in the contract. The agreement is the *accord* and the performance is the *satisfaction.*

Accretion (Chapter 2)—The depositing of soil onto the banks of a body of water, causing a property to become larger.

Actual authority (Chapter 15)—A principal has actually given an agent the authority to act on the principal's behalf.

Actual possession (Chapter 8)—An element of adverse possession—using real property in the same way a true owner would use it.

Adaptation test (Chapter 1)—With respect to determining if an item is a fixture, test to determine the extent to which the item was adapted for use in the piece of real property or to what extent the realty was adapted for this item.

Adequacy of consideration (Chapter 6)—The parties to the contract strike their own deal and are bound by it. The courts will not go back and change the terms of the contract. Any consideration, no matter how small, is adequate to form a binding contract.

Administrator (Chapter 14)—A person who manages the estate of one who dies without a will.

Adverse possession (Chapter 8)—The process by which one who is a trespasser long enough (21 years in Ohio) becomes an owner of real property.

Affidavit (Chapter 11)—A written sworn statement. Making a false affidavit can result in perjury.

Agent (Chapter 15)—Someone who is authorized to act on behalf of another person and has the power to bind that other person in a contract.

Agricultural property (Chapter 1)—Property that is used to raise crops and animals such as farms or ranches.

Air rights (Chapter 2)—The rights of a property owner that include everything from the surface of the land upward but that are subject to the rights of the government.

Ancestry (Chapter 16)—A person's ethnic heritage.

Ancillary administration (Chapter 14)—A probate matter to deal with real property that is opened in a state other than the decedent's state of domicile.

Ancillary trustee (Chapter 15)—A person appointed by the Ohio Division of Real Estate to wind up the business of a brokerage.

Apparent authority (Chapter 15)—Authority that is created when a principal does something that makes a third party reasonably believe that an agency relationship exists.

Appurtenant (Chapter 2)—Adjacent.

Appurtenant easement (Chapter 2)—A permanent property right that gives a person the right to use a specific part of an adjacent property for a specific purpose.

Area variance (Chapter 5)—A zoning variance that allows for property use that is slightly outside the rules regarding lot size, building size, setback, and other restrictions based on size or measurements. Contrast with *use variance*.

Assignee (Chapters 6 and 7)—The person to whom a contract or lease is assigned.

Assignment (Chapter 6 and 7)—The process by which rights and duties under a contract or lease are transferred to another person.

Assignor (Chapter 6)—The party assigning a contract.

Attachment test (Chapter 1)—With respect to determining if an item is a fixture, test to determine how permanently an item is attached to the realty.

Attorney opinion letter (Chapter 11)—A method of buyer title protection in which an attorney expresses a legal opinion as to the quality of title. If the opinion is not correct, the recipient of the letter may have a claim for malpractice against the attorney giving the opinion letter.

Attorney-in-fact (Chapter 14)—A person who is given power to act on behalf of another under a power of attorney.

Baseline (Chapter 9)—An east–west line of constant latitude that crosses a principal meridian in the rectangular coordinate system and associated with a particular principal meridian.

Beneficiary (Chapter 14)—In a trust, one who receives the benefits of the trust assets and who has beneficial ownership of them.

Bilateral contract (Chapter 6)—Contract in which each side has made promises about what they will do in the future. The exchange of an offer promise for an acceptance promise. Contrast with *unilateral contract*.

Bill of sale (Chapter 8)—A document used to transfer ownership of personal property.

Blanket mortgage (Chapter 4)—A mortgage that covers more than one piece of property.

Blockbusting (Chapter 16)—The process by which real estate professionals use concerns about the changing demographics of a neighborhood to obtain listings.

Borrower (Chapter 12)—One who borrows money.

Breach of contract (Chapter 6)—Failure to fulfill the duties required by the contract.

Building codes (Chapter 5)—A set of rules that specify the minimum standards for construction of buildings and other structures.

Capacity (Chapter 6)—The right and power to enter into a contract.

CC&Rs (Chapter 4)—See *covenants, conditions, and restrictions*.

Certificate of Transfer (Chapter 4 and 14)—A document issued by the Probate Court certifying as to the owner of real property that was transferred on account of death.

Chattels (Chapter 1)—Another name for personal property.

Closing (Chapter 3 and 13)—The process by which a transaction is consummated, documents are signed, and money changes hands, sometimes called settlement.

Closing Disclosure (Chapter 13)—A document that replaces the HUD-1 form, making it easier for the borrower to compare loan offerings.

Closing protection insurance (Chapter 13)—Insurance paid for by a borrower that protects against "theft, misappropriation, fraud, or other failure to properly disburse settlement, closing, or escrow funds" by the escrow agent.

Cloud on the title (Chapter 11)—An irregularity in the chain of title that causes some doubt as to the true owner of the property.

Codicil (Chapter 14)—An amendment to a will.

Collateral (Chapter 8 and 12)—An interest in real or personal property that is used as security for a loan or other obligation.

Commercial lease (Chapter 7)—The rental of real property for purposes other than places for people to live.

Commercial property (Chapter 1)—Land that is used for business to include stores, office buildings, and shopping malls, and other places where goods are sold or services rendered.

Commitment for title insurance (Chapter 11)—A document prepared by a title company promising to issue a policy of title insurance on particular property.

Common area (Chapter 4)—An area held as a tenancy in common with all the owners of a condominium or other jointly held real property.

Community property (Chapter 4)—All property acquired during a marriage with each spouse owning an undivided one-half interest. Only applies in states that recognize community property rights, not including Ohio.

Compensatory damages (Chapter 6)—The ordinary measure of damages for contract breach; to calculate this type of damage, subtract what the non-breaching party actually received under the contract from what the party should have received. The intent is to compensate the person who did not receive what was agreed upon in the bargain.

Condemnation (Chapter 5)—See *eminent domain*.

Conditional use (Chapter 5)—A deviation from zoning rules that allows land uses that are strictly inconsistent with a zoning plan but otherwise benefit the area, such as grocery stores and churches in an area otherwise zoned for residential use.

Condominium (Chapter 4)—A group of dwelling places, similar to an apartment, where the property is divided into units and the living spaces are individually owned. Subject to CC&Rs.

Conforming use (Chapter 5)—Use of property that is consistent with zoning regulations.

Consideration (Chapter 6)—One of the four elements required for a valid contract. What the parties have bargained for in the contract or what each side gives up, not what they receive. Sometimes referred to as a legal detriment.

Constructive eviction (Chapter 7)—A breach of the implied warranty of habitability that effectively gives the tenant no choice but to leave the rented property.

Continuous (Chapter 8)—An element of adverse possession—using real property without any break in possession.

Contract breach (Chapter 6)—Occurs when a party does not fulfill the duties required by a contract.

Contract for deed (Chapter 8)—See *land contract*.

Contract forfeiture (Chapter 8)—Under a land contract, the legal process by which the vendee loses all payments made to the vendor as a result of a default on the land contract.

Contract formation (Chapter 6)—Creation of a contract that creates enforceable promises, called duties. Requires four elements: capacity, offer, acceptance, and consideration.

Contract performance (Chapter 6)—Duties of the contract that are required to be fulfilled.

Conveyance (Chapter 7)—The transfer of property rights from one person to another.

Conveyance tax (Chapter 10)—A tax that is collected by the county on certain conveyances of real property in Ohio.

Cooperative (Chapter 4)—A group of residence units, much like a condominium, that is owned by a corporation with the residents being the shareholders. Allows for much more control over the selection of persons who are to be residents.

Corner (Chapter 9)—A point on the boundary of real property where the border changes direction.

Counteroffer (Chapter 6)—Rejection of an offer coupled with making a new offer with different terms. A counteroffer is no more binding than an offer.

Covenant of quiet enjoyment (Chapter 7)—An implied promise that the owner or tenant will not be disturbed and can occupy the premises without interference by others claiming a right to the property.

Covenants, conditions, and restrictions (Chapter 2)—Private land-use restrictions on property rights that are created by an agreement among homeowners or by a developer.

Creditor (Chapter 12)—See *lender.*

Cumulative zoning (Chapter 5)—A zoning regulation that divides property zones into layers, or strata. Property can be used in a manner that is consistent with the zoning regulations of the current layer or any higher layer. Contrast with *exclusive zoning.*

Curtesy (Chapter 4)—A husband's rights to part of his wife's property after her death; now simply included in dower.

Death beneficiary (Chapter 14)—In a trust, one who receives the benefits of the trust assets upon the death of the trustor.

Debtor (Chapter 12)—See *borrower.*

Decedent (Chapter 14)—A person who has died.

Deceit (Chapter 15)—See *misrepresentation.*

Declaration of condominium (Chapter 4)—A document that forms a condominium and lays out the CC&Rs of that particular condominium.

Declining value policy (Chapter 11)—A title insurance policy with coverage that decreases over time.

Deed (Chapter 10)—An official document used to transfer property interests.

Deed of trust (Chapter 12)—The security interest held by the lender in a title theory jurisdiction. (Ohio is not a title theory jurisdiction.)

Deed restrictions (Chapters 5 and 10)—Specific restrictions in a deed, which can include maintaining views, type of fences, cutting down trees, garden sheds, paint colors, number and kind of pets permitted.

Defeasible fee estate (Chapter 3)—Another name for a qualified fee estate.

Descent and distribution (Chapter 14)—The state law that specifies how property is to be distributed when a person dies without a will.

Disparate impact (Chapters 5 and 16)—An act that seems neutral on its face but has the effect of disproportionately affecting a protected class.

Disparate treatment (Chapters 5 and 16)—An act that directly discriminates against a protected class such as race, color, national origin, religion, gender, age, or disability on the basis of membership in the class.

Doctrine of part performance (Chapter 6)—Provides an exception to the statute of frauds, as it applies to a contract being in writing. If parties have substantially performed the contract, then a court can enforce the oral contract even though the statute of frauds would require a written contract.

Doctrine of relation back (Chapter 13)—Principle that something done at a later time will be treated as if it were done earlier.

Dodd–Frank Act (Chapter 13)—A federal law that was enacted to put controls on residential real estate lending. Its stated purpose is to "assure that consumers are offered and receive residential mortgage loans on terms that reasonably reflect their ability to repay the loans and that are understandable and not unfair, deceptive, or abusive."

Domicile (Chapters 1 and 14)—The location of the permanent legal residence of a person. One may have multiple residences at the same time, but only one place of domicile.

Dominant tenement (Chapter 2)—A property with easement rights to use another's property.

Dower (Chapter 4)—The right of a spouse to a potential one-third life estate in all real property held by the other spouse during their marriage after that spouse's death.

Dual agency (Chapter 15)—The same real estate agent represents both the buyer and the seller in a transaction. While not recommended, this is legal in Ohio.

Durable power (Chapter 14)—A power of attorney that remains in effect after the disability of the person granting the power.

Duress (Chapter 6)—Causing a person to enter into a contract by threat or physical harm.

Duty (Chapter 6)—The agreed performance of each party in a contract.

Earnest money (Chapter 6)—Deposit of money made to seller by buyer to demonstrate buyer's sincerity in wanting to purchase the property.

Easement (Chapter 2)—A permanent property right for a specific purpose whereby one person is allowed access to another person's property. Easements are said to "run with the land," meaning that they transfer to the new owner when the property changes hands.

Easement by necessity (Chapter 2)—A means of surface access to a parcel of land that otherwise has no access route; must be granted by court order.

Easement by prescription (Chapter 2)—An easement that is created by a person trespassing for such a long time (in Ohio, for 21 years) without the servient tenement objecting to the trespassing so that a right is created.

Easement in gross (Chapter 2)—An easement held by a person (such as a utility company) rather than by a dominant tenement, so that the person has access to the servient tenement, but this right can transfer to another person (such as a new utility company).

Eminent domain (Chapter 5)—The power held by local, state, and federal government to force the sale of private property for public purposes.

Equitable title (Chapter 8)—Under a land contract, right of the vendee to possess the property, which prohibits the vendor from selling the property to another.

Equity of redemption (Chapter 12)—The right of a borrower to cure a default and stop a foreclosure action at any time before the court confirms the foreclosure sale.

Erosion (Chapter 2)—The wearing away of soil at the water's edge that decreases the amount of property owned by the landowner.

Escheat (Chapter 8)—The process by which property passes to the State of Ohio when the owner dies without any heirs.

Escrow agent (Chapter 13)—A neutral third party who accepts money, documents, and other items and holds them in trust, then disburses them according to instructions given by buyers, sellers, and lenders.

Escrow closing (Chapter 13)—A closing process in which money, documents, and other items are delivered to an escrow agent to be held in trust until all of the conditions necessary to close the transactions are satisfied.

Escrow instructions (Chapter 13)—Instructions given to an escrow agent by buyers, sellers, and lenders identifying the conditions to be satisfied before a transaction is closed and the process by which it is to be closed.

Estate for years (Chapter 7)—A lease of real property for some specific period of time with a definite beginning and ending date.

Estate from year-to-year (Chapter 7)—A lease of real property that continues from one time period to successive time periods.

Eviction (Chapter 7)—The legal process by which a tenant who no longer has the right to be on the rented property is removed.

Exception (Chapter 10)—In the context of a deed, a description of rights that are not being conveyed because the grantor does not hold the rights.

Exclusionary zoning (Chapter 5)—Zoning regulations designed to exclude certain people.

Exclusive (Chapter 8)—An element of adverse possession—the property is used by the adverse possessor only and not the true owner.

Exclusive buyer's agent (Chapter 15)—A real estate agent who represents only buyers.

Exclusive seller's agent (Chapter 15)—A real estate agent who represents only sellers.

Exclusive zoning (Chapter 5)—A zoning regulation that requires property to be used in accordance with the zoning rules for a particular area. Contrast with *cumulative zoning*.

Executed contract (Chapter 6)—A contract where all of the duties have been fully performed. This term is sometimes used to describe a written contract that has been fully signed by all parties. The context in which the term is used determines which meaning is intended.

Executor (Chapter 14)—A person who manages the estate of one who dies with a will.

Executory contract (Chapter 6)—A contract with some duties that have not been fully performed.

Express contract (Chapter 6)—A contract that has been stated in words, either written or oral.

Fee simple absolute (Chapter 3)—The most complete ownership of property; one in which the owner holds all of the available rights to the property.

Feoffment (Chapter 3)—An ancient ceremony that was once used to transfer ownership of real property and to preserve the knowledge that the transfer took place; the modern equivalent is the closing.

Fiduciary deed (Chapter 10)—A deed given by a fiduciary, such as an executor of an estate or the sheriff in a foreclosure sale. A fiduciary deed only guarantees that the person giving the deed is a fiduciary, that they have the authority to give the deed, and that they have done everything that is required of them in connection with the deed.

Fiduciary duty (Chapter 14)—A duty of high ethical relation and trust.

First substantive contact (Chapter 15)—Either (1) the buyer is prequalified for financing, (2) the real estate agent receives specific information from the buyer, (3) the property is shown to the buyer (except in an open house situation), (4) the agent discusses an offer with the buyer, or (5) the agent submits an offer to purchase realty to a seller.

Fixture (Chapter 1)—An item of personal property that has been attached to the real property in such a way that it becomes a part of the real property.

Flat lot (Chapter 7)—The tenant is required to remove the buildings and return the property to vacant land, perhaps planting grass.

Forcible entry and detainer (Chapter 7)—See *eviction.*

Foreclosure (Chapter 12)—The legal process by which a lender causes the property held as collateral to be sold at a sheriff's sale in the event of a default.

Foreign real estate (Chapter 17)—Real estate located outside the state of Ohio.

Foreign real estate dealer (Chapter 17)—The equivalent of an Ohio broker but who is licensed to deal with real estate located outside the state of Ohio.

Foreign real estate salesperson (Chapter 17)—The equivalent of an Ohio real estate agent but who is licensed to deal with real estate located outside the state of Ohio.

Formal closing (Chapter 13)—A closing in which all of the parties are present at the same time in the same place.

Fraud (Chapters 6 and 16)—Lying (or failing to disclose something you have a duty to disclose), intending that someone will rely on it; they do rely and are harmed.

FSBO (Chapter 17)—Stands for "for sale by owner," pronounced "fizz-bow."

Fundamental rights (Chapter 16)—Rights that receive a high degree of protection, such as the right of free speech, the right to travel, the right to peaceably assemble, the right to practice religion, among others.

Future interest (Chapter 3)—A right that gives the interest holder the right (or potential right) to possess the property in the future.

General warranty deed (Chapter 10)—A deed that essentially guarantees that title to the realty is perfect.

Good Faith Estimate (Chapter 13)—A document used before October 2015 to indicate the estimated costs associated with a loan. Replaced by the Loan Estimate form.

Grantee (Chapter 10)—The person receiving property.

Grantee index (Chapter 11)—An index maintained by the county recorder that shows, for each grantee, how that person received an interest in property.

Grantor (Chapter 10)—The person transferring property.

Grantor index (Chapter 11)—An index maintained by the county recorder that shows, for each grantor, how that person transferred an interest in property.

Gross lease (Chapter 7)—The tenant pays rent and the landlord is responsible for property taxes, maintenance, and insurance on the property (but not its contents).

Ground lease (Chapter 7)—A lease of vacant commercial land, with the expectation that the tenant will construct a commercial building on the property.

Groundwater (Chapter 2)—Water under the surface of the earth. Groundwater is considered part of the property and can be used by the property owner so long as the use does not interfere with adjacent property owners.

Holdover tenancy (Chapter 7)—A tenant who once had the right to be on rental property no longer has the right to be there, but remains anyway.

Homeowners' association (Chapter 4)—An organization in which owners of homes or condos are the members. This organizations manages the owners and enforces CC&Rs. Usually overseen by a board elected by unit owners. Owners typically pay a monthly assessment or dues, which are used for maintaining the common area and the property.

Hostile (Chapter 8)—An element of adverse possession—the property is used without the permission of the true owner.

HUD-1 (Chapter 13)—A document used before October 2015 to show all the sources of money at a closing and how the money was disbursed. Replaced by the Closing Disclosure form.

Immediately available funds (Chapter 12)—Money that is cash or cash equivalent, such as a cashier's check.

Implied at law (Chapter 6)—A contract that is implied by the actions of the parties, not expressly stated. For example, if somebody goes to see a doctor, they are implying that they will pay the fee, even though it is not expressly stated.

Implied authority (Chapter 15)—Authority that is incidental to actual authority and is inferred by the agency relationship.

Implied contract (Chapter 6)—See *Implied at law.*

Implied warranty of habitability (Chapter 7)—An implied guarantee by the landlord that the premises are fit for humans to live there, included in every residential lease but not commercial leases.

Impossibility of performance (Chapter 6)—A situation in which it is not possible for anyone to fulfill the duties of a contract. For example, destruction of the contract's subject matter or death of someone who is to provide a personal service.

Improved land (Chapter 1)—Land that has some structure on it such as a house, barn, or other structure.

In rem action (Chapter 11)—A lawsuit directed against property, as opposed to a person.

Inactive license (Chapter 15)—A broker or real estate license that has been returned to the Ohio Division of Real Estate during a time that the licensee cannot practice real estate.

Inchoate (Chapter 4)—Incomplete; not fully formed.

Industrial property (Chapter 1)—Land that is used for manufacturing and fabrication. Factories, industrial parks, and the like are all examples of industrial property.

Intent test (Chapter 1)—With respect to determining if an item is a fixture, test to determine if an item was intended to become part of the realty at the time of attachment.

Intercreditor agreement (Chapter 12)—An agreement between lenders setting priority of payments from the proceeds of a foreclosure sale.

Intestacy (Chapters 4 and 14)—Dying without a valid will.

Intestate succession (Chapter 14)—The distribution of property of one who dies without a will.

Inverse condemnation (Chapter 8)—A claim brought by a landowner against the government claiming that the governmental action effectively took the value of the property away from the owner.

Involuntary transfer (Chapter 8)—A transfer of ownership of real property without the consent of the owner.

Jim Crow laws (Chapter 16)—State and local laws enacted after the end of the Civil War to perpetuate racial segregation.

Joint tenancy with right of survivorship (Chapter 4)—A type of ownership in which two or more people own an undivided interest in the property and co-tenant's share of the property will pass to any remaining co-tenants.

Just compensation (Chapter 5)—Determination of fair market value of property taken through eminent domain.

Laches (Chapter 5)—A concept in equity that causes the right to enforce restrictions to be lost if there is a delay in enforcing such restrictions.

Land contract (Chapter 8)—A form of seller financing where the seller retains title to the property until all of the payments have been made.

Latent defect (Chapter 15)—A property defect that is not obvious or that could not be discovered by a reasonable inspection.

Leasehold interest (Chapter 2)—A collection of property rights that are held by an apartment tenant; includes right to be there and to exclude others; also limits rights, such as no right to sell the property or to leave it to another person in a will.

Legal description (Chapter 9)—The method by which real property is uniquely identified by describing its boundaries.

Legal detriment (Chapter 6)—See *consideration*.

Lender (Chapter 12)—One who loans money.

Lender's policy (Chapter 11)—A policy of title insurance that protects only the interests of a lender who financed a real property transaction.

License on deposit (Chapter 15)—A broker's license that has be returned to the Ohio Division of Real Estate so that the person can act as a real estate agent and not a broker.

License revocation (Chapter 15)—The permanent termination of a real estate license.

License suspension (Chapter 15)—A temporary termination of a real estate license.

Licenses (Chapter 2)—A temporary, revocable right to go onto the real property of another.

Lien theory (Chapters 8 and 12)—The concept that a mortgage is a form of lien on the property in favor of the lender and not a form of title to the property. (Ohio is a lien theory state.) Contrast with *title theory.*

Life beneficiary (Chapter 14)—In a trust, one who receives the benefits of the trust assets during the lifetime of the trustor.

Life estate (Chapter 3)—A current right to possess and use real property for so long as that person is alive.

Life estate pur autre vie (Chapter 3)—A life estate measured by the life of another; typically created when a life estate interest is sold.

Life interest (Chapter 3)—The current possessory right held by one who has a life estate interest in real property.

Limited real estate salesperson (Chapter 17)—A person only deals who with real property associated with cemetery interment rights.

Limited warranty deed (Chapter 10)—A deed that provides guarantees only with respect to things that were done by the grantor or during grantor's ownership of the property.

Liquidated damages (Chapter 6)—An amount of money that the parties agree upon and write in the contract in the event that there is a breach of the contract. Liquidated damages are awarded instead of and not in addition to compensatory damages.

Lis pendens (Chapter 12)—A notice that is filed with the county recorder that a lawsuit is pending challenging title to the property.

Littoral rights (Chapter 2)—Real property rights that determine a landowner's use of nonmoving water, such as lakes and ponds, if the landowner's property borders the moving water.

Livery of seisin (Chapter 3)—A concept from the feoffment ceremony that is roughly equivalent to "delivery of possession." The new owner thereby is able to "seize" or hold the property.

Living trust (Chapter 14)—A trust that is created while the trustor is alive, as contrasted to a testamentary trust.

Loan commitment (Chapter 12)—A document issued by a lender in which it agrees to lend money upon certain conditions, such as signing a promissory note and a mortgage.

Loan Estimate (Chapter 13)—A document that replaces the Good Faith Estimate form, used to disclose the estimated costs of a loan. The Loan Estimate form is designed to be more readable than the Good Faith Estimate.

Measuring life (Chapter 3)—In a life estate, the person whose life will determine the duration of the right to possess the property.

Merger (Chapter 2)—A way to terminate an easement, in which both the dominant and servient tenements are owned by the same owner.

Meridian (Chapter 9)—A line running north–south of constant longitude.

Metes and bounds (Chapter 9)—A method of describing the boundaries of real property using angles, directions, and distances.

Misrepresentation (Chapter 15)—The first two elements of fraud, namely, (1) lying or failing to disclose a material fact (2) with the intent that a person will rely on it.

Mitigate damages (Chapter 6)—To take actions to prevent the damages from getting any larger. A nonbreaching party has a duty to mitigate damages.

Mortgage (Chapter 12)—A real property interest held by a lender that enables it to use the collateral to satisfy a loan in the event of a default.

Mortgage insurance (Chapter 12)—An insurance policy, usually paid for by the borrower, that protects the lender in the event of a default.

Mortgagee (Chapter 12)—One who gives a mortgage to the lender; the borrower.

Mortgagor (Chapter 12)—One who receives the benefit of a mortgage; the lender.

Mutual mistake (Chapter 6)—Both the offeror and offeree are mistaken about a material aspect of the contract, which makes the contract void.

Net lease (Chapter 7)—The tenant pays a portion of the taxes, fees, and maintenance costs for the property in addition to the rent.

Nonconforming use (Chapter 5)—Use of property that was in full compliance with the zoning regulations, but is no longer in compliance due to a change in the regulations. The property can continue to be used in its current manner, but cannot be expanded or changed.

Nonfreehold (Chapter 7)—An interest in real property that gives a person the right of possession, but not ownership.

Notice statute (Chapter 10)—A recording statute scheme that gives priority of title to the person with the most recent claim, but only if that person did not have notice of an earlier claim.

Novation (Chapter 6)—The parties agree to substitute someone else for a party who wishes to withdraw from the contract.

Objective standard (Chapter 6)—Standard for determining a person's intent to be bound in a contract; would a reasonable person believe that the party intended to be bound?

Offer (Chapter 6)—A proposal to enter into a contract, made by an offeror to the offeree. An offer has four elements: promise, communication, sufficient terms, and intent to be bound.

Offeree (Chapter 6)—The person to whom an offer is made.

Offeror (Chapter 6)—The person who makes the proposal to enter into a contract.

Ohio Division of Real Estate (Chapter 15)—The administrative agency that deals with the regulation of brokers and real estate agents; analogous to the administrative branch of the federal government.

Ohio Real Estate Commission (Chapter 15)—The administrative agency that sets standards, conducts hearings, and oversees the Ohio Division of Real Estate; analogous to the legislative and judicial branches of the federal government.

Open and notorious (Chapter 8)—An element of adverse possession—the use of the property by the adverse possessor must not be hidden; the true owner could discover the use by inspecting the property.

Option contract (Chapter 6)—An agreement not to revoke an offer for some period of time; an option contract requires separate consideration from the offer.

Option to renew (Chapter 7)—A lease provision that gives a tenant the opportunity to renew the lease, either under the original terms or new terms that are described in the lease.

Oral contract (Chapter 6)—A contract agreed upon verbally rather than in writing.

Owner affidavit (Chapter 11)—A method of buyer title protection in which a seller provides a sworn statement as to the quality of title.

Owner's fee policy (Chapter 11)—A policy of title insurance that protects the interests of the owner of real property.

Parol evidence (Chapter 6)—Oral testimony that is offered to contradict or supplement a final, complete written contract.

Partition (Chapter 8)—A legal remedy used to settle property disputes when there are multiple owners who cannot agree. The court can divide the property into parcels and transfer ownership of each parcel to the respective owners. If the property cannot be divided, the court can order the property sold and the proceeds divided among the owners.

Patent defect (Chapter 15)—A property defect that is obvious or that could be discovered by a reasonable inspection.

Per stirpes (Chapter 14)—"By right of representation"—a distribution of probate assets such that a predeceased person's share will pass to his or her heirs.

Percentage lease (Chapter 7)—A commercial lease that requires the tenant to pay rent in the form of a fixed amount each month, together with a percentage of the gross retail sales.

Perfection (Chapter 12)—The process by which a lender obtains the power to seize collateral in the event of a default on a loan.

Performance (Chapter 6)—Duties that are to be carried out in a contract.

Periodic tenancy (Chapter 7)—See *estate from year-to-year*.

Personal property (Chapter 1)—Property that is not real property. Anything that is not more or less permanently attached to real property is personal property.

Personal representative (Chapter 14)—The general term for one who manages an estate. See *administrator* and *executor*.

Personal service (Chapter 6)—A contract where the essence of the bargain is that a specific person will perform the contract.

Personalty (Chapter 1)—Another word used for *personal property*.

Plat map (Chapter 9)—A map used to describe a subdivision and lots within the subdivision. A plat map indicates the name of the subdivision, a drawing of the individual lots contained within it, any easements, the names of streets, building setbacks, etc.

Point of beginning (Chapter 9)—The starting point of a property border using metes and bounds.

Police power (Chapter 5)—State and local governmental power to reasonably and nondiscriminatorily promote safety, public health, and general welfare.

Possessory (Chapter 4)—Having possession or having the nature of possession.

Power of attorney (Chapter 14)—A legal document that gives a person the power to act on behalf of someone else.

Present interest (Chapter 3)—A right that gives the interest holder the right to currently possess the property.

Principal (Chapter 15)—The person who is represented by an agent.

Principal meridian (Chapter 9)—A north–south line of constant longitude used in the rectangular coordinate system associated with a particular base line.

Private land-use restriction (Chapter 4 and 5)—A restriction on how an owner can use their land that is created other than by a governmental entity.

Privity of contract (Chapter 7)—The relationship between parties created by virtue of a contract.

Privity of estate (Chapter 7)—The relationship between parties by virtue of holding interests in real property.

Probate (Chapter 14)—Literally "to prove"—but generally understood to mean the process of dealing with an estate.

Probate asset (Chapter 14)—An asset that does not automatically pass to another person upon death of its owner.

Profit (Chapter 2)—A temporary, revocable right to go onto the real property of another to remove something from the property.

Promissory note (Chapter 12)—The document that provides evidence of a loan and the duty to make payments.

Property index (Chapter 11)—See *tract index.*

Property rights (Chapter 1)—The bundle of rights associated with property.

Propriety lease (Chapter 4)—A lease between a cooperative corporation and an owner-tenant that sets the conditions for the right to occupy a particular unit.

Prorations (Chapter 13)—A method of allocating future costs fairly between the buyer and seller.

Public domain (Chapter 9)—Belonging to the people of the United States.

Public land-use restrictions (Chapter 5)—Involuntary restrictions placed on the use of real property by governmental entities.

Public nuisance (Chapter 5)—Something that threatens public safety, health, welfare, morals, or that becomes a public annoyance.

Public purpose (Chapter 5)—In connection with eminent domain, those things that benefit the public in general.

Punitive damages (Chapter 6)—Damages designed to punish. Sometimes awarded for intentional torts but not for mere breach of contract.

Qualified fee estate (Chapter 3)—A possessory estate that places some restrictions on the use of the property, such as property that is given to a city, but on the condition that is only used for a park. If the city tries to use the property for some other purpose, the grantor (or the grantor's heirs) can act to regain ownership and possession of the property.

Quiet title action (Chapter 8)—A lawsuit brought to establish ownership and title to the real property where the ownership is at issue.

Quitclaim deed (Chapter 10)—A deed that transfers any interest that the grantor may have, which may include no interest at all.

Race statute (Chapter 10)—A recording statute scheme that gives priority of title to the first person to record, irrespective of whether that person knew of an earlier claim.

Race-notice statute (Chapter 10)—A recording statute scheme that gives priority of title to the first person to record, but only if that person did not have notice of an earlier claim.

Range (Chapter 9)—Measurement of distance from the baseline in the rectangular coordinate system.

Ratification (Chapter 15)—A relationship created when a principal accepts the benefits of an act of a person who was not an agent of the principal at the time.

Real estate agent (Chapter 17)—See *real estate salesperson.*

Real estate broker (Chapter 17)—Someone who is licensed to engage in the business of selling, exchanging, purchasing, and renting real estate.

Real estate salesperson (Chapter 17)—A person associated with a real estate broker who is licensed to engage in the same acts as the broker, but under the broker's supervision.

Real property (Chapter 1)—Location on the planet earth and everything that is more or less permanently attached to that location.

Realty (Chapter 1)—Another term used for *real property.*

Reasonable person (Chapter 6)—A hypothetical person used as a legal standard; a person who exercises the degree of attention, knowledge, intelligence, and judgment that society requires of its members for the protection of their own and of others' interests.

Recording deeds (Chapter 10)—The process of filing a deed with the county recorder's office to put the world on notice as to the existence of the deed.

Rectangular coordinate system (Chapter 9)—A method of describing property boundaries in a grid pattern, akin to placing a sheet of graph paper over a map.

Redlining (Chapter 16)—The practice by which a lender refuses to lend money in certain geographic areas, because of perceived lower property values caused by the ethnic composition of the area.

Release (Chapter 7)—The termination of legal liability under a lease or contract.

Remainder (Chapter 3)—The future interest that follows a life estate.

Rent to own (Chapter 8)—A form of seller financing where a portion of a tenant's rental payments is applied to an option to purchase the property.

Rental agreement (Chapter 7)—A document that creates a landlord–tenant relationship; also called a lease.

Reservation (Chapter 10)—In the context of a deed, a description of rights that are not being conveyed because the grantor is retaining the rights.

Residential lease (Chapter 7)—The rental of a place where people live.

Residential property (Chapter 1)—Places where people live; places of domicile such as single-family houses, duplexes, apartments, and such.

RESPA (Chapter 13)—Short for Real Estate Settlement Procedures Act, the statute that controlled real estate closings. RESPA was modified by provisions of the Dodd–Frank Act.

Retaliatory eviction (Chapter 7)—The action of a landlord who attempts to evict a tenant because the tenant has taken some lawful action.

Reversionary interest (Chapter 3)—The future interest that follows a qualified fee estate.

Riparian rights (Chapter 2)—Real property rights that determine a landowner's use of nonnavigable moving waters, such as streams or creeks, if the landowner's property borders the moving water.

Round table closing (Chapter 13)—See *formal closing.*

Rule in Shelley's Case (Chapter 3)—A rule from a case in the 16th century that treated creating a life estate in A, with the remainder in A's heirs as a transfer of fee simple absolute to A. This situation originally dealt with a scheme to avoid taxes on the transfer. Ohio abolished the Rule in Shelley's Case in 1953—thus, a life estate in A with the remainder in A's heirs will not now be treated as a transfer of fee simple absolute.

Run with the land (Chapter 2)—Property rights that automatically transfer to a subsequent property owner when the property is sold or otherwise transferred.

Secondary market (Chapter 12)—The financial market in which investors purchase previously issued financial instruments, such as mortgage loans.

Section (Chapter 9)—A rectangular plot of land in the rectangular coordinate system, which usually contains 640 acres and is frequently divided into fractional parts.

Secured transaction (Chapter 12)—A transaction that involves collateral to help guarantee performance of duties in the transaction.

Separate property (Chapter 4)—Property held individually by a spouse. Includes property acquired before the marriage, as well as gifts and inheritances received during the marriage.

Servient tenement (Chapter 2)—A property that is burdened with an easement.

Settlement (Chapter 13)—See *closing.*

Settlor (Chapter 14)—See *trustor.*

Severalty (Chapter 4)—A type of ownership in which there is only one owner.

Special warranty deed (Chapter 10)—See *limited warranty deed*.

Specific performance (Chapter 6)—A remedy that the court can use in certain instances to order the parties to perform their duties under the contract. Specific performance requires that the subject matter of the contract be unique and money damages would not be adequate.

Split agency (Chapter 15)—A brokerage business model in which real estate agents are allowed to be dual agents, and which also allows two different agents in the brokerage to represent the buyer and seller.

Split agency but no dual agency (Chapter 15)—A brokerage business model that allows two different agents to represent the buyer and seller but does not allow dual agency.

Spot zoning (Chapter 5)—An act by a zoning board with respect to a particular parcel of land in a way that is not compatible with the use of the surrounding area. Spot zoning is an illegal use of police power.

Standing to sue (Chapter 16)—The right of a person to bring a lawsuit because that person has a direct interest in the outcome of the case.

Statute of frauds (Chapter 6)—A statute that requires that certain kinds of contracts be memorialized in a writing, signed by the party to be charged, with sufficient content to evidence the contract.

Statutory survivorship deed (Chapter 4)—A deed that establishes that the property will automatically pass to the surviving owners upon the death of another owner. Requires the use of specific language set out in a statute.

Steering (Chapter 16)—The practice by which real estate agents guide potential buyers to or away from certain areas based on the buyer's membership in a protected class.

Subjective standard (Chapter 6)—Deals with the intent to be bound in a contract. The subjective standard is what the offeror intended with regard to being bound to a contract. However, intent is measured by the objective standard which is asking would a reasonable person believe the offeror intended to be bound by a contract.

Sublease (Chapter 7)—The process by which a tenant essentially becomes a landlord and rents all or part of a rented premises to a new tenant.

Subletting (Chapter 7)—See *sublease*.

Subordination agreement (Chapter 12)—See *intercreditor agreement*.

Substantially performed (Chapter 6)—A contract is said to be substantially performed if the contract or performance is somehow deficient, but is so nearly equivalent so as to be unreasonable to deny the existence of the contract or the completeness of performance.

Subsurface rights (Chapter 2)—Ownership of everything from the property boundaries at the surface of the earth to the center of the earth.

Subtenant (Chapter 7)—The new tenant in a sublease.

Survey (Chapter 9)—A system by which a surveyor plans, designs, and establishes real property boundaries.

Survey marker (Chapter 9)—A marker, typically set in concrete, which represents a precise, known location on the face of the earth.

Tacking (Chapter 8)—In adverse possession, the requirement of continuousness can be satisfied by subsequent adverse possessors.

Taking (Chapter 5)—See *eminent domain*.

Tenancy at sufferance (Chapter 7)—A tenant who remains on property after the tenant no longer has the right to be there.

Tenancy at will (Chapter 7)—A lease of real property that exists so long as the landlord and the tenant desire the relationship to exist.

Tenancy by the entirety (Chapter 4)—A type of ownership available only to married couples in which the marriage itself is the owner of the property. This prevents creditors of either spouse from reaching the underlying property. Abolished in Ohio on April 4, 1985, but existing tenancies continued to exist.

Tenancy in common (Chapter 4)—A type of ownership in which two or more people own an undivided interest in the property. This is default ownership when two or more persons own real property in Ohio.

Term tenancy (Chapter 7)—See *estate for years*.

Testate (Chapter 14)—Dying with a will.

Testator (Chapter 14)—A person who makes a will.

Three-day notice (Chapter 7)—Part of the eviction process in Ohio; a notice from a landlord to a tenant to pay rent within three days or vacate the premises.

Time is of the essence (Chapter 6)—Any dates or timing in the contract are considered to be an essential and material part of the transaction and will be strictly enforced.

Title (Chapter 8 and 10)—The ownership interest in real property.

Title abstract (Chapter 11)—A history of ownership and encumbrances to real property starting with the original owner and all subsequent conveyances.

Title defect (Chapter 10)—Some flaw in title, such as a lien, encroachment, judgment, or serious error in a document.

Title examination (Chapter 11)—The process of searching the public records of the various offices to determine the owner and if there are any liens or other defects.

Title examiner (Chapter 11)—A person who conducts title examinations.

Title guarantee (Chapter 11)—A method of buyer title protection in which a guarantee is given as to the accuracy of a title search.

Title insurance (Chapter 11)—A policy issued by a title company that insures the title to property is good.

Title report (Chapter 11)—A report issued by a title examiner that details what was found in a title search.

Title search (Chapter 11)—See *title examination.*

Title theory (Chapter 8 and 12)—One of two approaches to a bank having collateral in land. In a title theory, the bank has an ownership interest in the property and need not use foreclosure to exercise its rights. (Ohio is not a title theory state.) See *lien theory.*

Township (Chapter 9)—In the rectangular coordinate system, a square of 6 miles on each side, created by the intersections of north–south and east–west lines. The term can also refers to a political subdivision of a county in Ohio.

Tract index (Chapter 11)—An index maintained by some county recorders that lists all recorded documents related to a particular tract of land.

Transfer (Chapter 7)—The process by which real property rights are shifted from one person to another.

Triple net lease (Chapter 7)—A lease in which the tenant pays all of the taxes, insurance, and maintenance costs for the property in addition to the rent.

Trust (Chapter 14)—An arrangement where assets are held for the benefits of others.

Trustee (Chapter 14)—In a trust, the person who holds legal title to the trust assets and manages the trust assets for the benefit of the beneficiaries.

Trustor (Chapter 14)—A person who creates and funds a trust.

Truth in lending (Chapter 13)—A document used before October 2015 to disclose interest rates associated with a loan. Replaced by the Loan Estimate form.

Underwater (Chapter 13)—A loan where the value of the collateral is less than the amount owed.

Undue influence (Chapter 6)—One person exerts some force or power over another to cause that person to enter into a contract; different from *duress* in that no physical harm is threatened or exerted.

Unenforceable contract (Chapter 6)—A contract that is missing something that is necessary to make it enforceable.

Unilateral contract (Chapter 6)—A contract that requires some performance in exchange for a promise; a unilateral contract can only be accepted by performing what is required by the offer. For example, a reward offer for finding a lost dog can only be accepted by actually finding the dog, not by promising to do so.

Unilateral mistake (Chapter 6)—Either the offeror or offeree are mistaken about a material aspect of a contract. A unilateral mistake does not excuse performance.

Unimproved land (Chapter 1)—Land that is more or less in its natural state. Grasslands, vacant lots, forests and the like are all examples of unimproved land.

Unity of interest (Chapter 4)—A requirement of a joint tenancy with right of survivorship in which all owners must have an equal ownership interest in the property.

Unity of possession (Chapter 4)—A requirement of a joint tenancy with right of survivorship in which all owners must have right to possess the entire property; an undivided interest in the whole of the property.

Unity of time (Chapter 4)—A requirement of a joint tenancy with right of survivorship in which all owners must have acquired ownership of the property at the same time.

Unity of title (Chapter 4)—A requirement of a joint tenancy with right of survivorship in which all owners must have the same title to the property; if a condition applies to one owner, it must apply to all owners.

Use variance (Chapter 5)—See *conditional use*.

Valid contract (Chapter 6)—A contract that contains all of the necessary elements of a contract: capacity, offer, acceptance, and consideration.

Variance (Chapter 5)—A permanently allowed deviation from the zoning requirements that attaches to a particular parcel of land.

Vendee (Chapter 8)—In a land contract, the person purchasing the property.

Vendor (Chapter 8)—In a land contract, the person selling the property.

Void contract (Chapter 6)—A purported contract that is not a contract at all. It never was a contract and will never be a contract.

Voidable contract (Chapter 6)—A contract that can be canceled by one or more parties.

Voluntary transfer (Chapter 8)—The transfer of real property with the owner's consent.

Walk-through (Chapter 13)—An activity where the buyer's agent arranges for the agent and the buyer to have access to the property for the purpose of inspecting the condition of it before closing.

Waste (Chapter 3)—The duty of a person who has less than a fee simple interest in real property to preserve the property for the benefit of the person that holds the rest of the rights in the property. Waste basically includes damages other than ordinary wear and tear.

Will (Chapter 14)—A legal document that expresses the wishes of how a person would like his or her assets to be distributed upon death.

Writ (Chapter 7)—A court order.

Written contract (Chapter 6)—A contract that has been reduced to writing.

Zoning (Chapter 1 and 5)—The exercise of states' police power that divides land into different areas that are classified according to use. Is intended to keep like uses of land together and improve the conditions of an area by limiting the permissible uses within a particular zoning district.

Index